196.

Cricket and the Victorians

Cricket and the Victorians

KEITH A.P. SANDIFORD

Published by
SCOLAR PRESS
Gower House
Croft Road
Aldershot
Hants GU11 3HR
England

Ashgate Publishing Company
Old Post Road
Brookfield
Vermont 05036
USA

British Library Cataloguing in Publication Data
Sandiford, Keith A.P.
    Cricket and the Victorians
    I. Title
    306.483

    ISBN 1-85928-089-7

Library of Congress Cataloging-in-Publication Data
Sandiford, Keith A.P., 1936–
    Cricket and the Victorians/Keith A.P. Sandiford.
        p. cm.
    Includes bibliographical references (p.   ) and index.
    ISBN 1-85928-089-7
    1. Cricket—Social aspects—Great Britain—History—19th century.
    I. Title
    GV928.G7S26 1994
    796.358'0941—dc20   94-15034
                            CIP

ISBN 1 85928 089 7

To my Yeading cousins, Clyde and Elaine King –
without whose hospitality and generosity
this enterprise would surely have failed

Contents

Preface

This study has sprung from my two major interests: history and cricket. The one has been my profession for almost 30 years and the other has been my passion for as long as I can remember. It has also been inspired by three works in particular: Harry Edwards, *Sociology of Sports* (Illinois, 1973); C.L.R. James, *Beyond a Boundary* (Sportsmans Book Club, 1964); and Tony Mason, *Association Football and English Society 1863–1915* (Sussex, 1980).

It was Edwards who first impressed upon me the paramount significance of all sport in a socio-cultural context. He convincingly demonstrated how sports in the United States not only reflected, but even helped to shape and buttress, American attitudes and values. About 30 years ago, James posed an intriguing question when he pointedly asked: *What do they know of cricket who only cricket know?* His very useful message was that it was impossible to understand the game without looking intelligently beyond the playing field. Following the example set by James, my own question now is: What do they, who know nothing of sport, really know about the Victorians? I am convinced that the Victorians will never be properly understood until their obsession with sport has been carefully investigated. And Mason, in his excellent study of British soccer, has supplied the model. I have deliberately tried here to examine some of the themes which Mason so relentlessly pursued.

The decision to undertake serious research in the area of Victorian sport was the direct result of several conversations I had with my former student and colleague Dr Morris Mott, who is now an associate professor of history at Brandon University. During the mid-1970s Morris (for his PhD from Queen's University) was investigating the development of 'manly' sports in Manitoba. It was he, in effect, who suggested that I should turn my talents away from diplomatic history and towards a field for which, in his judgment, I was far better suited temperamentally. This work is thus the offspring of that suggestion. Morris has also been very helpful in drawing attention to some of the more fundamental questions that I might otherwise have neglected. For his help I am grateful. I must also offer a warm word of thanks to Professors Peter Bailey, John Finlay, John Kendle and Edward Moulton who have not only read and criticized some of my earlier writing but have rendered yeoman service by periodically discussing several aspects of Victorian leisure. From these discussions I have profited enormously. Beyond the Canadian boundary, such scholars as Dr Richard Cashman, Dr Brian Stoddart, Dr John Twigg and Dr Wray Vamplew have also offered considerable encouragement and support over the years.

Great debts, as is well known, are accumulated in the writing of any manuscript. Many of mine are acknowledged in the numerous references which accompany the text. But there are those of a more subtle kind which are nevertheless of equal importance. My Antiguan friend, Mr Herbert Spencer, will not find his name among my footnotes, although his spirit is assuredly there. Over the past quarter of a century, we have spent count-less hours discussing the importance of cricket while looking critically at its past and fretting ruefully over its future. Herbie's encouragement has been a telling factor here. My former secretary, Ms Blanche Miller, cheer-fully performed the myriad tasks which go into the preparation of articles for publication; and her successor, Ms Karen Morrow, has done the same for the present manuscript. I owe them a special debt of gratitude. Above all, my cousins, Clyde and Elaine King, who have since returned to Barbados, must surely have earned a medal of some kind. They blithely endured my constant cricket chatter during the many summers I spent with them in Yeading while pursuing my research. Without the million kindnesses they bestowed upon me in Middlesex, this book would not have been possible at all.

Many sections of this work have already appeared, in one form or another, in a variety of journals. I am grateful to the editors of *Albion*, the *Australian Cricket Journal*, the *British Journal of Sports History*, *Historical Reflections*, the *International Journal of the History of Sport*, the *Journal of the Cricket Society*, the *Journal of Social History* and the *Journal of Sport History* for their kind permission to reprint passages previously published by them.

Winnipeg, Canada
October 1993

CHAPTER ONE

Prolegomena

Cricket was much more than just another game to the Victorians. Indeed, they glorified it as a perfect system of ethics and morals which embodied all that was most noble in the Anglo-Saxon character. They prized it as a national symbol, perhaps because – so far as they could tell – it was an exclusively English creation unsullied by oriental or European influences. In an extremely xenophobic age, the Victorians came to regard cricket as further proof of their moral and cultural supremacy.

It is difficult to exaggerate the importance of cricket in Victorian life. It was a ritual as well as recreation, a spiritual as well as a sporting experience. Its values and its language came to be freely used by politicians, philosophers, preachers and poets. Its influence on the imagery of Newbolt and Kipling was pronounced, and Lord Palmerston, that most English of all Prime Ministers, occasionally made use of his cricketing vocabulary in some of his most telling epigrams.[1] The game itself, as Leslie Frewin, Benny Green and Tony Mangan have shown, inspired a healthy volume of Victorian verse as well as fiction.[2] Not surprisingly, therefore, it also evoked a good deal of popular art and music during the nineteenth century.[3]

It can be argued that, in focusing on cricket, the Victorians were merely perpetuating a Georgian legacy. The game had really been modernized during the Hanoverian age. By 1840 it had more or less crystallized into the form in which it is still being played today.[4] The Victorians could, as a consequence, treat cricket with the same awe and reverence that they reserved for ancient and durable institutions. They lived in a revolutionary world of constant flux and, despite their buoyant optimism and insufferable arrogance on the surface, they were always anxious about their present and their immediate future. The great technological changes by which they were enveloped left them with both a sense of pride and a feeling of insecurity. It was, in Walter Houghton's view, this unsettling sense that their old world was visibly crumbling beneath them which formed the basis of their inherent conservatism. Hence their devotion to Crown and cricket – two established and respectable institutions which could serve, each in its own way, as agents of social and organic harmony.[5]

The Victorians played cricket with a greater intensity than ever the Georgians did, largely because, in their view, they had cleansed it of its Georgian impurities. They removed gambling and corruption from the game in a deliberate and successful attempt to purify it. This was in keep-ing with their approach to life in general. The majority of them – particularly those belonging to the middle classes – were earnest, prim and evangelical. Such puritanism stood in stark contrast to the licentiousness of their immediate predecessors. In many ways, indeed, it was a violent reaction against what the Victorians had themselves condemned as Georgian laxity. The Georgians had played cricket, as they had done every-thing else, with spectacular exuberance and panache. This was certainly not in keeping with the Victorian spirit and temper, with its emphasis on sobriety and moderation. Whereas the Georgians had played cricket largely for their own enjoyment, the Victorians did so for their spiritual and mental regeneration. Georgian enthusiasm gave way to Victorian earnestness – even though the basic form of cricket, to a considerable extent, remained virtually unaltered.

So clean had the Victorians washed the Georgian game that the term 'It's not cricket' came gradually into general usage.[6] It was a loaded and emotive phrase both in the nineteenth century and the twentieth. It was meant to denote any despicable act or thing which was immoral, ungentlemanly and/or improper. It had much to do, that is to say, with a regrettable lack of 'good form' and/or 'fair play'. 'Keep your end up' gradually became a general call for a positive contribution to a worthy cause. And 'playing the game of life with a stiff upper lip and a straight bat' was the customary advice given to the vast bulk of young men by their late-Victorian fathers, beseeching them to conduct themselves always in a correct and courageous manner. Such linguistics have serious sociological implications. They tell us a good deal about the Victorian concept of the meaning of cricket. In the Victorian mind, cricket was the ideal form of recreation (using this term in its truest classical sense), in which the chivalrous Christian participated. The notion of the chivalrous cricketer was of paramount importance in an age completely dominated by the cult of muscular Christianity.

All classes of Victorians were encouraged to play cricket because it was seen by the social and cultural leaders of the day as the perfect recreative pursuit. Physicians recommended it as the securest guarantee against illness; and educators encouraged participation in the game out of the profound conviction that it produced better men as well as scholars. This idea was perhaps best expressed by Dr George Ridding, one of the most famous headmasters of the Victorian age, who once said: 'Give me a boy who is a cricketer and I can make something of him.'[7] It was a sentiment wholeheartedly shared by many public school teachers in the second half of the nineteenth century, when cricket actually became an essential feature of the public school curriculum.[8]

As with most matters relating to culture, mores and social attitudes, leadership in this cricketing cult came from the aristocracy, the church and the Crown. Queen Victoria herself encouraged her sons to play the game and hired a professional cricketer, F.W. Bell, to coach them.[9] She also played a prominent role in the foundation of the Home Park Cricket Club in 1850, when she placed a field at the foot of Windsor Castle at the disposal of local residents. Since then, a member of the royal family has always been that club's patron.[10] The Prince of Wales, following in the footsteps of his father, became the patron of the Marylebone Cricket Club (MCC) and held a similar position with the Surrey County Cricket Club.[11] Prince Christian Victor played the game with a high degree of skill and His Royal Highness the Duke of Albany was only seven years old when he was enrolled as a member of Esher Cricket Club.[12] Members of the royal family were constantly reported as being present at some of the great Victorian cricket festivals, and are known also to have contributed generously to the Dr W.G. Grace Testimonial Fund in 1895.[13]

Neither the Queen nor Albert, the Prince Consort, took an active part in cricket, but they certainly gave it their stamp of approval. This was of major importance in an age when aristocrats as well as commoners were still willing to follow the guidance of the monarchy in matters cultural. Not surprisingly, the nobility also served as patrons of cricket clubs at all levels and did much to keep the game alive in almost every county. Many Members of Parliament were members also of the MCC, as its president, W.E. Denison, observed with pride in 1892.[14] Six years previously, *Cricket*, one of the best sports journals of the day, had also marvelled at the high percentage of MPs who had played the game or were still in some ways connected with it.[15] In the Conservative Cabinet of 1886, for instance, cricket was well represented by Lord George Hamilton and Edward Stanhope. A. Akers-Douglas, Lord Harris, W. St John Broderick, Walter Long, Col. Walrond and the Earl of Latham, all of whom were well-known cricketers, were also promoted to important posts outside the Cabinet.[16]

There was, in short, a direct link between Victorian politics and Victorian cricket. Even the rather puritanical Richard Cobden, best remembered now for his role in Corn Law repeal, allowed his name to be used as patron of the North of England Cricket Club in 1846.[17] Four years later, he had 'no hesitation in allowing my name to be used as one of the patrons of the Wakefield Mechanics' Institution Cricket Club'. Cobden viewed cricket as 'a healthful, manly recreation' and 'the most innocent of all out-of-door amusements'.[18] The Members of Parliament frequently arranged matches among themselves. In July 1863, for instance, the Opposition achieved a moral victory over Her Majesty's Government by scoring 259 runs in a single innings at Lord's, the headquarters of the MCC. The ministers mustered only 46 in their first turn and were struggling desperately at 136 for seven wickets in their second when play ended for the day. Friendly cricket matches were also arranged quite often in those days between the legislators and the leading bureaucrats.[19] In fact, cricket interests in the Victorian parliament were so strong that, in 1888, they easily killed a section of the Great Central Railway Bill which threatened the famous Lord's cricket ground with possible extinction.[20] They were strong enough, too, to permit the swift passage of Sir John Lubbock's Bank Holiday Act in 1871 and thus allow the immortal W.G. Grace to thrill massive holiday crowds for the next 30 years.[21] The Lubbocks themselves were long-standing members of the MCC.

If the links between cricket and politics were thus very vital and direct in those days, even more so were the links between cricket and religion, cricket and class, cricket and technology, and between cricket and Victorian culture itself. As literally millions of pounds were spent on the game during the last third of the nineteenth century, when leagues and associations sprang up like mushrooms everywhere, cricket also became inextricably linked with Victorian economics and commerce.

It is arguable, indeed, that the Victorians devoted more time, thought, energy and money to cricket than to such questions as religion and politics, which have traditionally dominated the history books. Yet, almost inexplicably, professional historians for many years neglected cricket altogether. G.M. Trevelyan, for example, found it possible to write a sizeable and illustrated history of Britain without devoting a single paragraph to cricket. He remained convinced that the French aristocracy could have avoided the great Revolution in 1789 had they played cricket on a regular basis with their underlings. Yet, in his own text on England, he contented himself with a few brief references to the game.[22] As late as 1973, as the American historian William Baker has observed, H.J. Dyos and Michael Wolff could edit a two-volume study of the Victorian city without focusing on any aspect of leisure or recreation.[23]

This neglect of such a prominent theme as sport led C.L.R. James, the West Indian historian, philosopher, novelist, music critic, cricket correspondent and political activist, to denounce Trevelyan and the social historian G.D.H. Cole, among others, for their callous treatment of cricket and cricketers. In James's view, the greatest Victorian of them all was Dr W.G. Grace, the celebrated cricketer, whose bearded image was easily the most recognizable and the most popular among nineteenth-century Englishmen. Grace's cricket career directly touched more people then, and has continued to influence more lives even now, than did the political career of any of his contemporaries. James did not see how it was possible for anybody to write a huge volume on English social history without even once referring to the 'Champion'. To James, this was surely most unprofessional since, so far as he could judge, the cult of cricket lay at the very base of Victorianism.[24] He might well have asked: 'What do they know of England who do not cricket know?' His own well-known epi-gram, '*What do they know of cricket who only cricket know?*', suggests the obverse – that cricket is intelligible only when placed within a wider context. His famous *Beyond a Boundary* was also aimed directly at those journalists who wrote volumes about the game without looking beyond the cricket field.[25]

Ironically, it is to these same journalists that the professional historian must now look when attempting to do what James was recommending. Any attempt to place cricket in a broader Victorian framework must begin with a synthesis of contemporary press reports and the countless books written by journalists ever since. Until very recently, social historians neglected sport because in their view as well as that of laymen, it merely involved forms of play. History was a much more serious business, involving work, industry and worship. This narrowness of approach was not confined to historians; it was at one time characteristic of all social science.

Happily, this attitude has changed dramatically, thanks in no small measure to men like James, and social scientists over the last 20 years or so have seriously been analysing play, sport, leisure and recreation. There is now a healthy volume of literature on the anthropology, philosophy, psychology and sociology of fun and games. Historians now know that it is hardly possible to write intelligibly about work without also dealing intelligently with play; and it is universally recognized that sport is one of the most important features of any society's culture. These basic notions have spawned a sizeable body of seminal works on the question of British leisure.[26]

What historians must now do is build on these solid foundations by investigating individual sports and games with greater care. The example here has been well set by Tony Mason, Wray Vamplew and James Walvin, who directed their attention to soccer and horse racing and effectively demonstrated how particular sports can be placed within a broader socio-economic context.[27] It was Mason, perhaps, who succeeded best in performing this task. He produced a very careful analysis of soccer clubs, players and crowds during the late Victorian and Edwardian periods. He threw a useful ray of light on the socio-economic backgrounds of the spectators as well as the soccer professionals. He stressed the role of the academic institutions, pubs and churches in the development of English soccer and examined its economics in much greater depth than had previously been attempted. Despite his unduly modest and cautious attitude, Mason was able to demonstrate how, and why, soccer became so vital a feature of Edwardian life. His work is at once a model and a source of inspiration to the sociologists of sport.

In pursuing his study of soccer, Mason complained about the paucity of his primary sources. But he was far more fortunate than he knew, for there is probably more primary material on Association football than on all the other organized sports in the period on which he focused. Several football clubs became incorporated and formed limited liability companies towards the end of the Victorian age. As such, they had to keep records, however sparse such materials may now appear to the researcher. Cricket clubs did not generally behave in this manner. Even the county cricket clubs tended to be hand-to-mouth operations run by small committees who were accountable to very few people. They published brief annual reports which sometimes appeared in the local newspapers. Otherwise club records for nineteenth-century cricket are frustratingly limited.

Mason was left to depend on the press for the vast bulk of his information. He did not think that this was altogether satisfactory. But the cricket historian, in search of primary materials, is even more completely at the mercy of contemporary journalists. He/she has a slight advantage, however, in that more Victorian cricketers than footballers left memoirs. The cricket coverage in the Victorian press was also considerable. But by far the greatest asset is the extensive body of cricket literature that is readily available. The game has generated more books, and better written books on the whole, than any other. These abundant secondary sources need to be synthesized and properly integrated.

To understand fully what cricket meant to the Victorians, it is necessary to focus initially on the impact of the Georgian legacy, and on this theme useful books have been written by men like G.B. Buckley, J. Nyren, P.F. Thomas and H.T. Waghorn. These authors have provided not only details about matches, clubs and players, but have also left scores of anecdotes which help to illustrate the relationships between wealthy patrons and plebeian performers on the field.[28] They were themselves more interested in cricket than in social history, however. Their works must therefore be supplemented by those of J. Ford, Brian Harrison and R.W. Malcolmson, who have drawn especial attention to the role of peers and publicans in the evolution of Georgian cricket in an age dominated by gambling and corruption.[29]

While it is clear that the Victorians were continuing a Georgian tradition when they played organized cricket, the historian must still seek a satisfactory explanation for the dramatic boom which the game enjoyed after 1860. One of the most vital forces which gave rise to it, as to the sports revolution in general, was undoubtedly the popularity of the cult of athleticism. On this theme some excellent work has already been done by scholars such as Bruce Haley, Tony Mangan and David Newsome.[30]

Some additional clues can definitely be found in a careful study of the histories of clubs at various levels. The county cricket clubs, in this connection, have been excellently served. A veritable army of modern journalists and enthusiasts has produced useful histories of county cricket which have contributed materially to our understanding of the development of the game at the first-class level. It is true that they concentrate more on the events which took place on the field, rather than away from it, but they are nevertheless very good on such important topics as cricket technique, economics, the impact of technology and amateur–professional relationships.[31] From among this imposing list Leslie Duckworth's *The Story of Warwickshire Cricket* must be singled out for special mention. It not only deals with the year-to-year performance of the county cricketers on the field, but contains much useful administrative and financial material and is especially helpful on such important topics as crowds and benefits.

Within the recent past, such publishing firms as Crowood Press, Christopher Helm and Partridge Press in London have added to the number of county cricket stories by producing an impressive array of 'official' histories, with thoughtful introductions and/or forewords by former cricket stars attached to the respective counties. The authors have clearly had freer access to the available club records and have, for the most part, put them to good use – correcting factual errors made by previous writers and filling many vital gaps. The social historian will find particularly useful the studies presented by Brian Bearshaw, Derek Hodgson, David Lemmon, Peter Roebuck and John Shawcroft.[32]

Several local clubs have also been honoured with histories, many of which are brief pamphlets celebrating a centenary or some unusual achievement. They provide a good sample from which sound conclusions can be drawn on significant topics, such as the social structure of teams and the relationships between local patrons and players.[33] Among this group, the most valuable perhaps are the works of Chris Aspin, Richard Binns, A.J. Forrest, George L. Greaves, Gerald Howat, J.L. Hurst and H.F. and A.P. Squire.[34] These books tell us much about social control and class distinctions, Victorian snobbery and paternalism. They also demonstrate that in many villages the cricket club was the focus of an intense loyalty and parochialism. This is also apparent from John Kay's studies on league cricket, a subject about which not enough has yet been written.[35]

The Victorians, in their earnestness, left thousands of autobiographies and monographs. Those who were involved with cricket were no different in this respect from contemporary political leaders. For example, James Pycroft, an Anglican priest, and Charles Box and Fred Gale, two cricket journalists, produced several studies on Victorian cricket.[36] Many players, such as William Caffyn, Richard Daft, C.B. Fry, W.G. Grace, Lord Harris, A.E. Knight, A.A. 'Dick' Lilley, K.S. Ranjitsinhji, Walter Read and

Sir Pelham Warner, among others, left recollections and reminiscences from which a good deal of social history can be gleaned.[37] Arthur Haygarth's monumental *Scores and Biographies* is also an invaluable source, especially on the socio-economic backgrounds of Victorian professional cricketers.[38]

Beyond this mass of Victorian literature, the historian also has at his disposal countless books by twentieth-century commentators who, like James, were very conscious of the role of cricket in English culture. Of these the most famous perhaps are John Arlott and Neville Cardus, even though their best work is mainly relevant to the post-Victorian age.[39] For the purposes of historical sociology, the books by Benny Green, Gerald Brodribb, G.D. Martineau and A.A. Thomson throw the most useful light on the Victorians. Green performed a great service by editing the majority of the volumes of *Wisden*, writing a quaint and somewhat irreverent but incisive history of the game, and producing an excellently edited anthology to demonstrate how close was the relationship between literature and cricket. There is also an amazing wealth of vital information on amateurs, professionals and administrators in his 1986 edition of the major obituaries appearing in *Wisden Cricketers' Almanack* between 1892 and 1985.[40] Brodribb and Martineau are helpful precisely because of their emphasis on the unusual and the odd – as much off the field as on it.[41] And Thomson's studies, albeit confined largely to the north, are nevertheless of incalculable worth.[42]

There are, in addition, many general cricket histories of varying merit. The majority are popular works deliberately aimed at a wide and general audience. A typical example is Trevor Bailey's *A History of Cricket*, published by Allen and Unwin in 1979. While it purports to be a history of the game, it looks too narrowly at its evolution in England during the twentieth century and pays too little attention to cricket developments elsewhere. This, in fact, had been the ambitious project undertaken about a decade earlier by Major Rowland Bowen, who sought valiantly to deal with the growth and development of cricket everywhere. His book, and *English Cricket* by Christopher Brookes, are the most serious of the general histories. While Bowen tried to cast a much wider net, Brookes was mainly concerned with the plight of English professional cricketers. He took pains to demolish some of the myths surrounding the origins of the game, to lament the treatment of cricket professionals over the years and to criticize the MCC for its general lack of leadership and foresight during the Victorian period.[43]

Among the popular histories, by far the most successful is the old classic by H.S. Altham and E.W. Swanton, which has gone through several editions. Its treatment of Victorian cricket is very good. It shows evidence not only of solid research but a thorough grasp of the sociological implications of the game.[44] Many years after collaborating with Altham to update the history which the latter had first published in 1926, Swanton edited the magisterial *World of Cricket* which, to the social historian, is probably more vital than all the other cricket histories combined. This work was updated and reprinted in 1980 under the title of *Barclays World of Cricket*. Encyclopedic in intention and scope, this magnum opus was further revised and expanded in 1986 'to coincide with the bicentenary of MCC'. E.W. Swanton, George Plumptre and John Woodcock, the main editors, succeeded in assembling a fine team of researchers and writers to produce in this massive volume a vital body of information which no social historian, working alone, could possibly have unearthed.[45]

Positive contributions to Victorian cricket historiography have also been made by Richard Cashman, David Frith, Alan Gibson, Maurice Golesworthy, Robin Marlar, John Marshall, Christopher Martin-Jenkins, Ric Sissons and Roy Webber. Cashman has added significantly to our knowledge and understanding of the development of cricket in Australia and India during the Victorian age. His fine biography of Spofforth necessarily throws light also on late nineteenth-century England, whither the 'Demon' had migrated to spend the later part of his life.[46] Most of Frith's books relate to cricket in the twentieth century, but his good biography of Andrew Stoddart, who captained England both at cricket and rugby, is relevant to Victorian studies. So, too, is his interesting examination of the game during the period 1890–1914. In writing about slow and fast bowlers over the years, Frith also makes perceptive observations about the evolution of cricket techniques during the nineteenth century.[47] Gibson performed a yeoman service with his careful research on all the cricket captains of England. His *Jackson's Year*, though focusing primarily on the Edwardian age, contains revealing information on late-Victorian cricketers like 'Dick' Attewell of Nottinghamshire and William Brockwell of Surrey.[48] Golesworthy's encyclopedia is a very handy reference, with useful entries on the major clubs, counties and players of the Victorian era.[49] Marlar, in a fascinating introduction to an old work by Fred Lillywhite on the first cricket tour undertaken by an English team, paints vivid pictures of the professionals who accompanied Lillywhite to Canada and the United States in 1859.[50] Marshall's books on some of the famous cricket grounds in England are very helpful. They contain valuable details about crowds, players, administrators, pavilions, benefits and finances. For similar reasons the modern researcher should also be grateful for his history of Sussex cricket, published in 1959.[51] Useful information on the leading Victorian cricketers is provided by Martin-Jenkins in his bulky but attractive *Who's Who* of international players.[52] Ric Sissons has produced a wonderful study of the professional cricketer through the ages and has added significantly to our knowledge of the professional's lot during the early and mid-Victorian periods. His work builds splendidly on the foundations established so securely in the early 1970s by William Mandle, another Australian historian.[53] And Webber has written very well on the early Australian tours to England as well as the beginnings of the county championship.[54]

In recent years, the social historian has been much assisted by the keen researches of the Association of Cricket Statisticians, led by Philip Bailey, Robert Brooke, Philip Thorn and Peter Wynne-Thomas. This enthusiastic team has ferreted out almost all the personalities who performed in first-class cricket matches during the Victorian age. They have compiled lists of players for the majority of the counties. They also collaborated to produce the mammoth and indispensable *Who's Who* of all those who played first-class cricket in England up to 1983. Although individual entries have necessarily to be brief and to focus narrowly on cricket performance, the directory is most useful because it allows the historian to track down even the most obscure professionals who fell by the wayside after performing briefly for first-class counties.[55]

Among all the various writers who have done much to shape our under-standing of the role of cricket in Victorian life, the three to whom we owe perhaps the greatest debt are William Mandle, Eric Midwinter and Wray Vamplew. In two excellent pioneering articles, Mandle taught us a great deal about Victorian professionals and nineteenth-century approaches to the general question of professionalism in sport. In another instructive essay, he made a number of incisive comments about superstardom and hero-worship in the Victorian age while assessing the unique position which W.G. Grace occupied.[56] Midwinter, in a short but solid biography, succeeded in placing W.G. more squarely in his historical context than any of Grace's previous biographers had been able to do.[57] Vamplew, a naturalized Australian, has made several key contributions. His main strength lies in his ability to analyse cricket from the perspective of an economic historian, while most of the other scholars focusing on that sport have either been social historians or historical sociologists. Vamplew's excellent article on crowd behaviour and controls in the late-Victorian period broke new ground. He was the first writer to delve deeply beneath crowd misconduct to determine some of its basic causes. He then produced a number of germinal essays on the economics of late-Victorian sport, before emerging with his remarkable *tour de force* on professional sport in Britain during 1875–1914.[58]

Any critical study of Victorian cricket must begin with a careful examination of these seminal works. But it must yet depend, to an even greater extent, on the local newspapers and the numerous sporting journals which flourished in Britain after 1870. For the earlier period,

Bell's Life in London is indispensable. It had little competition in those days and its cricket reports are often the sole surviving pieces of evidence. Later in the Victorian age, the *Athletic News, Cricket,* the *Cricket Field* and *Wisden Cricketers' Almanack* are the most vital mines of information. Among these, *Wisden* must always command the greatest respect. Established in 1863 by John Wisden, a professional cricketer, this annual publication has survived until today and is everywhere regarded as the cricketer's bible. *Wisden* has established an enviable reputation for its accuracy and it is impossible to write very much about cricket over the past 130 years without referring to it frequently. This *Cricketers' Almanack* is an absolutely essential source. Also very useful are the *Badminton Magazine,* the *Midland Athlete* and the *Sportsman.* The *Cricket and Football Times* is excellent as far as it goes, but its files in the Colindale Library are incomplete. The leading daily newspapers, like *The Times,* the *Manchester Guardian* and the *Daily Telegraph,* also devoted considerable space to cricket. Apart from the private records of the cricket clubs themselves, these are the most important primary sources, replete with the kind of information that is the very meat and potatoes of social history.

Burrowing through the voluminous files of the Victorian sporting press is hard work, but it is also tremendously rewarding. These sources enable us to recreate a fairly composite picture of the nineteenth-century cricketing world – especially when they are judiciously used alongside the memoirs of such late Victorians as Sir Home Gordon, Sir Henry Leveson Gower and E.H.D. Sewell.[59] Also available, of course, are the numerous cricket books written by that remarkable Edwardian commentator, Frederick S. Ashley Cooper.[60]

In his study of soccer, Mason arrived at a number of hesitant conclusions because he was too conscious of his dependence on the press and the periodicals. He nevertheless demonstrated how these sources can best be utilized. His own handling of the Ibrox tragedy of 1902, when hundreds of spectators were injured, is perhaps his major triumph in this regard.[61] Mason very skilfully showed how newspaper reports could serve as useful guides in a serious analysis of the socio-economic background of soccer crowds. It is true that we are at the mercy of bourgeois observers here. But this has been the essence of historiography from time out of mind. When we read orthodox accounts of British political history or foreign policy before the First World War we are, in effect, digesting secondhand accounts of bourgeois intellectuals.[62] For too long the British proletariat, like its equivalents elsewhere, remained an inarticulate majority. But this circumstance has not hindered the writing of countless volumes of excellent history. We have to exercise caution in our analysis of crowds whose size at spectator sports, before the advent of turnstiles, could not accurately be gauged. It was not always easy for a reporter to estimate the numbers in attendance when the crowd exceeded 5000. It is still historically significant, nevertheless, to learn that early Victorian crowds were even approximately that large. Considering that transportation was enormously difficult before the building of railways, that few cities in Britain boasted 50000 inhabitants during the early Victorian period, and that facilities were seldom adequate to accommodate more than a handful of spectators, any crowd in the neighbourhood of four or five thousand indicated extraordinary interest and enthusiasm prior to 1850. Even as late as 1875 a gathering in excess of 10000 often provided enormous problems for the organizers of a sporting event.

There is less need to be suspicious of Victorian reporters' commenting on the social structure of the audience or the behaviour of the crowd. They were so class-conscious and so obsessed with respectability that they tended to be more observant in such matters than we are now. Perhaps it may be said that their innate snobbery led them sometimes to conclude that cricket crowds were more aristocratic and 'respectable' than was probably the case. This, however, is hard to prove. Equally difficult to prove is that their snobbishness led them to associate unruly behaviour with a lack of proper breeding. Even so, it is noteworthy that rowdyism at soccer matches and on the race course, which prompted occasional reprimands from the press, was usually attributed to the lower orders.[63] How fair this was is hard to judge from this distance. Suffice it to say that crowd composition and conduct were themes which constantly formed the core of newspaper sports reports. Historians should be grateful for that.

What, then, can a new book on Victorian cricket provide that is not already available in published form? It can, first of all, integrate and synthesize, in a novel and necessary fashion, a wide variety of rich cricket literature. *Cricket and the Victorians*, aimed primarily at the student of social history, is intended to illuminate the various and complex ways in which the game was linked to other facets of Victorian culture. Not many authors of cricket literature, with the notable exception of Brookes, Cashman, Green, James, Mandle, Midwinter, Sissons, Brian Stoddart and Vamplew, have deliberately set out with this object in view.

The main purpose of this study is to assess the meaning and role of cricket in Victorian life; to throw additional light on the relationships between and among those individuals who organized, watched and played the game; to emphasize the influence of the Georgian legacy which has so often been neglected by serious scholars; to analyse the impact of muscular Christianity which fed, and in turn fed on, the powerful cricketing craze; to evaluate the contributions of the church, the academic institutions, Dr W.G. Grace, Victorian women and the MCC to the evolution of the modern game; to examine critically the nineteenth-century attitude towards professionalism in sport, while stressing the influence of the professionals in the development of cricket throughout the Victorian era; to comment briefly on the economics of nineteenth-century cricket, while looking also at the size, composition and conduct of cricket crowds during the Victorian age; to assess the impact of industrial technology on cricket technique; and to examine the complex ways in which the national sport linked the colonies to the metropolis.

It is only by pursuing such themes as these that the historian can place cricket effectively within the broader socio-cultural context. Throughout this study, too, cricket is intended to be seen as but a segment of the great movement towards mass leisure which affected the whole of British society during the second half of the nineteenth century. Perhaps by focusing in this way on an individual sport, the book can, it is hoped, lead towards a better understanding of those social attitudes and changing economic circumstances that inspired the Victorians to reshape their patterns of play, leisure and recreation.

The Victorian age is an uncommonly long one, stretching for our current purposes from approximately 1835 to about 1900. As perhaps the most dynamic age in the history of England, it witnessed revolutionary changes in most facets of English life. During that span there were also many millions of Victorians occupying a variety of rungs on a complicated social ladder. These realities present enormous problems for any analyst, but should not prevent the historian from arriving at some well-considered generalizations and drawing some general conclusions about the Victorians and Victorianism.

Notes

1. E.g. Palmerston to Russell, 1 May 1864, Russell Papers, PRO 30/22/15B, fol. 245: claiming to have scored 'a notch off my own bat', when he had spoken rather sternly to the Austrian ambassador without the Cabinet's authorization. Cited in K.A.P. Sandiford, *Great Britain and the Schleswig-Holstein Question*, 1848–64 (Toronto, 1975), 103.
2. L. Frewin, *The Boundary Book* (London, 1962); *The Poetry of Cricket* (London, 1964); and *The Best of Cricket Fiction* (London, 1966). B. Green, ed., *The Cricket Addict's Archive* (Newton Abbot, 1977), 1–83. J.A. Mangan, *Athleticism in the Victorian and Edwardian Public School* (Cambridge, 1981), 141–206.
3. N. Gale, *Cricket Songs* (London, 1894). R. Simon and A. Smart, *The Art of Cricket* (London, 1983).
4. H.S. Altham and E.W. Swanton, *A History of Cricket* (London, 1948), 27–70.
5. This point is well developed by W.E. Houghton, *The Victorian Frame of Mind* (Yale University Press, 1966), 1–89. But it is also noteworthy that although Houghton does refer once (p. 204) to 'muscular Christianity', he

does not have much to say about the cult of athleticism in general or cricket in particular.

6.   W.J. Lewis, *The Language of Cricket* (Oxford, 1938), 57. See also M. Rundell, *The Dictionary of Cricket* (London, 1985), *passim*.
7.   Quoted in N.G. Annan, *Roxburgh of Stowe* (London, 1965), 11.
8.   *Ibid.*, 11–13. T.W. Bamford, *Rise of the Public Schools* (London, 1967), 80–83. A.G. Bradley *et al.*, *A History of Marlborough College* (London, 1923), 250–66. L. Cust, *A History of Eton College* (London, 1899), 244. B.E. Haley, *The Healthy Body and Victorian Culture* (Harvard University Press, 1978), 161–68. P.C. McIntosh, *Physical Education in England since 1800* (London, 1952), 9, 62–69. W.S. Patterson, *Sixty Years of Uppingham Cricket* (London, 1909), 51–55. And especially J.A. Mangan, *Athleticism in the Victorian and Edwardian Public School* (Cambridge, 1981), 68–96.
9.   W.F. Mandle, 'The Professional Cricketer in England in the Nineteenth Century', *Labour History* (1972), 23:8.
10. E.W. Swanton, ed., *The World of Cricket* (London, 1966), 580.
11. *Wisden Cricketers' Almanack* 1870 (London, 7th edition), 17, 66. [Hereinafter *Wisden*.]
12. *Athletic News*, 12 August 1889, 1. *Cricket Field*, 7 May 1892, 3. G.F.H. Berkeley, *My Recollections of Wellington College* (Newport, 1946), 74.
13. See, e.g., *Cricket Field*, 24 August 1895, 423.
14. *Ibid.*, 18 June 1892, 118.
15. *Cricket*, 15 April 1886, 57.
16. *Ibid.*, 5 August 1886, 325.
17. C. Box, *The English Game of Cricket* (London, 1877), 73.
18. Richard Cobden to the Editor of *The Times*, 20 September 1850. Cited in Marcus Williams, ed. *Double Century: 200 Years of Cricket in 'The Times'* (London, 1985), 37.
19. See, e.g., *Cricketers' and Sporting News*, 25 June 1867, 2. *The Times*, 6 July 1863, 5.
20. Swanton, ed., *World of Cricket*, 732.
21. A.A. Thomson, *The Great Cricketer: W.G. Grace* (London, 1968), 32. J.A. Walvin, *Leisure and Society, 1830–1950* (London, 1978), 64–67.
22. G.M. Trevelyan, *English Social History* (London, 1958), 316–17, 407–08, 549. Nor is there much more on cricket in his four volumes of *Illustrated English Social History* (London, 1952).
23. W.J. Baker, 'The Leisure Revolution in Victorian England: A Review of Recent Literature', *Journal of Sport History* (1979), 6: 77. H.J. Dyos and Michael Wolff, eds, *The Victorian City: Images and Realities*, 2 vols (London, 1973).
24. C.L.R. James, *Beyond a Boundary* (Sportsmans Book Club, 1964), 157–83.
25. *Ibid.*, preface.
26. E.g., P.C. Bailey, *Leisure and Class in Victorian England: Rational Recreation and the Contest for Control, 1830–85* (London, 1978). H. Cunningham, *Leisure in the Industrial Revolution* (London, 1980). J. Golby and A.W. Purdue, *The Civilisation of the Crowd: Popular Culture in England 1750–1900* (London, 1984). J. Hargreaves, *Sport, Power and Culture* (Cambridge, 1986). J.M. Hoberman, *Sport and Political Ideology* (London, 1984). J. Lowerson and J. Myerscough, *Time to Spare in Victorian England* (Sussex, 1977). R.W. Malcolmson, *Popular Recreations in English Society, 1700–1850* (Cambridge, 1973). M. Marrus, *The Rise of Leisure in*

Industrial Society (St Charles, 1974). H.E. Meller, *Leisure and the Changing City* (London, 1976). S. Parker, *The Sociology of Leisure* (London, 1976). K. Roberts, *Contemporary Society and the Growth of Leisure* (New York, 1978).

27. T. Mason, *Association Football and English Society 1863–1915* (Sussex, 1980). W. Vamplew, *The Turf: A Social and Economic History of Horse Racing* (London, 1976). J. Walvin, *The People's Game: A Social History of British Football* (Newton Abbot, 1975).

28. G.B. Buckley, *Fresh Light on Eighteenth Century Cricket* (Birmingham, 1935); and *Fresh Light on Pre-Victorian Cricket* (Birmingham, 1937). J. Nyren, *The Young Cricketer's Tutor* (London, 1833); and *Cricketers of My Time* (London, 1833). P.F. Thomas, *Old English Cricket* (London, 1929). H.T. Waghorn, *Cricket Scores 1730–1773* (London, 1899); and *The Dawn of Cricket* (London, 1906).

29. J. Ford, *Cricket: A Social History, 1700–1835* (Newton Abbot, 1972). B. Harrison, *Drink and the Victorians: The Temperance Question in England 1815–1872* (London, 1971). Malcolmson, *Popular Recreations.*

30. B.E. Haley, 'Sports and the Victorian World', *Western Humanities Review* (1968), 12: 115–25; and *The Healthy Body.* Mangan, *Athleticism.* D. Newsome, *Godliness and Good Learning* (London, 1961).

31. E.g., H.S. Altham *et al.*, *Hampshire County Cricket* (London, 1958). R.L. Arrowsmith, *A History of County Cricket: Kent* (Sportsmans Book Club, 1972). W.R. Chignell, *A History of the Worcestershire County Cricket Club* (Worcester, undated). J.D. Coldham, *Northamptonshire Cricket: A History* (London, 1959). L. Duckworth, *The Story of Warwickshire Cricket* (London, 1974). J. Kay, *A History of County Cricket: Lancashire* (Newton Abbot, 1974). J.M. Kilburn, *A History of Yorkshire Cricket* (Sportsmans Book Club, 1971). A.W. Ledbrooke, *Lancashire County Cricket* (London, 1954). L. Newnham, *Essex County Cricket 1875–1976* (Colchester, undated). G. Ross, *The Surrey Story* (London, 1957). J. Shawcroft, *A History of Derbyshire County Cricket Club* (London, 1972). E.E. Snow, *A History of Leicestershire Cricket* (London, 1949). E.M. Wellings, *A History of County Cricket: Middlesex* (Newton Abbot, 1973).

32. See, e.g., B. Bearshaw, *The Official History of Lancashire County Cricket Club* (1990). A. Hignell, *The History of Glamorgan County Cricket Club* (1988). D. Hodgson, *The Official History of Yorkshire County Cricket Club* (1989). C. Lee, *The Official History of Sussex County Cricket Club* (1989). D. Lemmon, *The Official History of Middlesex County Cricket Club* (1988); *The Official History of Worcestershire County Cricket Club* (1989); and *The Official History of Surrey County Cricket Club* (1989). D. Moore, *The History of Kent County Cricket Club* (1988). P. Roebuck, *The Official History of Somerset County Cricket Club* (1991). J. Shawcroft, *The Official History of Derbyshire County Cricket Club* (1989). A. Woodhouse, *The History of Yorkshire County Cricket Club* (1989). P. Wynne-Thomas, *The History of Hampshire County Cricket Club* (1988).

33. E.g., H. and E. Bagshaw, *Great Oakley Cricket: The History of a Village Club* (Northampton, 1964). D.H. Benson, *Harborne Cricket Club 1868–1968* (Birmingham, 1969). K.J. Cole, *Two Hundred Years of Dorking Cricket 1766–1968* (London, 1969). B. Devereux, *Nottingham Forest Amateur Cricket Club 1876–1976: A Century of Cricket* (Nottingham, 1976). G.L. Eames, *Bromley Cricket Club 1820–1970* (Bromley, 1970).

G. Harbottle, *A Century of Cricket in South Northumberland 1864–1969* (Newcastle upon Tyne, 1969). F.R.D'O Monro, *The History of the Hampstead Cricket Club* (London, 1949). A.L. Parsons, *Durham City Cricket Club History* (Durham, 1972). G. Quin, *Cricket in the Meadow: A Short History of the Amersham Cricket Club 1856–1955* (Chesham, 1956). J.H. Rees, *One Hundred Years of Cricket in Gowerton 1880–1980* (Swansea, 1980). The Saltaire Cricket Club, *Souvenir Centenary Booklet 1869–1969* (Saltaire, 1969). B.J. Wakley, *The History of Wimbledon Cricket Club 1854–1953* (Bournemouth, 1954). A. Woodhouse *et al.*, *Cricketers of Wombwell* (Bradford, 1965).

34.   C. Aspin, *Gone Cricket Mad: The Haslingden Club in the Victorian Era* (Manchester, 1976). R. Binns, *Cricket in Firelight* (Sportsmans Book Club, 1955). A.J. Forrest, *Village Cricket* (London, 1957). G.L. Greaves, *Over the Summers Again: A History of Harrogate Cricket Club* (London, 1976). G. Howat, *Village Cricket* (London, 1980). J.L. Hurst, *Century of Penrith Cricket* (Cumberland, 1967). H.F. and A.P. Squire, *Henfield Cricket and its Sussex Cradle* (Hove, 1949).

35.   J. Kay, *Cricket in the Leagues* (London, 1970); 'League Cricket', in E.W. Swanton, ed., *World of Cricket*, 680–711; and 'League Cricket – The North and the Midlands: The Story to 1964', in E.W. Swanton, ed., *Barclays World of Cricket* (London, 1986), 571–75.

36.   Box, *English Game*. F. Gale, *Public School Matches* (London, 1867); *Modern English Sports: Their Use and Abuse* (London, 1885); *Life of Hon. Robert Grimson* (London, 1885); *The Game of Cricket* (London, 1887); *Sports and Recreations in Town and Country* (London, 1888); and *Echoes From Old Cricket Fields* (London, 1896). J. Pycroft, *The Cricket Field* (London, 1851); and *Oxford Memories* (London, 1886).

37.   W. Caffyn, *Seventy-One Not Out* (London, 1899). R. Daft, *Kings of Cricket* (Bristol, 1893); and *A Cricketer's Yarns* (London, 1926). C.B. Fry, *The Book of Cricket* (London, 1900); and *Life Worth Living* (London, 1939). W.G. Grace, *Cricket* (Bristol, 1891); *The History of a Hundred Centuries* (London, 1895); and *Cricketing Reminiscences and Personal Recollections* (London, 1899). Lord Harris, *A Few Short Runs* (London, 1921). A.E. Knight, *The Complete Cricketer* (London, 1906). A.A. Lilley, *Twenty-Four Years of Cricket* (London, 1912). K.S. Ranjitsinhji, *The Jubilee Book of Cricket* (London, 1897). W.W. Read, *Annals of Cricket* (London, 1896). Sir P.F. Warner, *Cricket in Many Climes* (London, 1900); *Book of Cricket* (London, 1946); *Gentlemen vs Players* (London, 1946); *Lord's 1787–1945* (London, 1946); and *Long Innings: An Autobiography* (London, 1953).

38.   A. Haygarth, *Scores and Biographies*, 15 vols (London, 1862–76).

39.   J. Arlott, *From Hambledon to Lord's* (London, 1948); *The Middle Ages of Cricket* (London, 1949); *Concerning Cricket* (London, 1949); and *Rothmans Jubilee History of Cricket 1890–1965* (London, 1965). N. Cardus, *A Cricketer's Book* (London, 1926); *Cricket* (London, 1930); and *English Cricket* (London, 1945).

40.   B. Green, ed., *Cricket Addict; Wisden Anthology 1864–1900* (London, 1979); *Wisden Anthology 1900–1940* (London, 1980); *Wisden Anthology 1940–1963* (London, 1982); *The Wisden Book of Obituaries* (London, 1986); and *A History of Cricket* (London, 1988).

41. G. Brodribb, *All Round the Wicket* (London, 1951); *Next Man In* (Sportsmans Book Club, 1953); and *Hit For Six* (Sportsmans Book Club, 1961). G.D. Martineau, *The Field is Full of Shades* (Sportsmans Book Club, 1954); *Bat, Ball, Wicket and All* (Sportsmans Book Club, 1954); and *They Made Cricket* (Sportsmans Book Club, 1957).

42. A.A. Thomson, *Pavilioned in Splendour* (London, 1956); *Odd Men In* (Sportsmans Book Club, 1959); *Hirst and Rhodes* (Sportsmans Book Club, 1960); *Cricket Bouquet* (London, 1961); *Cricket: The Golden Ages* (Sportsmans Book Club, 1962); *The Great Cricketer: W.G. Grace* (London, 1968); and *Cricket: The Wars of the Roses* (Sportsmans Book Club, 1968).

43. T. Bailey, *A History of Cricket* (London, 1979). R. Bowen, *Cricket: A History of its Growth and Development Throughout the World* (London, 1970). C. Brookes, *English Cricket: The Game and its Players Through the Ages* (Newton Abbot, 1978).

44. Altham and Swanton, *A History of Cricket*.

45. E.W. Swanton, ed., *Barclays World of Cricket* (London, 1980); rev. and considerably expanded in 1986. The 3rd edition represents a great improvement over the original *World of Cricket*, published in 1966.

46. R. Cashman, *Patrons, Players and the Crowd: The Phenomenon of Indian Cricket* (New Delhi, 1980); *'Ave a Go, Yer Mug! Australian Cricket Crowds from Larrikin to Ocker* (Sydney, 1984); and *The 'Demon' Spofforth* (New South Wales, 1990).

47. D. Frith, *The Fast Men* (Newton Abbot, 1976); *My Dear Victorious Stod* (London, 1977); *The Golden Age of Cricket 1890–1914* (London, 1978); and *The Slow Men* (New South Wales, 1984).

48. A. Gibson, *Jackson's Year* (Sportsmans Book Club, 1966); and *The Cricket Captains of England* (London, 1970).

49. M. Golesworthy, *The Encyclopaedia of Cricket* (Sportsmans Book Club, 1964).

50. F. Lillywhite, *The English Cricketers' Trip to Canada and the United States in 1859* (London, 1860; repr. in 1980 by World's Work Ltd, with an introduction by R. Marlar).

51. J. Marshall, *Lord's* (London, 1970); *Headingley* (Newton Abbot, 1972); *Old Trafford* (Newton Abbot, 1973); and *Sussex Cricket: A History* (London, 1959).

52. C. Martin-Jenkins, *The Complete Who's Who of Test Cricketers* (London, 1983). This is a rev. version of the study which first appeared in 1980.

53. R. Sissons, *The Players: A Social History of the Professional Cricketer* (London, 1988).

54. R. Webber, *The Australians in England* (London, 1953); *The County Cricket Championship* (Sportsmans Book Club, 1958); and *The Phoenix History of Cricket* (Sportsmans Book Club, 1961).

55. P. Bailey, P. Thorn and P. Wynne-Thomas, *Who's Who of Cricketers* (London, 1984). See also, e.g., the *Derbyshire Cricketers 1871–1981* (1982); *Hampshire Cricketers, 1800–1982* (1983); *Kent Cricketers 1834–1983* (1984); *Northamptonshire Cricketers 1905–1984* (1985); *Yorkshire Cricketers 1863–1985* (1986); *Essex Cricketers 1876–1986* (1987); *Glamorgan Cricketers 1888–1987* (1988); *Lancashire Cricketers 1865–1988* (1989); and *Sussex Cricketers 1815–1990* (1991), produced by the Association of Cricket Statisticians during a ten-year span.

56. W.F. Mandle, 'The Professional Cricketer'; and 'Games People Played: Cricket and Football in England and Victoria in the late Nineteenth Century', *Historical Studies* (1973), 15: 511–35. See also his 'W.G. Grace as a Victorian Hero', *Historical Studies* (1981), 19: 353–68.

57. E.C. Midwinter, *W.G. Grace: His Life and Times* (London, 1981).

58. W. Vamplew, 'Sports Crowd Disorder in Britain, 1870–1914: Causes and Controls', *Journal of Sport History* (1980), 7: 5–20; 'Playing for Pay: The Earnings of Professional Sportsmen in England 1870–1914', in R. Cashman and M. McKernan, eds, *Sport: Money, Morality and the Media* (New South Wales, 1982), 104–30; 'Profit or Utility Maximisation? Analysis of English County Cricket before 1914', in W. Vamplew, ed., *Economic History of Leisure* (South Australia, 1983); 'Close of Play: Career Termination in English Professional Sport 1870–1914', *Canadian Journal of the History of Sport* (1984), 15: 64–79; 'Not Playing the Game: Unionism in British Professional Sport 1870–1914', *British Journal of Sports History* (December 1985), 2: 232–47; and *Pay Up and Play the Game: Professional Sport in Britain, 1875–1914* (Cambridge, 1988).

59. Sir H. Gordon, *Background of Cricket* (London, 1939). Sir H. Leveson Gower, *Off and On the Field* (London, 1953). E.H.D. Sewell, *Cricket Under Fire* (London, undated).

60. F.S. Ashley Cooper, *Gentlemen vs Players* (Bristol, 1900); *Chats on the Cricket Field* (London, 1910); *Edward Mills Grace, Cricketer* (London, 1916); *Eton vs Harrow at the Wicket* (London, 1922); *Kent County Cricket* (London, 1923); *Nottingham Cricket and Cricketers* (Nottingham, 1923); *Derbyshire County Cricket* (London, 1924); *Gloucestershire County Cricket* (London, 1924); *Hampshire County Cricket* (London, 1924); *The Hambledon Cricket Chronicle, 1772–96* (Nottingham, 1924); and *Cricket Highways and Byways* (London, 1927).

61. Mason, *Association Football*, 155–57.

62. The majority of Victorian cricket reporters might not have been properly described as 'intellectuals', but any list which includes Charles Box, C. Stewart Caine, C.B. Fry, Fred Gale, Rev. H.S. Holmes, Archie MacLaren, Charles H. Pardon, Arthur Porritt, A.W. Pullin and Rev. Pycroft must certainly be considered bourgeois.

63. See, e.g., *The Times*, 3 May 1871, 12. The *Sporting Mirror*, 25 July 1892, 6. The *Athletic News*, 5 January 1886, 4.

CHAPTER TWO

The Georgian Legacy

Social historians have rightly stressed the tremendous impact of industrialization on all aspects of British life and their example has been followed in recent years by most of the pioneers in the study of leisure. Hugh Cunningham, however, emerged over a decade ago with a very wise and timely word of caution: while we cannot fail to notice the influence of urbanization and its concomitant stresses, we should not undervalue the force of continuity. Indeed, he concluded that there was more continuity than innovation in British leisure patterns during the nineteenth century.[1] Nowhere can this thesis be better demonstrated than in the history of Victorian cricket, which was one of the three major sports that changed least in the post-Hanoverian age. The other two were boxing and horse racing. But at least in boxing the end of the long-winded bare-knuckle contest, with its endless rounds and knock-downs, was enough to mark a significant turning-point, as was the division of the combatants according to weight. The acceptance of the more gentlemanly Queensbury Rules separated Georgian forms of pugilism from modern boxing. The reforms implemented by the Jockey Club during the nineteenth century were also important enough to leave an indelible imprint on horse racing.

The Victorians inherited a sophisticated brand of cricket which they did surprisingly little to transform. By 1835, the implements of the game had been modernized. Bats, balls and stumps were much the same then as they are now. The laws, first codified in 1744, and later repeatedly revised by the MCC, were not substantially different from those with which we are now familiar. A third stump had been found necessary before the end of the eighteenth century, and the curved bat had given way to the straighter version now still in vogue.[2]

In short, cricket as it was played at the beginning of the Victorian age was not much different from the game being played today. The more colourful costumes reflected the fashions of the Georgian era and the pitches were rather ill-prepared. The outfield was bumpy, bushy, rocky and dangerous. The modern pavilions had not yet been built. Grounds had not yet become enclosed and, in comparison with twentieth-century standards, the game was poorly organized at all levels. International competition was as yet unknown and the county championship belonged to the future. These were the areas in which the Victorian cricketers were to do their best and most innovative work.

It must be emphasized, however, that the Georgians left very solid cricket foundations upon which the Victorians could later build. Already, in fact, they had given up the original form of rolling the ball along the pitch and were experimenting with round-arm bowling. Their underhand bowlers had discovered effective ways of persuading the ball to spin and to break in controllable directions after pitching, and they knew enough about the science of bowling to appreciate the value of length and line. The new round-arm bowlers carried this science even further.

In response to the progressive challenges posed by the steadily shifting bowling styles and patterns, the Georgian batsmen emerged with additional scoring strokes and had already, by 1835, invented such modern strokes as the cut and the drive. Such stars as 'Silver' Billy Beldham, William Fennex and Harry Walker had also shown the value of footwork. The early Hanoverian style of rolling the ball as fast as possible along the turf had rendered footwork secondary. Most batsmen in the eighteenth century had consequently seen no need for mobility at the crease.[3] It was the introduction of underarm lobs, with leg breaks and off-spin, which steadily compelled the later Georgian batsmen to focus as much on length as on line. In essence, it was the steady advances made in the theory and science of bowling, with a new emphasis on varying the pace, pitch, trajectory and spin, that produced more and more sophisticated batting during the first third of the nineteenth century. The addition of the third stump, coupled with the promulgation of more stringent laws of obstruction, also forced the later Georgian batsmen to formulate superior strategies.

In a word, the Georgian cricket legacy included scientific underarm bowling, already moving towards the round-arm variety, and equally scientific batting techniques, despite the absence of modern pads and gloves for the batsman's protection. The emphasis, in Georgian cricket, was on the scoring of as many runs as possible. The object of the game was, and still is, to outscore the opponents in two innings. Two batsmen operated together as partners, each occupying a crease at either end of the pitch which was already 22 yards long. The batsmen had to place their hits into the gaps between the fieldsmen and cross safely to the opposite crease for runs to be scored. Thus a single run would take the hitter down to the bowler's end and leave his partner to face the bowling. Each bowler could deliver only four balls at one turn and each bowler's turn was called an 'over'. At the end of an over, a colleague then bowled from the opposite end. An expert batsman could thus monopolize the bowling by scoring a single run (or any *odd* number of runs) off the last ball of each over. The innings ended when the last surviving batsman ran out of partners.

The Victorians saw no need to change these basic features of Georgian cricket. They preserved the vast majority of the old rules, eventually allowing any bowler to use both ends of the pitch – so long as he did not bowl two overs in succession. As the century progressed, the Victorians increased the number of balls in one over from four to five and eventually to six. It was the Georgians, too, who established that the normal size of the cricket team should be 11 members. The Victorians copied this principle but continued for many years to allow weak teams to field as many as 22 players in second-class matches against strong elevens.[4] By the end of the century, however, matches between arithmetically unbalanced sides had become increasingly rare.

The game had reached this level of sophistication by the end of the Georgian era precisely because it had been played and promoted by aristocrats and capitalists. Cricket seems to have evolved essentially as a rural form of recreation dominated by workers and children. This, in the view of some historians at least, served to explain the paucity of early records and documents.[5] But, from early in the eighteenth century, it received encouragement from publicans, priests and squires and became so popular that the various laws by which it had historically and regularly been banned could never be effectively enforced.

Like most Georgian activities, cricket was the source of much gambling, corruption and chicanery. There was therefore considerable opposition to it – especially from the emerging Methodists, who felt that it was an immoral waste of energy and time. Some members of the wealthier classes objected to cricket because it seemed to encourage the intermingling of the élite and the multitude. There were also those individuals who regarded the game as at once a threat to private property and public order since it attracted crowds too large to be controlled by the local magistrates. There were others, of course, who objected to cricket on the ground that it was too often played in violation of the Sabbath. Many observers in the later Georgian period also felt that although the game was innocuous enough, it too easily lent itself to the worst forms of vice.[6] Such resistance failed to deter the growth of cricket in the eighteenth century. It had simply acquired too large and too influential a following by the time of George III's accession.

Foremost among those who promoted cricket in the eighteenth century was Frederick Louis, the Prince of Wales, who predeceased his father, George II, in 1751. It was he who established durable links between Crown and cricket that were to serve the game extremely well. Neither his father nor his son showed much enthusiasm for the sport, but his brother, the infamous 'Butcher' Cumberland, and the majority of his grandchildren most certainly did.[7] George IV took a keen interest in cricket, as did his brothers the Dukes of York and Clarence. The latter, who was destined to ascend the throne with the title of William IV, served as the patron of the Royal Clarence Cricket Club, founded in 1828. Just before his death in 1837, he contributed £20 towards the founding of the Sussex County Cricket Club, in the hope of encouraging 'the manly exercise of cricket, as a game which so peculiarly belongs to this country'.[8] This tradition of royal involvement in British cricket was later continued by Albert, the Prince Consort, and the majority of Queen Victoria's offspring.

Cricket prospered because of royal support in an age when the monarchy was expected to offer leadership in social matters. But it would still not have been so triumphant had it not been for the enthusiasm of the Georgian aristocracy, especially in the southeast of England. The leading nobles in Kent, Hampshire and Sussex did most to keep the game alive in the eighteenth century.

In Kent the Duke of Dorset (who is reputed to have spent £1,000 per annum on his 'stable of professionals'), the Earl of Darnley and Sir Horatio Mann were the major cricket forces just before the Napoleonic age.[9] The Duke of Richmond and the Earls of Bridgewater, Burlington, Middlesex, Sandwich, Tankerville and Winchelsea did much to make cricket a fashionable sport in the southeast.[10] In this they were ably supported by wealthy squires such as Frederick Beauclerk, George Osbaldeston and William Ward – notwithstanding their character and reputation.[11] A vital role in the ascendancy of cricket was played also by the publicans who became very important promoters of the game. Several cricket clubs, in fact, revolved around the alehouses and inns which dotted the Georgian landscape. As Brian Harrison has remarked, it was the liquor interest which, as usual, led the way in providing recreation and leisure facilities for the multitude.[12] A very observant Victorian, Rev. James Pycroft, in trying to explain the early success of Kentish cricketers, put it down to the curious fact that cricket tended to follow the path of ale rather than whisky.[13] Richard Nyren, the famous innkeeper at the Bat and Ball, in Hambledon, was also prominent in the early history of cricket.[14]

The public schools played a significant role, too, in popularizing cricket towards the end of the Georgian era. Although the records are sparse, it is known that Eton and Harrow were opposing each other regularly before the end of the eighteenth century. Dr Keate, the renowned Eton headmaster, strangely tried his best to discourage the Eton–Harrow cricket rivalry in the 1820s even though he himself had played in a similar match in 1791. He signally failed. That contest became an annual fixture at Lord's after 1822. By the 1820s, Charterhouse, Rugby and Winchester were already playing cricket frequently and in earnest. Public school alumni continued to play the game in their manhood and did much to establish cricket as a respectable pastime.[15]

The same is true of the Universities of Cambridge and Oxford. Georgian undergraduates played a good deal of cricket before the annual classic at Lord's was established in 1827.[16] Graduates, who were among the social and political leaders of the period, gave much encouragement to the game in their old age.

The Georgian era thus witnessed the growth of cricket at the academic institutions and in clubs mainly sponsored by public houses. It also saw the birth of county cricket. As early indeed as 1697 there was mention in the *Foreign Post* of a Sussex XI; and in 1735 a match was arranged between the Gentlemen of Sussex and the Gentlemen of Kent, suggesting that certainly by the early part of the eighteenth century the workers and children in the southeast had lost their dominant position in English cricket. The game flourished in Sussex throughout the eighteenth century and even more so after the Prince of Wales (later George IV) presented Brighton with a cricket ground in the northern section of the town. The county was strong enough, in fact, to defeat the rest of England in two of three experimental matches played in 1827. Eventually, the first Sussex County Cricket Club was officially organized in 1836. It was re-formed in 1839, and again in 1857. By the beginning of the Victorian age, then, the idea of a county cricket club had taken firm root there.[17]

It was the same in Kent, which actually played its first game against Surrey in 1709 and participated in two matches against London in 1719. It also opposed Sussex for the first time in 1728. Kent played several games thereafter, first under the aegis of the Sackvilles, and later under that of the Blighs. Cricket seems to have been hardest hit there by the Napoleonic Wars, for there occurred 'a long break in the regular sequence of Kent matches' lasting from 1796 to 1834. After the departure of the Duke of Dorset, who was appointed ambassador to Paris in 1783, Kent also lacked the necessary patrons.[18]

Hampshire, Middlesex and Surrey had also taken the field by the 1730s.[19] Surrey became strong enough to defeat the rest of England by two wickets in a thrilling contest in 1749. Several matches were arranged by that county during 1773–1810 before a rather inexplicable and lengthy slump took place from 1810 to about 1845.[20] Hampshire cricket throve during the second half of the eighteenth century. That county soundly defeated Kent, Surrey and Sussex in the 1760s, by which time it was clearly the strongest team in England.[21]

The cricket boom in Hampshire during the Georgian period was due in no small measure to the rise of Hambledon, one of the most famous clubs in the history of the game. This historic institution owed its original success to a somewhat curious alliance between a publican and a priest. The legendary innkeeper, Richard Nyren, served for many years as its secretary and captain and was its acknowledged 'head and right arm'.[22] But he could never have established so powerful a cricket club without the assistance of the influential Rev. Charles Powlett, son of the Duke of

Bolton, who remained one of Hambledon's stewards throughout its glorious history.[23]

The great Hambledon Cricket Club, with its headquarters at Broadhalfpenny Down (before its migration to Windmill Down in 1782), dominated Georgian cricket for at least a generation. It was everywhere acknowledged as the leading force in the game before the emergence of the MCC during the Napoleonic age. It differed from the other strong teams of those days in that its original members all lived within a 20-mile radius of Broadhalfpenny Down. It did not, in other words, depend on the importation of players as was the custom among its major rivals.[24]

The majority of first-class Georgian teams, indeed, appear to have been makeshift combinations hastily assembled by well-to-do patrons to play for high stakes. There was little by way of structure or organization. This may well tell us something about the more informal approach of an essentially agrarian community. It is probably also a reflection of Georgian independence and individualism. Be that as it may, it was Hambledon which led the way in the establishment of a more modern club structure. Nyren served as its chief executive officer. Its members were elected and had to pay an annual subscription of three guineas, which was well beyond the means of the working classes. Hambledon members, albeit drawn from the ranks of the squirearchy, were nevertheless subject to fines and strict discipline.[25]

Hambledon prospered in the beginning because of these regulations and the influence of its patrons. Among its members it boasted the Dukes of Albemarle, Dorset and Lennox, and the Earl of Tankerville. Its aristocratic membership made it respectable as well as wealthy. It also played successful cricket partly because of that highly developed sense of parochialism which inspired its players to represent their native district to the best of their talents. In the ten years following 1771, they won 29 of 51 contests against first-class opposition, including sometimes even the rest of England. The club became markedly less successful when it began to import professionals from other districts. It also declined towards the end of the century with the death or retirement of its original supporters.[26]

Hambledon would perhaps have declined in any event once the MCC had been launched. This rival, founded in London in 1787, enjoyed all the advantages of proximity to the nation's capital.[27] It soon attracted the chief players and patrons in the country. Its influence sprang largely from its respectability. It was also a very successful club because it could afford to hire the best professionals. Yet, as Brookes has emphasized, it suffered for many years from the absence of a decent administrative structure and was too dependent on the entrepreneurial skill of Thomas Lord and James Dark.[28] It cannot, however, be denied that it enjoyed a lofty reputation and was expected to provide leadership, especially in the important field of interpreting and promulgating the laws of the game.

If cricket looked to the aristocratic Hambledon and then Marylebone for guidance at that time, it was not behaving in a peculiar manner. It was the landed squires and aristocrats who led the rest of the society in politics, fashion, leisure and agricultural improvements. They were an active rather than an ornamental élite. In cricket they played the game and encouraged others to do likewise. They also paid commoners rather handsomely to play it much better than they themselves were capable of doing.

Thus the majority of Georgian cricketers were not aristocrats at all. Many of them were not even gentlemen. Some of the best players in the eighteenth century were carpenters and wheelwrights like, for example, William Ashley, Andrew Freemantle and Thomas Sueter.[29] John Wells was a baker, Stephen Dingate a barber, Hodswell a tanner and Cutbush a clockmaker. It was, in fact, the hired hand who, in the service of the great patron, made the more telling contribution to the evolution of Georgian cricket.

Already the distinction between gentleman and player, amateur and professional, had become well established by 1835. In fact, the series between the Gentlemen and the Players at Lord's, which survived until 1962, was inaugurated in 1806. The professionals were so much better than the gentlemen that the latter had occasionally to be given all kinds of odds. Indicative of the imbalance at the beginning of the nineteenth century was the fact that only four amateurs played (and achieved very little) in the great match at Lord's in 1807 when Surrey defeated England.[30] Lord Frederick Beauclerk batted well enough to help the amateurs' cause for a while. But even the great Alfred Mynn, considered by many to be the most gifted cricketer prior to the advent of W.G. Grace, lacked the necessary support to redress the balance in the 1830s.[31] For years the players remained too good for the gentlemen. It took the extraordinary talents of the mighty Grace to produce more even competition after 1865.

The majority of professional cricketers in the Georgian era were skilled artisans, some of whom came from relatively 'prestigious' families at the local level. This is a point much emphasized by Brookes who is at pains to show that the great Georgian cricket teams included hardly any unskilled labourers at all. Many of the cricketers belonged to the lower middle classes or better. Peter Stewart, for example, was a publican; George Lee a brewer; and the Beldhams, Brett and Lambert were all farmers. Among the skilled tradesmen who were retained by cricket nabobs were Edward Aburrow, William Barber, Noah Mann, Richard Purchase, John Small and the Walkers – all of whom were engaged in 'respectable occupations'.[32]

Brookes thought it necessary to stress their socio-economic roots to show that the Georgians were no more egalitarian than the Victorians who came after them. It was, in his view, relatively easy for an aristocrat to mingle with a respectable artisan on the cricket field even if his sense of class and status might have been offended by having to play with and against a non-skilled worker. This might well have been true in some cases. It is well known, however, that a common interest, such as cricket or bridge, can often transcend socio-economic boundaries. In any case, as the Victorians were to demonstrate later on, intermingling on the cricket field did not necessarily entail the removal of class barriers.

At all events, it appears that the rise of professionalism in cricket during the Hanoverian period was due almost entirely to the aristocratic propensity for gambling. It became increasingly necessary to assemble the strongest possible team when matches were being played for astronomical stakes. Wagering reached its peak in Britain during the period 1720–1835.[33] It was much encouraged by the emergence of dice and cards, and perhaps reflected a certain sense of security after the political upheavals of the seventeenth century and the long struggles against Louis XIV of France. Many wealthy men, such as the Duke of York and Charles James Fox, are reputed to have squandered fortunes during this age of the betting craze. Cards, dice, cricket, boxing and horse racing were the fields which then offered the biggest temptations to the gamblers.[34]

In fact, all the great cricket matches of the Georgian age were played for high stakes. The stake was then the very essence of the game, far more important than the mythical ashes of our own time. The powerful Hambledon team of the 1770s, for instance, won £22,000 for its backers in recorded stakes as against the £10,000 which it lost.[35] Sometimes as much as 1,000 guineas was wagered on a single game, and Lord Frederick Beauclerk claimed to have made in excess of 600 guineas per annum for betting on cricket matches, in many of which he himself participated.[36] This was actually more than he could have derived at the beginning of the nineteenth century from his calling as a vicar of Redbourne.[37]

With so much money at stake, the game exposed itself to all kinds of chicanery and must surely have been prohibited by law during the Wesleyan era of moral retrenchment had it not been for the strength of the cricket interest in the British parliament. If the Evangelicals failed to suppress cricket, they at least succeeded in emancipating it from the stigma of corruption during the early Victorian age. Cricket, like boxing and horse racing, came under very critical scrutiny. The purifying of the game was part of the new morality which steadily governed the nation after 1835.[38] Thus could Frederick Gale, James Pycroft and Anthony Trollope heartily rejoice later on over the disappearance of dangerous betting from the cricket field.[39]

Georgian cricket inevitably reflected Georgian manners and morals. If

Beauclerk and Lambert were accused of bribery and corruption towards the end of the Hanoverian period, the same fate had befallen Sir Robert Walpole and others in the political arena at the beginning of it. Samuel Redgate, too, was typifying the habits and attitudes of his generation when, on one occasion in the 1830s, he drank a glass of brandy at the fall of each wicket when he dismissed three famous batsmen in the space of four deliveries.[40] He was an excellent bowler who was also a notorious alcoholic. His opponents therefore rendered him ineffective by freely passing the tankard, and his cricket career was one of unfortunate brevity as a consequence.[41]

To dwell, however, on the misfortunes and the misdeeds of players like Beauclerk, Lambert, Osbaldeston and Redgate would create a misleading picture of pre-Victorian cricket. If playing the game for high stakes led undoubtedly to immoral behaviour, it also produced some positive effects. It resulted, in the first place, in the rapid improvement of cricket technique. Secondly, it caused the rich patrons to treat their professional cricketers with unusual generosity and kindness. As a result, professionalism in cricket took very deep root and could not possibly be eradicated by the Victorians even though they never did take kindly to the notion of playing for pay.

Many patrons retained their cricketers, long after they had retired from the game, in nominal positions as estate or household servants. This was the happy fate, for example, of Budd, Dingate, Green, Pye and Waymark who were all eventually retained by the Duke of Richmond. The Duke of Dorset engaged Miller and Brown as gamekeepers and Minshul as a gardener. Boxall was employed by Stephen Amhurst in his later days 'as a tide waiter at Purfleet'.[42] Sir Horatio Mann enticed James Aylward from Hambledon to be his bailiff in Kent.[43] Rev. John Mitford employed old Fennex as a gardener on his estate in Suffolk thus providing him with a home in his last years.[44] The Earl of Tankerville, one of the early patrons of Surrey cricket, employed 'Lumpy' Stevens as a gardener and William Bedster as a butler. He also found employment on his estate for William Yalden, a noted wicketkeeper for Surrey and England in matches against Hambledon and Kent in the second half of the eighteenth century.[45]

Professional cricketers were, on the whole, much better treated by the Georgians than by their successors. There were fewer of them, as there were far fewer opportunities than those which opened up in the Victorian age, but they seemed subject to fewer stresses and strains. The Georgian player did not have to view his retirement from the game with the same sense of dread and anxiety as his Victorian counterpart. The eighteenth-century patron manifested as a rule a greater sense of loyalty and affection towards his retainers. It is therefore not surprising that so many Georgian professional cricketers lived so long. Fennex, for example, survived beyond 80; Budd died at 89; and Beldham lived almost to 100.[46] This sort of longevity stands out in stark contrast to the tragically early death which so many Victorian players were to suffer. No doubt the pressure of competing for a place in a much tougher market took its toll. Part of the problem here sprang from the fact that whereas the Georgian patrons bestowed their kindnesses on individual *players*, the great Victorian patrons were more generous in their treatment of cricket *clubs*.

That cricket was popular in the Georgian age is no longer open to doubt, but it is still very difficult for the social historian to deal confidently with its appeal to pre-Victorian crowds. There is too little evidence of actual attendance, and even less on crowd composition and behaviour. It seems clear, however, that cricket had already become a spectator sport by the nineteenth century. Hambledon is reputed to have attracted as many as 20000 in the 1780s.[47] Considering the difficulties of travel, however, and the absence of adequate facilities to accommodate such a crowd either at Broadhalfpenny Down or Windmill Down, such estimates must be regarded as ridiculously generous. More credible is the estimate of the size of the crowd which is reported to have watched a match free at Mallings, in Sussex, in 1830. The reporters thought that some 8000 persons were in attendance.[48] Such audiences inevitably forced the Georgians to invent gate receipts and to introduce the habit of charging admission fees in order to help pay the professionals. Thus when Sussex met the rest of England at Lord's in 1827, it was reported that approximately £250 was collected by charging the spectators 6d. each.[49]

The most that can now be said about Georgian cricket crowds is that they were in general noisier and less inhibited than their Victorian descendants. They took to the race course and the cricket field a certain carnival spirit and atmosphere which was then in keeping with the feast days and festivals of the agrarian calendar. They were perhaps more unmanageable than unruly, since few cricket grounds then boasted the necessary amenities for proper crowd control and accommodation. It seems clear also that no techniques existed for deliberately excluding the masses once the game had got under way. The evidence seems to indicate that all classes of people watched the important matches – especially since admission charges were irregular and perhaps even impossible to collect. It was almost pointless to insist on admission fees before the erection of the necessary fences, enclosures, pavilions, stands, boundaries and turnstiles. It must also be remembered that pre-Victorian crowds were materially restricted by the quality of the available transportation. Travel was extremely hazardous before the advent of the railway, and it was this as much as anything else which ultimately crippled Hambledon.

Notwithstanding these enormous handicaps, the Georgian cricket legacy was substantial. It was during this period that the game established most of its modern laws and features. The idea of county competition, essentially a pre-industrial concept, took very firm root. Club cricket competition, following the Hambledon model, has not yet disappeared. The great rivalries between Eton and Harrow, Cambridge and Oxford, North and South, and Gentlemen and Players all survived for considerable periods. Professionalism became so deeply embedded in Georgian cricket that the Victorians never even contemplated its suppression, although they valiantly tried to eliminate it from soccer and succeeded at least officially in restricting rugby union football to amateurs. The MCC, by the end of the Georgian period, had superseded Hambledon as the dominant cricket club, even if it was the latter which left the more enduring lessons about club structure and administration. The huge cricket stakes were steadily eradicated after 1835, but it was the great Georgian gamblers who demonstrated how cricket might in time be commercialized.

A significant feature of the Georgian legacy was the remarkable growth of women's cricket. There are several reports in the contemporary newspapers of important matches involving women. In June 1793, for example, a Married Women's XI defeated eleven Maidens by 80 runs in a contest on Bury Common which was staged apparently as a trial match for the selection of a Bury XI to challenge an All England women's team.[50] In October 1811, *The Times* followed the fortunes of a 'Cricket-match Extraordinary' at Ball's-pond, Newington, between the Women of Hampshire and the Women of Surrey, which the former won by '15 notches'. The females on this occasion were sponsored by 'two amateur Noblemen of the respective counties, for five hundred guineas a side'.[51] In September 1835, Eleven Single Women defeated Eleven Married Women by seven runs in a match at Parson's Green in Middlesex, thereby 'earning themselves £20 and a hot supper'.[52] But notices of such matches became increasingly rare thereafter.

Different notions about femininity persuaded the Victorians to abandon female cricket for about 50 years. They were very willing, however, to accept the other aspects of the Georgian cricket legacy. They adopted the Georgian infant, as it were, clothed it in uniquely Victorian garb, and passed it on to posterity with most of its Georgian elements basically intact. Thus can cricket still be seen, especially by twentieth-century North Americans, as a somewhat quaint and rustic anomaly in a highly urbanized age. Regrettably, there is a good deal of truth in this caricature.

During the eighteenth century, given the quality and condition of the pitches and the general level of play, cricket matches could be brought to a summary conclusion in a single day. Scores were low and it was not difficult to effect 20 dismissals within a matter of hours. As the science of batsmanship improved, however, individuals began to aim at centuries and the later Georgians occasionally had to return on a second day to complete an important match. As early as the 1760s, the great Hambledon CC was winning matches by as many as 200 runs and, in 1785, the White Conduit Club defeated the Gentlemen of Kent by 304.[53] On a memorable afternoon in July 1820, William Ward scored a mammoth 278 against Norfolk at Lord's to establish a new record for an individual innings.[54] But even in the face of these developments, the Victorians saw no need to alter the laws of cricket. When the science of groundsmanship improved to the point where pitches were as smooth as glass and batsmen could score more readily against the fastest bowlers, all the Victorians were prepared to do was to increase the amount of time necessary to play a first-class game. By the end of the nineteenth century, really big matches, which had previously occupied one or two afternoons, were now spread out over three days. All first-class matches played in England during the late Victorian era were thus scheduled to last about 18 hours.

The Australians, however, were no more enterprising. Recognizing that their pitches were conducive to somewhat higher scoring than was the norm in England, they simply extended the time in which to complete their first-class fixtures. Thus, as early as March 1877, they scheduled the second Test against England to last for four days.[55] It took five days to complete the only Test match played between those two countries during the 1887–88 tour and by 1891, it was agreed that Tests between England and Australia in Australia would be scheduled to last for 30 hours.[56] But it was not before 1930 that England could be persuaded to play even four-day Tests at home. When that series still remained tied 1–1 (with two draws) after four games, it took six days to complete the fifth Test which was, by prior agreement, 'played to a finish'.[57]

All of these regulations were but relics of a bygone era and they persisted after 1880, in spite of the disconcerting fact that an increasingly significant percentage of first-class matches were ending in draws. Had the Victorians not been overly committed to Georgian forms of cricket, they might well have seen the necessity to readjust the sport in keeping with the needs of an urban and industrial society. One obvious response to the growing confidence and expertise of the players and the groundsmen was to reshape cricket in such a manner as to guarantee a positive result within one afternoon of intense and businesslike play. Like soccer and all other modern sports, cricket could easily have been limited in time and space. The original allocation of 11 men and two innings could have been retained, while imposing limits on the number of balls delivered. Thus, a first-class match, scheduled to last for no more than two days, could have been restricted to a maximum of 60 or 70 overs an innings. An international Test match of greater importance could have been extended to three days, with each side being limited to 100 overs per innings. This would have guaranteed more enterprising play and allowed cricket, as a commercialized spectator sport, to compete on more even terms with soccer and horse racing in the late- and post-Victorian periods.

Even as late as 1913, however, the editor of *Wisden* could still argue that 'cricket does not stand in need of alterations . . . it must not be tampered with to please people who vainly think that it can have the concentrated excitement of an hour-and-a-half's football'.[58] It took many decades of financial misery on the part of English county clubs before cricket administrators could be persuaded to stage one-day matches of limited overs. This experiment, begun rather hesitantly among the counties in 1963, has now spread to all parts of the world. One-day Internationals have become an integral part of first-class cricket. But they are still regarded as separate from, and basically inferior to, the five-day Tests – notwithstanding the exciting quality of the play and the financial success of a sequence of World Cups since 1975.

Such was the awesome power of the impact of the Georgian legacy. By remaining so true to its pre-industrial origins, cricket has done much to stifle its own growth and popularity in the modern world. The Europeans have shown a clear preference for soccer and the Americans for baseball. Beyond the boundaries of a certain segment of the Commonwealth, cricket remains but a dull and cryptic ritual.

Notes

1. Cunningham, *Leisure in the Industrial Revolution*, 9–10.
2. Altham and Swanton, *A History of Cricket*, 27–32. Bowen, *Cricket: A History*, 68–78. D. Lemmon, *Surrey County Cricket Club*, 6.
3. Altham and Swanton, 48–49. Lemmon, *Surrey County Cricket Club*, 6. T. Lewis, *Double Century: The Story of MCC and Cricket* (London, 1987), 33, 48.
4. Altham and Swanton, 65–70.
5. See, e.g., Brookes, *English Cricket*, 9–23. Ford, *Cricket: A Social History*, 15.
6. Altham and Swanton, 38–39. Malcolmson, *Popular Recreations*, 105–06, 160–63.
7. Altham and Swanton, 34. Ford, 144–51. Lemmon, *Surrey County Cricket Club*, 6–8.
8. M. Williams, ed., *Double Century: 200 Years of Cricket in 'The Times'* (London, 1985), 22. Ford, 147–51.
9. Arrowsmith, *A History of County Cricket: Kent*, 16–24. Lewis, 37.
10. Altham and Swanton, 31–40. Ford, 51. Lemmon, *Surrey County Cricket Club*, 9–11. Lewis, 37–40.
11. Altham and Swanton, 59–64. Ford, 78.
12. Harrison, *Drink and the Victorians*, 48–49.

13. Pycroft, *The Cricket Field*.
14. Harrison, 49.
15. Altham and Swanton, 71–73. Cust, *History of Eton College*, 241–44.
16. Altham and Swanton, 73–74. G. Bolton, *History of the O.U.C.C.* (Oxford, 1962), 1–4. J.G.W. Davies, 'Cambridge University', in E.W. Swanton, ed., *Barclays World of Cricket*, 471–72.
17. A.E.R. Gilligan, 'Sussex Through the Years', *Wisden 1954*, 108–09. Marshall, *Sussex Cricket*, 1–49. C. Lee, *From the Sea End: The Official History of Sussex County Cricket Club* (London, 1989), 13–76.
18. Arrowsmith, 13–25. D. Moore, *The History of Kent County Cricket Club* (London, 1988), 23–24.
19. Altham *et al.*, *Hampshire County Cricket*, 11–12. But *cf* D. Lemmon, *History of Middlesex County Cricket Club* (London, 1988), suggesting (p. 21) that many of the so-called 'Middlesex' teams were hardly representative of that county during the eighteenth century.
20. Lemmon, *Surrey County Cricket Club*, 13. Ross, *Surrey Story*, 18–19.
21. Altham *et al.*, 13.
22. *Ibid.*, 15.
23. Brookes, 55–56.
24. *Ibid.*, 56–58. Altham *et al.*, 14–21.
25. Brookes, 58–59.
26. *Ibid.*, 59–60.
27. Ashley Cooper, *Hambledon Cricket Chronicle*, 162.
28. Brookes, 67–75. Lewis, 18–20.
29. Ford, 89.
30. Lewis, 62.
31. Altham and Swanton, 74–75.
32. Brookes, 60–66. See also Arrowsmith, 17–24.
33. Ford, 96–98. Lewis, 37–38.
34. Ford, 96–98.
35. Altham *et al.*, 16.
36. A.A. Thomson, 'Lord's and the Early Champions, 1787–1865', in Swanton, ed., *Barclays World of Cricket*, 8.
37. Marshall, *Lord's*, 6.
38. H.A. Harris, *Sport in Britain: Its Origins and Development* (London, 1975), 48.
39. Gale, *Game of Cricket*, 36–37. *Cricket Field*, 11 August 1894, 368. A. Trollope, ed., *British Sports and Pastimes* (London, 1868), 319.
40. Arrowsmith, 36.
41. Pycroft, *Oxford Memories*, 144.
42. Arrowsmith, 22–23. Brookes, 66. Lewis, 37.
43. Arrowsmith, 20.
44. Pycroft, *Oxford Memories*, 120. Altham and Swanton, 42.
45. Lemmon, *Surrey County Cricket Club*, 9–10. Lewis, 39.
46. Pycroft, *Oxford Memories*, 120.
47. Altham *et al.*, 16.
48. Ford, 124.
49. Lee, *Sussex County Cricket Club*, 71. Marshall, *Sussex Cricket*, 12–13.
50. Williams, ed., 11.
51. *Ibid.*, 13.
52. D. Lemmon, *Middlesex County Cricket Club*, 24.

53.   Altham and Swanton, 43, 53.
54.   Marshall, *Lord's*, 7.
55.   Arthur Wrigley, *The Book of Test Cricket* (London, 1965), 12.
56.   *Ibid.*, 43–45.
57.   *Ibid.*, 134.
58.   *Wisden 1913*, 234. Cited in K.A.P. Sandiford and W. Vamplew, 'The Peculiar Economics of English Cricket Before 1914', in *The British Journal of Sports History* (December 1986), 3: 323.

CHAPTER THREE

The Impact of Muscular Christianity

A spectacular sports explosion took place in Britain after 1850. This phenomenon was perhaps the most impressive feature of the leisure revolution which the Victorian age witnessed. It sprang mainly from the gradual improvement in the standards of living, the steady reduction of working hours and the development of a more positive attitude towards 'manly' exercises. The steady increase in the amount of free time at the disposal of workers was accompanied by the fear on the part of the élite that they might not be able to use it constructively. Hence the frantic search for 'improving' and 'rational' recreations which led to the formation of Friendly Societies and an assortment of clubs. Most of these institutions became increasingly involved in the organization of manly sports. The fact is that industrialization had significantly interfered with many of the traditional forms of popular recreation and thus created a vacuum in British social life. This void was gradually filled by music halls, seaside resorts and sports clubs.[1]

The late Victorians became even more sports-minded than their predecessors. They devoted considerable thought, time, money and energy to the development of such activities as archery, badminton, bowls, boxing, canoeing, dog racing, golf, hockey, horse racing, polo, rowing, soccer, swimming, tennis and yachting. Their continuing zeal for cricket was thus part of a wider sports upheaval.

The Victorians obviously enjoyed their new forms of entertainment but could not quite escape the feeling that play somehow contributed to delinquency. They therefore argued much about the meaning of sport in their lives. To some bourgeois minds, the sports explosion was a threat to social cohesion since it blurred the distinctions between the élite and the masses. The clergy, after considerable debate, resigned themselves to the sporting mania and tried to put it to constructive use.[2]

In this they were much encouraged by the Crown which was then still the most influential institution determining social modes of behaviour. Queen Victoria and Prince Albert were themselves very keen on sport and recreation. The Prince was fond of music and billiards and the Queen liked dancing and the theatre.[3] She also encouraged her children to be sports-minded and gave very positive support to their interest in cricket. Prince Albert served from 1846 to 1861 as the patron of the MCC and was the patron also of the Henley Regatta during the last ten years of his life.[4]

Quite clearly the Court believed that sport was respectable and constructive. The same view was taken by educators such as H.H. Almond, G.E.L. Cotton, C.J. Vaughan and H. Walford, who recognized that organized sports could serve as an effective instrument in bringing order and discipline to aggressive groups of rich, spoilt and rebellious brats. They regarded play as a useful tool for the building of adolescent character. It was Samuel Butler, the great headmaster of Shrewsbury from 1798 to 1836, who first tried to monitor play in an effort to develop manliness and discipline. His example was followed almost everywhere, most notably by Benjamin Kennedy at Shrewsbury, John Perceval at Clifton and Edward Thring at Uppingham.[5]

Most of the Victorian educators, in fact, became ardent apostles of the creed known as muscular Christianity. Briefly stated, this doctrine revolves around the basic notion that there is something innately good and godly about brute strength and power, so long as that energy is directed to noble purposes. Physical weakness is unnatural since it is only a manifestation of moral and spiritual inadequacy. It could be overcome by prayer, upright living, discipline and exercise.

The leading preachers of the gospel of muscular Christianity were Bishop Fraser, Thomas Hughes, Charles Kingsley and Charles Wordsworth. It was largely due to their teachings that godliness became more and more associated with manliness. By the 1870s the transition was complete.[6] In this process, the work of Thomas Hughes was of major importance. His *Tom Brown's Schooldays*, published in 1857, sold 11000 copies in its very first year. His glorification of the cult of athleticism was immensely popular. He equated manliness with robust power and raw courage, and thus articulated a philosophy which the majority of Victorians were anxious to uphold. He himself recognized some of the dangers inherent in such an ideology and tried to correct some of the damage with a more moderate *The Manliness of Christ*. The latter, however, made little impact. The later Victorians much preferred the classical Greek ideal of the perfect man being at once handsome, wise and mighty.[7]

Charles Kingsley, indeed, felt that a healthy mind was impossible without a robust body since so much depended upon the absolute harmony between body and soul. In a sense, he fused Thomas Carlyle's concept of the hero with Cardinal Newman's ideal of the perfect gentleman to emerge with his model of the muscular Christian, even though he himself did not like that particular term. Like Herbert Spencer, who considered athletic training even more important than the narrowly intellectual, Kingsley was prepared to argue that boys could acquire through sports all kinds of virtues which books would never be able to provide. He allowed his philosophy to be governed too much perhaps by physiological concepts.[8]

This stress on athleticism was not peculiar to the priests and philosophers of the late-Victorian generation. It often found eloquent expression in the sports journals of the period. The *Midland Athlete*, for example, gave wholehearted support to the doctrine: athletics not only built strength but helped also to produce mental sharpness and to cultivate spiritual qualities.[9] The editor of the *Athletic News* often expressed the same philosophy. His main concern, shared by the editor of the *Cricket and Football Times*, was that urbanization had tended to promote sedentary life which could prove very dangerous to public health – both in a physical and mental sense.[10]

It is impossible not to detect the pervasive influence of muscular Christianity in all branches of English literature during the second half of the nineteenth century. The Victorians revived the medieval concept of the chivalrous knight and emerged with the notion of the Christian cricketer. Godliness and manliness, spiritual perfection and physical power, became inextricably interwoven. It was not likely, in their view, that a feeble body could support a powerful brain. Hence, for instance, even Leslie Stephen, despite his physical frailty, could ironically pose as a staunch champion of muscular Christianity. His response to chronic illness was to become a fanatical athlete. Like most of his contemporaries, he sincerely believed that he could overcome all weakness by strengthening his physique.[11]

In this climate of opinion, it would probably have been impossible for the clerical and other leaders to resist the trend towards athleticism. As it was, all the Victorian churches accepted play as an 'adjunct to work'.[12] Even the Nonconformists, who had earlier tried to check the expansion of sport, revised their strategy and attempted to control it. They began to establish cycling clubs, sports teams and Pleasant Sunday Afternoon Societies wherever they could.[13] In fact, the Evangelicals came to use cricket as a propaganda weapon after 1880. By the turn of the century, Rev. Thomas Waugh could actually write *The Cricket Field of a Christian Life*. Cricket, morality and religion had become intermixed in the Victorian ethos. In Waugh's book, for instance, the Christian team is batting against Satan's devious and immoral bowlers who blatantly disregard the rules of the game. The godly batsman must therefore cope not only with the quality of the bowling itself but also with the attitude of the ungodly bowlers. It is significant, in analysing the late-Victorian frame of mind, to notice that Waugh chose to write about cricket rather than soccer and that his Christians were batsmen and not bowlers. He adopted, in other words, the Victorian habit of glorifying the bat at the expense of the ball, while also supporting the popular view that soccer led to too many emotional excesses.[14]

The Victorian clergy gave cricket their unqualified blessing. Several churchmen of all persuasions played the game and encouraged others to do likewise. Rev. James Pycroft, a curate of Dorset from 1856 to 1895, gave his life to reading and writing about cricket. Rev. A.P. Wickham kept wicket very well and very regularly for Somerset during the 1890s, having played for Marlborough and Oxford University in his younger days.[15] Rev. A.R. Ward contributed more than any single individual to the development of cricket at Cambridge University.[16] Cardinal Manning had, before his ordination, represented Harrow against Eton and Winchester.[17] Rev. G.L. Langdon, the first honorary secretary of the Sussex County Cricket Club, was the moving spirit behind its formation in 1839. A left-handed batsman, he appeared for Sussex against England at Brighton in 1840 and for the Gentlemen against the Players at Lord's in 1841.[18] Rev. C.G. Lane played cricket for Westminster when only 13 and went on to represent Oxford University and Surrey during the period 1856–61.[19] Dr John Peel, the Dean of Worcester and brother of the great Sir Robert, permitted the Worcestershire County XXII to play against an All England XI on his estate at Waresley in 1838, and Rev. R. Peel (presumably a relative) was one of the founders of Worcester City and County Cricket Club in 1855.[20]

The relationship between Victorian cricket and religion was thus very close and direct. The influence of the churches was doubly profound since a number of clergymen also served as headmasters in the public schools, where they implemented their ideas of muscular Christianity and tried to train outstanding civic leaders by exposing them to organized sports. In their view, all the requisite civic virtues could best be inculcated in a physical education programme that made cricket, soccer, rugby and rowing almost essential features of the public school curriculum. So important had the physical aspects of Victorian secondary education become that Thomas Hughes, for example, was assigned to teach boxing, cricket and rowing, in addition to law and public health, at the Working Men's College.[21]

All the major public schools, in fact, began to hire professional cricketers to coach their students. As early as 1823 a professional bowler was engaged by Harrow whose example was followed by Eton not long afterwards.[22] At first the public schools depended mainly on amateur coaching as members of the academic staff and some of the enthusiastic alumni taught the boys to play. Old Harrovians such as Robert Grimston, Frederick Ponsonby and I.D. Walker devoted many years to this kind of service. Among the most famous of the amateur coaches at Eton were G.R. Dupuis, R.A.H. Mitchell and C.M. Wells. Rev. William James Earle, meanwhile, did much to promote the cause of cricket at Uppingham from 1850 to 1881. He often played as a member of the school XI and was joined regularly in such a capacity by the headmaster himself, Edward

Thring.[23] Masters also took cricket very seriously at Winchester, where M.C. Kemp took charge of the game; and even at a small private school like Farnborough, cricket was very earnestly played at the turn of the century.[24]

In short, the Victorian public schools made cricket something of a cult from the 1830s onward and it had become an essential feature of the curriculum by the 1860s.[25] So powerful was this cricketing craze that some of the strongest headmasters could do nothing to resist it. At Uppingham, for instance, the great Thring could write in his diary, on 28 May 1872: 'I do not want the cricket to get too powerful in the school here, and to be worshipped and made the end of life for a considerable section of the school.' It was, nevertheless, Thring himself who consented to the yearly appointment of a cricket professional at Uppingham before that same year was over. By the early 1870s all the major schools, including Brighton, Charterhouse, Marlborough, Repton, Sherborne, Shrewsbury and Tonbridge, had long been employing regular professionals. At Eton, in fact, there were already two permanent professionals in addition to two cricket masters.[26]

It was in 1872 that H.H. Stephenson, who had led the first English touring team to Australia in the winter of 1861–62, was finally engaged as the senior resident professional at Uppingham. There he remained for almost a quarter of a century, establishing an enviable reputation as a gentleman and a teacher of cricket. By the time of his death in 1896, he had become something of a legend in the Uppingham district. His teams were highly successful and included such renowned players as G.R. Bardswell, S. Christopherson, A.P. Lucas, Gregor MacGregor, W.S. Patterson, S.S. Schultz, the Steels (D.Q. and H.B.) and C.E.M. Wilson.[27]

Although Stephenson was to become the most famous perhaps of Victorian public school coaches, his appointment to Uppingham was rather belated, since Thring had been so reluctant to follow the contemporary trend. The idea of a resident professional had long become a tradition at other schools. Rugby, for example, had hired Deacon of Nottinghamshire in the late 1830s as its first regular professional.[28] In the 1850s it had also profited much from the services of John Lillywhite, who was succeeded there by Alfred Diver and Walter Price. The popular Yorkshire and England professional Tom Emmett, too, spent many years coaching at Rugby after his brilliant first-class cricket career was over. By 1849, Westminster already had a cricket coach for several weeks annually. Later it was served faithfully by Tom Mantle, its senior professional from 1862 to 1883. James Lillywhite went to Marlborough in 1853, before proceeding to Cheltenham in 1855. He died in harness there 30 years later. Charles Brampton also proved himself a capital coach at Marlborough where he spent 20 years (1859–79) turning out such excellent cricketers as F.M. Lucas, C.O.H. Sewell, A.G. Steel and C.P. Wilson.[29]

By the 1860s public school cricket had become systematized and there was much competition for the services of the better professionals in the spring before the start of the summer schedule of matches in which MCC, some of the counties and the itinerant elevens then participated. Many schools therefore began their cricket season in late March or early April.[30] This meant that, in addition to the permanent professional, other cricketers were engaged for short periods each year – especially during the last quarter of the century when the county cricket championship had become more formalized. Thus by the 1890s, while James Wootton of Kent, for example, was the regular professional at Winchester, Tom Richardson of Surrey and Victor Barton of Hampshire also appeared for a few weeks at that school.[31] William Caffyn, the famous Surrey and England professional who had also coached for some years in Australia, observed in 1895 that many schools like Eton, Cheltenham and Wellington often boasted more than one full-time professional. Caffyn himself, over a lengthy career, coached at Brighton, Cheltenham, Clifton, Eton, Haileybury, Wellington and Winchester.[32] John Painter of Gloucestershire also coached at several public schools before his death in 1900.[33]

It is difficult to exaggerate the importance of cricket in the development of the Victorian public schools. Some inkling of its perceived value at that time may be gleaned from the fact that, at Eton, Oscar Browning could be dismissed by Dr Hornsby for his alleged opposition to games.[34] Edward Bowen, a housemaster at Harrow from 1859 to 1901, was given 'three days special leave' in 1888 to compose a poem in celebration of F.S. Jackson's mighty deeds against Eton at Lord's that summer.[35] Roxburgh ended his days at Charterhouse as a Trinity Exhibitioner, but as a consequence of his indifference to sports, had never been created a monitor.[36] E.C. Wickham, who 'believed in cricket even more genuinely than did most of the great headmasters of that time', more or less transformed Wellington College into a cricket nursery under the tutelage of John Relf, a Nottingham professional.[37] At Radley, the playing fields became almost as important as the chapel.[38] And at Marlborough, G.E.L. Cotton established cricket as firmly as he did the classics.[39] Indeed, all the Victorian alumni who left memoirs or histories of their public schools have attested to the vital importance of cricket by devoting lengthier chapters to that game than to the more academic aspects of the curriculum.[40]

This emphasis on cricket naturally meant that the inter-school competition flourished. Among all the public school rivalries, the most glorified was the yearly meeting between Eton and Harrow at Lord's. By the 1860s this event had already become the most important social occasion on the

Victorian cricket calendar each summer. This series, inaugurated in 1822, very soon assumed (and for a long time retained) all the airs and trappings of a medieval pageant. Also very popular were the Charterhouse vs Westminster, Marlborough vs Rugby and Cheltenham vs Marlborough confrontations.

It is by no means surprising then that the public schools came to serve as the great cradle of Victorian amateur cricket. Between 1827 and 1854, Eton alone produced 63 university 'blues', Winchester 43, Harrow 34, and Rugby 23.[41] When the county championship became regularized later on, the public schools provided the vast majority of first-class amateur cricketers. The public school stress on cricket led to a dramatic improvement in the standard of amateur play and did much to redress the balance between the Gentlemen and the Players after 1865.

The public school alumni took their superior skills to the universities also. The great Oxford–Cambridge rivalry went back to the Georgian period, as we have seen, but neither the standard of play nor the general interest in the university matches was originally very high. Even as late as 1848, *Bell's Life in London* devoted no more than a few lines to the university contest at Lord's.[42] All of this was to change dramatically by the 1860s. Following the example set by the great public schools, the universities began to engage professionals to coach their students. In 1862, for instance, C. Rogers was hired by Balliol College, while Henry Curtis joined the Oxford University ground staff.[43] By the 1860s, too, the annual Oxford–Cambridge match at Lord's was attracting over 5000 spectators.[44] By 1880, the Cambridge University Cricket Club was hiring over a dozen professionals each spring. In 1895 it announced as many as 18 such engagements.[45]

The notion that cricket encouraged the development of sterling spiritual qualities led to its ascendancy at the universities also. Even the difficulties with respect to establishing their own home grounds failed to stem the tide. The MCC offered Oxford and Cambridge an annual subsidy after 1881, in which year the Oxford University Cricket Club finally established its headquarters at the Parks. It was not before 1893 that Cambridge managed to purchase the beautiful ground at Fenner's.[46]

The early development of university cricket owed a great deal to Rev. James Pycroft, Charles Wordsworth and Rev. A.R. Ward. Indeed, it was Ward who did most to acquire Fenner's for Cambridge and to make that institution a driving force in later Victorian cricket. It was he who, in 1876, negotiated a 35-year lease of Fenner's from Caius College. He also did much to finance and build the new pavilion there. His greatest virtue lay in an unparalleled ability to raise funds for university cricket. When he died in 1884, after having served as president and treasurer of the Cambridge University Cricket Club for 11 years, he left the club's finances in a very healthy state.[47]

The universities inevitably spawned many excellent cricketers. From Victorian Cambridge alone came Stanley Jackson, Gilbert Jessop, A.O. Jones, A.P. Lucas, Alfred Lyttelton, K.S. Ranjitsinhji, Charles Studd and S.M.J. Woods. Victorian Oxford produced B.J.T. Bosanquet, H.K. and R.E. Foster, C.B. Fry, K.J. Key, G.J. Mordaunt, T.C. O'Brien, C.J. Ottaway, L.C.H. Palairet, G.O. Smith, E.F.S. Tylecote and A.J. Webb.[48] Many graduates played good county cricket and some of them, such as Fry, Jackson, Jessop and Ranjitsinhji, became famous international stars. The universities also produced many outstanding cricket administrators, like Lord Harris, Lord Hawke, Sir Henry Leveson Gower, Sir Francis Lacy and Sir Pelham Warner, who had all been fine players as well.

The academic institutions left an indelible mark on Victorian cricket. Like the churches, they promoted and popularized the game, giving it a measure of respectability it would otherwise have lacked. They provided the sport with administrative leadership at all levels, especially through the ability of their alumni to infiltrate and dominate the MCC as well as the county cricket committees which sprang up after 1860. They eventually served on a variety of town councils, public boards and royal commissions, through all of which they continued to transmit and to implement their notions of muscular Christianity. It is not therefore astonishing that the famous Clarendon Commission in 1864 should support the idea that cricket was a positive force capable of fostering such virtues as loyalty, courage and team spirit.[49]

The public schools and the universities, like the churches, founded countless cricket clubs in the second half of the nineteenth century. Over a hundred such institutions are listed in Haygarth's *Scores and Biographies*. The list includes Accidentals, Active Fleas, Anomalies, Cambridge Quidnuncs, Dingle Wanderers, Eton Ramblers, Free Foresters, Gnats, Harrow Blues, Harrow Wanderers, Incogniti, Inexpressibles, Kentish Stars, Knickerbockers, Oxford Harlequins, Staffordshire Rangers, Suppositions and Uppingham Rovers. These were all amateur clubs composed exclusively of gentlemen and tended, like the celebrated I Zingari, to be nomadic without fixed headquarters.[50] As membership of any of these clubs was expressly by invitation only, they remained somewhat snobbish and élitist and were totally detached from the proletariat. Even so, they made a notable contribution to cricket by spreading it to all parts of the kingdom. The alumni of the great academic institutions made an even more vital contribution to the development of cricket in the late-Victorian age by their willingness to donate large sums of money for the leasing of land and the building of pavilions. It is estimated that, by 1900, old Harrovians alone had provided some 20 acres for cricket and 50 for soccer. In the summer of 1866, when Harrow wanted to purchase additional fields, its alumni succeeded in raising £6,000 for that purpose in little more than six weeks.[51]

It has to be admitted, however, that the academic institutions of the Victorian era did not exert as powerful an influence over the development of cricket as they assuredly did in the emergence of soccer. It was the public schools and the universities which did most to codify the rules of Association football and, by 1870, to set it apart quite clearly from the Rugby game. These institutions provided leadership and legislation and gave soccer the kind of encouragement that was vital to its very survival. Soccer was very much the product of muscular Christianity in the public schools after 1850. It is thus the offspring of an industrialized society.[52]

Cricket, on the other hand, was too well developed by the time of Hughes, Kingsley and Spencer. It already had its traditions, regulations, rules and rituals. With very few of these could the spirit of muscular Christianity interfere. Yet, paradoxically, the muscular Christians adopted cricket as their special game and bestowed upon it a sanctity that no other sport can come close to matching in the modern age. The Victorians, almost to a man, viewed cricket as the game least tainted by human foibles. It became so closely identified in their minds with religion, morality and public health that it could loom large in every discussion from education to imperialism. It had to be encouraged in the academic institutions because it was an indispensable aid to intellectual pursuits. It was equally a part of the white man's burden as it had become an integral feature of the process of imperial assimilation. For this latter purpose, it came to be used most effectively by bureaucrats, like Arthur Grimble later on, who introduced it to the Pacific Islands as a civilizing agent. Lord Harris, as the Governor of Bombay in the 1890s, also thought that cricket could bridge the gulf between Anglo-Saxon and Indian, Anglican and Hindu.[53]

If cricket thus had the magical power to cement bonds of friendship over the far-flung empire, then surely it could perform similar miracles among the working classes at home. This philosophy became dominant, as muscular Christianity entrenched itself. Thus all the voluntary organizations, Sunday schools, church societies, Old Boys' associations, Rational Recreation movements and the YMCA took part in the marvellous proliferation of cricket clubs in the late-Victorian age. Even the parsimonious town council in Bristol, as Helen Meller has shown, was deeply affected by muscular Christianity.[54]

Naturally, all Victorian cricketers sincerely believed that their game was a special one above all others. W.G. Grace had no doubt that it could advance the cause of civilization and hold together, as by a common bond, peoples of vastly differing backgrounds.[55] C.B. Fry expressed the view that 'there is something in the game that smothers pretence and affectation, and gives air to character'. To him, the special virtue of cricket was precisely that it could bring out the best features of human character. It was a 'form of recreation free from all tendency to degrade either those who play or those who pay'.[56] And, early in the twentieth century, Albert Knight could view the game as a virtual panacea for a multitude of ailments.[57]

Several of their contemporaries felt exactly the same way as the Victorian cricketers did. Rev. G.J. Chester, in a sermon delivered at Sheffield in 1859, saw cricket as tending to promote purity of life as well as health of body. It could also serve, in his judgment, 'to break down the barriers which unchristian pride has built up between class and class, and to cement bonds of goodwill and brotherly feeling'.[58] Lord William Lennox, as early as 1840, was already referring to cricket as the 'national game' which 'preserves the manly character of the Briton, and has been truly characterized as a healthful, manly recreation, giving strength to the body and cheerfulness to the mind'.[59] To Edward Thring, cricket was more than a game: it was the greatest bond of English speaking people.[60] The Bishop of Hereford, in a typical eulogy of W.G. Grace in 1915, remarked that the good Doctor 'was the best known of all Englishmen and the King of that English game least spoilt by any form of vice'.[61]

This singular attachment to cricket, as representing the most splendid features of Anglo-Saxonism, remained with the British long after the Victorian and Edwardian periods had ended. As late as 1944, for instance, the poet Edmund Blunden could still see cricket as the great catalyst in British society. He agreed with G.M. Trevelyan that the peasants would never have burnt the castles of the nobility in France had the two classes played cricket together.[62] It is quite clear then that muscular Christianity gave cricket a stimulus and a momentum which sustained it over a considerable timespan. It gave rise immediately to a huge cricket explosion which saw the multiplication of clubs at all levels and within each county. County matches escalated and professional leagues sprang up in the north where they have survived to this day.

The emphasis on muscular Christianity, however, strengthened the tendency towards male chauvinism and led the Victorians for several decades to disparage female participation in athletics. Manly exercises were considered too strenuous for ladies and the latter gradually found themselves restricted mainly to indoor recreation. It was not before the late 1880s that a reaction against this trend could set in. Thus, although their Georgian predecessors had played an active role in the game, Victorian women, on the whole, did not. They encouraged their menfolk to play the game and they themselves watched it in large numbers at the first-class level. But their role in the development of Victorian cricket must be seen as negligible. There is no evidence to show that they were actively involved in the game even at the club and village levels. Alfred Shaw, the great bowler for Nottinghamshire and England, certainly thought that they were not as keen cricket fans as their Australian counterparts whom he had seen on several trips 'down under' during the 1880s.[63]

There can be no doubt that the ladies supported the game at the county level and formed a fair percentage of the regular attendance. In February 1886, for instance, there were 336 ladies among the members of the Lancashire County Cricket Club. This number rose to 575 by 1890. As the total membership increased during this period from 1852 to 2310, this means that the female component increased from approximately 18 to 25 per cent of the total. At the other end of the scale, the Essex County Cricket Club encountered difficulty in enticing ladies to enrol. Of its 1209 members in 1895, only 112 (or just over 9 per cent) were female. Among its 1824 members in 1898 there were 136 ladies, and there were still only 156 of them (i.e. less than 7 per cent) in a total of 2283 one year later.[64]

Whatever the actual percentage of female members in individual county clubs, all Victorian cricket reports refer to the presence of thousands of ladies at first-class matches. They were always conspicuously plentiful at the Oxford–Cambridge and Eton–Harrow confrontations. In July 1894, for instance, hundreds of them went to Lord's to support their young heroes despite torrents of rain which made play seem unlikely. This prompted one journalist to observe that the crowd included many 'sisters and cousins and aunts'.[65] The ladies were well represented also at the great festivals, which many of them treated as fashion shows. Like the school-boys, they were admitted at reduced rates, and during the Canterbury Week the highlight each year was Ladies' Day. Even when the weather was dreary, Ladies' Day (Thursday) seemed somehow to attract unusual numbers. In 1871, Ladies' Day drew 7000 spectators, more than half of whom were female; and in 1879, 'although the weather was far from summerlike', in *Wisden*'s words, 'the visitors flocked in from far and near'.[66]

Until late in the century, however, Victorian women did not generally play cricket. A pronounced and protracted slump occurred in female cricket from the 1830s onward. Georgian women had been far more active in the game and had indeed contributed significantly to its modern development by pioneering round-arm bowling. George Knight and Thomas Willes, who were among the first men to use this type of delivery, had copied it from their female relatives.[67] But the Victorian women did not really re-enter the ranks until the 1880s. Even when the female students at Cambridge and Oxford were playing tennis and hockey, they were discouraged from playing at the manly sport of cricket. It was felt at those institutions (and others like them) that the manliness required of cricket contrasted too sharply with the orthodox notions of feminine weakness and passivity. Up to 1914, in fact, none of the Oxford colleges had ever produced a female cricket XI.[68]

The turning point really came with the founding of the White Heather Club in 1887. This was a rather aristocratic institution and its social structure might well have accounted for its success. It was led by the Marchioness of Willingdon, Lady Milner, the Countess of Brassey, Lady de la Warr and Lady Abergavenny. It began with only eight members but grew within four years to 50, and included such superb players as the four Misses Lofts, Mrs Catley, Miss Hornby, Miss Le Fleming and Miss Georgie Waters.[69]

Several female cricket clubs appeared in England thereafter, and there also surfaced very briefly the 'Original English Lady Cricketers', a semi-professional group who played a number of exhibitions between their 'blue' and 'red' teams. As professionalism among ladies was then considered grossly improper, they had to play under assumed names. One of them, Miss Flora Blanch Lyon, adopted the pseudonym Miss Westbrook. An excellent stroke-player, she was the captain of the 'reds'. Over one very short period in 1890, she scored 66 at Wolverhampton, 62 at Northants, 65 not out at Leamington, and continued the streak with a brilliant 88 not out. One of the reporters who followed this group marvelled at the proficiency of the ladies, who 'did not burlesque the manly sport of cricket' but in fact played the game 'in a thorough [sic] legitimate manner, having been properly coached by some of the best leading professionals of the day'.[70]

The details surrounding this enterprising club, which had its head-quarters in Staffordshire, are now quite hazy. It vanished after a single season although it seems to have drawn good crowds and played bright cricket. Some 15000 spectators, for example, are estimated to have watched their exhibition in Liverpool on the Police Athletic Ground at Easter. The reports of their play were somewhat mixed, but many conservative pundits offered positive comments and the *Illustrated London News* as well as the *Cricketer's Annual* concluded that the women had shown that they had as much right as men to play the national game. The *Buckinghamshire Examiner* offered the opinion that the experiment had 'demonstrated that ladies could play cricket very well'. The young ladies were invited to tour Australia that winter but their parents demurred, having somehow reached the conclusion, in Netta Rheinberg's words, that 'the people of that country were too wild and unruly for their Victorian daughters'.[71] The male manager apparently absconded with the funds and the girls thereupon disbanded.

On the whole, the Victorian male cricketers themselves did not seem to welcome the experiment. W.G. Grace, for one, did not lament its demise. He actually rejoiced to see that 'interest in their doings did not survive long'. In his judgment, cricket was not a game for women who

were really not 'constitutionally adapted to the sport'.[72] One might have
expected the 'Champion', whose female relatives are reputed to have
played the game very skilfully indeed, to have evinced a more sympathetic
attitude. His own daughter, Bessie, was thought to be, at 14, as adept a
cricketer as most boys her age.[73]

W.G.'s views on the subject were shared by Richard Daft, another
famous Victorian cricketer, who, in his weekly column in the *Athletic
News*, considered it impossible for women to compete on even terms with
men. Their physique as well as their apparel were too obviously against
them. Daft recommended reducing the pitch to 20 yards, shortening and
lightening the normal bat, and reducing considerably the weight of the
ball. 'By these means,' he wrote, 'I think the game might be played by
ladies to advantage.' Many of these suggestions were eventually adopted
by the women, though Daft himself remained pessimistic about ladies'
cricket since he thought that they had in any case an excellent alternative
in lawn tennis.[74]

There is no doubt that Daft and Grace spoke for the majority of
Victorian male chauvinists. Most of the reporters who followed the
women's game at that time ridiculed their efforts. Effeminacy, after all,
was one of the major targets against which muscular Christianity itself
was directed. It was also too easy to ridicule the women when, on one
occasion in 1884, they were beaten by 16 runs in a match at Salisbury by
men who bowled and fielded left-handed and then batted with broom-
sticks. 'A Male Reporter' described, in very condescending terms, a game
between two women's teams at Eastbourne in 1887, when the residents
were dismissed for 68 runs, of which Mrs Coombes scored 42 with '14
chances'. The Visitors were then bowled out for a paltry 43. A report of
a similar game at Drewsteignton in 1890 by 'A Male Onlooker' was,
predictably, no less sexist in tone. In 1895, in a women's cricket match on
the ground of the East Melbourne Club, England defeated Australia by a
score of 103 to 44, and Miss Day McDonnell hit a breezy 62 not out. But
one male reporter was left to regret that 'as a display of cricket, the game
was disappointing'.[75] The fact is that the Victorians were still convinced,
as the editor of the *Cricket Field* put it in 1892, that 'A girl cannot stand
the hard knocks which must often come, and her hands were never
intended to be bruised and battered. That some girls can play a good game
proves nothing, and the best of them could never stand up against a fast
bowler, even if a fast bowler could be induced to try the experiment.'[76]

Male chauvinism, however, failed to prevent the feminist revival. By
1887, the *Athletic News* was able to remark that 'Ladies cricket in the
North seems to be rather popular, judging from the reports of the various
matches that have crept into the papers of late.' Such well-known names
as Appleby, Key, Marriott, Stevenson and Walker were appearing

regularly among the female score cards.[77] By the 1890s, the recently established female schools and colleges had accepted the notion that organized games were very important in the healthy development of both minds and bodies. Miss June Frances Dove, headmistress of St Leonard's School, became the foremost preacher of this gospel, and the girls' secondary schools began to promote such sports as cricket, cycling, hockey and tennis. The bicycle, in fact, became everywhere a symbol of the newly discovered freedom. By the end of the century, Princess Helena College, the St Leonard's School, Wimbledon House School and Wycombe Abbey were all turning out female cricketers who were eager to continue playing the game after their graduation. Several institutions, including Girton College and Dartford Physical Training College, were also producing good cricketers. The Nausicaa Club and the St Quentin Cricket Club were already prospering in London; and fine teams were operating also at Addlestone, Epping and Walton-on-Thames. The Derbyshire Ladies, calling themselves the 'Dragonflies', surfaced briefly also and won a notable match against the White Heather in 1896, thanks to the brilliance of Miss Fitzherbert, who scored 53, and Miss Thornewill who took 12 wickets for 69 runs. Clifton Ladies also appeared, under the captaincy of Miss Ethel Lomas, and profited often from the powerful hitting of Miss Bessie Grace.[78]

Some superb female cricketers performed noteworthy feats at the turn of the century. Miss Wright once scored 106 in a total of 142 at Sidmouth, and Miss Leslie Crawford, playing for the Ladies of Caterham, achieved a great century in 1899. Miss Mabel Bryant, representing the Visitors against the Residents of Eastbourne in 1901, smashed 224 not out in 135 minutes and then, bowling with exceptional fire, took 5 wickets in each of her opponents' innings.[79]

This resurgence in female cricket was in keeping with similar developments in late-Victorian leisure and recreation. After allowing their menfolk to monopolize the athletic field for about half a century, women took up cycling, golf and tennis with extraordinary zeal. In golf, for instance, Victorian women had for many years been kept away from the main courses by prevailing ideas on propriety, the ungainliness of feminine garments and by men's low estimate of their ability. But in the 1890s, in defiance of male chauvinism and female fashions, the St Rule Ladies Golf Club was founded and women's golf was established on a national footing in Scotland by 1903.[80] This came as no surprise to that reporter for the *Athletic Sports and Games* who had observed in May 1896 that women had the capacity to be excellent golfers since they were often superior to men in pluck, patience and manual dexterity.[81]

By the Edwardian age, women's cricket, cycling, golf, hockey and tennis had all become respectable. Already women's cricket was being played in Australia and New Zealand. The first women's cricket match in Australia took place in 1886 and the first intercolonial match there was staged in 1891. But it was not before 1926 that the Women's Cricket Association (WCA) was founded to facilitate regular and organized women's cricket in England.[82] There is a certain irony about the history of women's cricket in England. It failed to make more rapid progress after 1890 because it appealed mainly to the élite and lacked the support and encouragement of the lower classes. It would not, however, have broken down the sexist barriers in Victorian England at all had the support of the upper classes been lacking.

If muscular Christianity ultimately failed to keep Victorian women in their place indefinitely, it certainly triumphed in the face of much serious criticism. Matthew Arnold, Thomas Carlyle, Wilkie Collins, John Ruskin, *Punch* and the *Saturday Review* remained convinced that the doctrine could do more harm than good by its exaltation of brawn over finesse. Wilkie Collins, for instance, had tried in his *Man and Wife* published in 1870, to point out the dangers of glorifying brute strength; but the sporting press deplored his heresy and his novel languished in obscurity while the works of Hughes and Kingsley sold millions.[83] Kipling, too, made no headway with poems which criticized the means rather than the ends of the new athleticism. The fact is, as N.G. Annan has emphasized, some critics, such as George Bernard Shaw and H.G. Wells, were so bitter in their denunciations that they tended to be ignored. Even more moderate spokesmen, such as Dean Farrar and Matthew Arnold, could not hope to succeed.[84] The cult of athleticism flourished because it became the focus of Victorian jingoism, especially after the Crimean War, the Anglo-Chinese Wars and the Indian Mutiny. Muscular Christianity fed, as well as fed on, the emerging notions of social Darwinism with its stress on the survival of the fittest. Athleticism, manliness, jingoism, militarism, imperialism and militant nationalism were all integral parts of that pronounced xenophobia which prevailed throughout the Victorian age.

It was against this background that Matthew Arnold was reacting, in his *Culture and Anarchy*. Not only was he rejecting Hughes's image of his father's Rugby in *Tom Brown's Schooldays*, but he much feared that while organized games were good in themselves, they were really only a means and not an end. In his view, physical education had become tragically over-valued.[85] Herbert Spencer, too, began to fear that muscular Christianity was leading to violence, aggressive imperialism and inevitably towards war. His *Facts and Comments*, written during the Boer War, is thus substantially less sympathetic to the cult of athleticism than his *Education: Intellectual, Moral and Physical*, first published in 1861.[86]

Only a minority of Victorians, however, reacted like Matthew Arnold and Herbert Spencer. As Mangan has so convincingly demonstrated, the cult of athleticism completely triumphed during the last three decades of the nineteenth century. By 1900, all the major public schools were equipped with lavish courts, fields, pools and gymnasia. Ideology and coercion were both employed to establish this 'huge games-playing machine' throughout the country. The stark contrast between the dingy classrooms and the spacious playing fields symbolized not only the increasing wealth of the Victorians but the dominant values of the new system as well. The gospel of athleticism was freely articulated in school songs, newspaper editorials, novels, poems and theses on education.[87]

It was not until after the First World War that the cult of athleticism finally came under significant fire. By this time the pacifists could argue that it had been one of the fundamental causes of that global catastrophe. But, in Victorian Britain, muscular Christianity flourished, as it did almost everywhere else, because it fitted in so neatly with that spirit of aggressive nationalism that was then so prevalent.

Notes

1.   Bailey, *Leisure and Class*. R.C.K. Ensor, *England 1870–1914* (Oxford, 1936), 164–67. E. Grayson, *Corinthians and Cricketers* (Sportsmans Book Club, 1957), 18. Lowerson and Myerscough, *Time to Spare*. Malcolmson, *Popular Recreations*, 158–71. J.K. Walton, *The English Seaside Resort: A Social History 1750–1914* (New York, 1983), 1–4. Walvin, *Leisure and Society*, 11–20. G.M. Young, ed., *Early Victorian England: 1830–65* (Oxford, 1934), I: 236–37.

2.   P.C. Bailey, 'A Mingled Mass of Perfectly Legitimate Pleasures', *Victorian Studies* (Autumn, 1977), 21: 7–28.

3.   E. Burton, *The Early Victorians at Home* (Newton Abbot, 1973), 213–53. A. Hardy, *Queen Victoria Was Amused* (London, 1976). G. Rowell, *Queen Victoria Goes to the Theatre* (London, 1978).

4.   R. Burnell, *Henley Regatta: A History* (London, 1957), 30. *Wisden 1870*, 17.

5.   R.D. Altick, *Victorian People and Ideas* (New York, 1973), 143. D. Bowen, *The Idea of the Victorian Church* (Montreal, 1968), 213–31. Mangan, *Athleticism*. McIntosh, *Physical Education*, 26–103.

6.   Haley, 'Sports'; and *The Healthy Body*. McIntosh, *Physical Education*, 40–103. Newsome, *Godliness and Good Learning*.

7.   J.W. Diggle, *Godliness and Manliness* (London, 1887). T. Hughes, *Tom Brown's Schooldays* (London, 1857); and *The Manliness of Christ* (London, 1894). McIntosh, 41.

8.   Haley, *The Healthy Body*, 68–119. R. Holt, *Sport and the British: A Modern History* (Oxford, 1989), 93. C. Kingsley, *Health and Education* (London, 1874).

9.   *Midland Athlete*, 4 May 1881, 395; and 11 May 1881, 423.

10. *Athletic News*, 30 July 1876, 1; 14 October 1876, 4; and 19 November 1879, 4. *Cricket and Football Times*, 24 February 1881, 205.

11.   N.G. Annan, *Leslie Stephen: His Thought and Character in Relation to His Time* (London, 1951), 29.
12.   Bailey, *Leisure and Class*, 18–20. K. Inglis, *The Churches and the Working Classes in Victorian England* (London, 1963), 75–9.
13.   Inglis, *The Churches*, 75–85. P. Scott, 'Cricket and the Religious World in the Victorian Period', *Church Quarterly* (July, 1970), 3: 134–44.
14.   Scott, 140–43.
15.   *Ibid.*, 134–44. *Wisden 1893*, 63. B. Green, ed., *Wisden Book of Obituaries*, 984.
16.   Swanton, ed., *World of Cricket*, 175–76.
17.   *Cricket*, 1 August 1895, 312. *Wisden 1893*, xxxiii.
18.   Green, ed., *Wisden Book of Obituaries*, 534. Lee, *Official History of Sussex County Cricket Club*, 76. Marshall, *Sussex Cricket: A History*, 37. See also *Cricket Field*, 27 January 1894, 10.
19.   Green, ed., *Wisden Book of Obituaries*, 531. *Wisden 1893*, xxxv-xxxvi.
20.   D. Lemmon, *Worcestershire County Cricket Club*, 8. N. Stone, 'The Rise of Worcestershire', *Wisden 1963*, 125.
21.   Altick, *People and Ideas*, 143. Bowen, *Idea of the Victorian Church*, 231. McIntosh, 26–103.
22.   Altham and Swanton, *A History of Cricket*, 120.
23.   Patterson, *Sixty Years of Uppingham Cricket*, 7–10.
24.   Leveson Gower, *Off and On the Field*, 17, 35–36.
25.   N.G. Annan, *Roxburgh of Stowe* (London, 1965), 13. Cust, *A History of Eton College*, 244. R. Bowen, *Cricket: A History*, 82. McIntosh, 26–40.
26.   Patterson, 48–69.
27.   *Ibid.*, 68–97. Leveson Gower, 139. *Cricket Field*, 1 June 1895, 141–42.
28.   *Cricket Field*, 28 January 1893, 10.
29.   *Athletic News*, 17 June 1895, 1. *Cricket*, 8 May 1884, 104–05. *Cricket Field*, 31 December 1892, 429. Altham and Swanton, 120. Haygarth, *Scores and Biographies*, X: 194. Leveson Gower, 139. W.H.D. Rouse, *A History of Rugby School* (London, 1898), 327.
30.   Altham and Swanton, 120.
31.   *Cricket Field*, 10 November 1894, 485.
32.   *Ibid.*, 6 April 1895, 49.
33.   *Cricket*, 20 September 1900, 417.
34.   McIntosh, 53.
35.   Mangan, *Athleticism*, 180.
36.   Annan, *Roxburgh of Stowe*, 11.
37.   Berkeley, *Recollections of Wellington College*, 44–51, 63–79.
38.   A.K. Boyd, *The History of Radley College 1847–1947* (Oxford, 1948), 89.
39.   Bradley *et al.*, *History of Marlborough College*, 166–72.
40.   E.g., A.C. Ainger, *Memories of Eton Sixty Years Ago* (London, 1917). Berkeley, *Recollections*. Cust, *Eton College*. Rouse, *Rugby*.
41.   Altham and Swanton, 119.
42.   *Ibid.*, 124.
43.   *Illustrated Sporting News*, 12 April 1862, 33.
44.   See, e.g., *Cricketers' and Sporting News*, 9 July 1867, 2.
45.   *Cricket and Football Times*, 11 March 1880, 249. *Cricket Field*, 6 April 1895, 47.
46.   Altham and Swanton, 158–59. See also Swanton, ed., *Barclays World of Cricket*, 471–77.

47. J.G.W. Davies, 'Cambridge University', in Swanton, ed., *Barclays World of Cricket*, 472–73.
48. *Ibid.*, 473–74, 476–77.
49. McIntosh, 47.
50. Haygarth, VI: 395.
51. Haygarth, IX: 525–26. McIntosh, 54.
52. J. Walvin, *The People's Game*, 31–49. P.M. Young, *A History of British Football* (Sportsmans Book Club, 1969), 73–101.
53. Green, ed., *Cricket Addict*, 27–33. A. Grimble, *A Pattern of Islands* (London, 1952). Lord Harris, *A Few Short Runs*.
54. C. Binfield, *George Williams and the YMCA* (London, 1973), 306. Cunningham, *Leisure in the Industrial Revolution*, 27–28, 44, 114, 179, 181–82. Meller, *Leisure and the Changing City*, 161–236.
55. Grace, *Cricketing Reminiscences and Personal Recollections*, 183–84.
56. Cited in R.H. Lyttelton *et al.*, *Giants of the Game*, with an introduction by John Arlott (Newton Abbot, repr. 1974), 117–18.
57. Knight, *Complete Cricketer*.
58. G.J. Chester, *The Young Men at Rest and at Play* (London, 1860), 7.
59. Box, *English Game*, 75.
60. McIntosh, 62.
61. Altham and Swanton, 134. Cited also in Meller, 230.
62. E. Blunden, *Cricket Country* (London, 1944), 67.
63. *Cricket Field*, 21 May 1892, 42.
64. *Cricket*, 25 February 1886, 31; 26 February 1891, 18; 9 May 1895, 123; 14 April 1898, 53; and 20 April 1899, 70.
65. *Cricket Field*, 21 July 1894, 310.
66. *Wisden 1872*, 60; and *Wisden 1880*, 95.
67. *Cricket*, 13 May 1886, 121. Box, 349–50. Brodribb, *All Round the Wicket*, 199–201. Ford, *Cricket: A Social History*, 152–61. Marshall, *Sussex Cricket*, 23. Martineau, *They Made Cricket*, 59–63, 82–83.
68. K. E. McCrone, *Playing the Game: Sport and the Physical Emancipation of English Women 1870–1914* (Lexington, 1988), 42.
69. *Ibid.*, 144. N. Joy, *Maiden Over: A Short History of Women's Cricket* (London, 1950), 23–33. Martineau, 209. Swanton, ed., *World of Cricket*, 1133–134.
70. *Athletic Star*, 2 June 1890, 5; and 23 June 1890, 1.
71. Swanton, ed., *World of Cricket*, 1134.
72. Grace, *Reminiscences and Recollections*, 218–19.
73. *Athletic News*, 9 September 1876, 5. *Cricket Field*, 7 May 1892, 5.
74. *Athletic News*, 8 August 1892, 1.
75. *Ibid.*, 24 September 1884, 1. *Cricket*, 24 November 1887, 460; 25 September 1890, 417; and 2 May 1895, 105.
76. *Cricket Field*, 17 September 1892, 364.
77. *Athletic News*, 10 May 1887, 1.
78. *Cricket*, 27 April 1899, 90–91. Joy, 26–33. McCrone, 72–77.
79. Joy, 29. Swanton, ed., *World of Cricket*, 1134.
80. G. Cousins, *Golf in Britain: A Social History* (London, 1975), 65–70.
81. *Athletic Sports and Games*, May 1896, 7.
82. Joy, 30–31. Swanton, ed., *World of Cricket*, 1135.
83. See, e.g., *Athletic News*, 14 October 1876, 4; and 7 September 1881, 4. McIntosh, 63–64.

84. Annan, *Roxburgh of Stowe*, 14. Newsome, 35–37, 238–39. Haley, *Healthy Body*, 168–80.
85. M. Arnold, *Culture and Anarchy* (London, 1869).
86. H. Spencer, *Education: Intellectual, Moral and Physical* (London, repr. 1949); and *Facts and Comments* (New York, 1902).
87. Mangan, *Athleticism*.

CHAPTER FOUR

The Great Cricket Explosion

One of the most remarkable features of English cricket history is the dramatic fashion in which the game expanded during the second half of the nineteenth century. County matches in the Georgian age had been irregular affairs organized on private grounds by wealthy patrons. The sport lacked administrative structures and everything was therefore left entirely to private enterprise. Travel was then so difficult and hazardous that the movement of players and teams was greatly restricted. Spacious cricket grounds with adequate facilities for participants and spectators were almost nonexistent. These obstacles to cricket expansion were all removed during the Victorian age.

In 1840 there were only 15 county cricket clubs. This number rose to 25 in 1860. By 1870 all but five counties had cricket clubs. Between 1836 and 1863, the total number of county games played approximately trebled. Between 1860 and 1900 this trend continued. Old county cricket clubs, such as those in Kent, Sussex and Surrey, were thoroughly reorganized and new ones sprang up all across the United Kingdom, including Clakmannanshire, Denbighsire and County Donegal in Ireland.[1] By 1873 nine clubs were competing for the first-class county cricket championship. This number rose to 14 by 1895, 15 by 1899 and 16 by 1905. In 1921, Glamorgan was admitted into the competition.[2] The county championship, as presently known, was thus established by the Victorians. The Minor Counties Competition, inaugurated in 1895, was reorganized on a sounder basis and officially recognized in 1901.[3]

The emergence of major, minor and second-class county cricket is thus a Victorian phenomenon. The age also witnessed an incredible upsurge of club cricket. Haygarth has drawn attention to scores of cricket clubs which were established by public school alumni and university graduates between 1845 and 1870. Above and beyond this galaxy of genteel and nomadic clubs, others arose in almost every centre of British life. By 1900, virtually each town, village and hamlet boasted its local cricket heroes. There was thus, by the time of Queen Victoria's death, a form of amateur cricket appealing to every conceivable class and taste. In addition, there came the professional leagues in the north which survived well into the twentieth century. The MCC, which played only a handful of matches in the early 1860s, competed in 46 by 1869, and 196 by 1900.[4]

There is thus overwhelming evidence in support of a spectacular cricket explosion. It was caused, in part, by the impact of muscular Christianity which extolled the virtues of cricket above all other sports. Also important was the advent of railways, locomotion and macadamized roads, which considerably reduced the time and hazards involved in travel. The increasing prosperity of the society, the gradual extension of leisure time even for the working classes, the great publicity and encouragement given to all branches of sport by the press, the more positive attitudes on the part of educators and priests towards sport and recreation, and the tendency of private philanthropists and civic bodies to focus more on the utility of parks and playing fields all contributed in significant ways to the gradual ascendancy of cricket in the period after 1865.

Like other sports in the late-Victorian era, cricket profited immeasurably from the ongoing process of urbanization. Between 1871 and 1901 the percentage of the English population living in urban centres increased from 61 to 77, thereby producing superior markets for commercialized sport. Real wages in Britain increased by an estimated 60 per cent during the last three decades of the nineteenth century and thus permitted the workers greater opportunities for attending sporting events. The introduction of additional holidays and the regular Saturday half-day, which further reduced the industrial work week, also provided working-class Britons with more time to devote to recreation. These factors help to explain why, by 1880, there were as many as 214 cricket clubs in Birmingham alone and, by 1890, 224 in Liverpool.[5] The *Athletic News* also estimated that more than 1000 men were affiliated with the Notts Forest Association in 1887.[6] When the Fifty Guineas Cup was first offered for competition in Sheffield in 1880, no fewer than 40 clubs had signed up before the end of January. A similar trophy was then being contemplated in Leeds where cricket clubs had sprung up in large numbers; and cups of that sort were already being contested in Derbyshire, Leicestershire and Nottinghamshire.[7]

By the end of the century, the cricket field had become a traditional village tradition. As no one was then prepared to doubt the importance and necessity of cricket at the club level, many clubs were kept afloat by great patrons and local townsmen who provided the teams with equipment and took care of the grounds and pavilions. Most of the money for leases and renovations was provided by civic leaders and even when cricket clubs were founded as members of professional leagues for the purpose of making a profit, they were sustained by local charity more often than not. Generally speaking, southern clubs did not fare as well financially as those in the north, but even there it had become axiomatic by the end of the century that it was necessary for a club to play football in the winter to balance its books. This is one of the greatest ironies of the cricket explosion: clubs sprang up and stayed alive in a highly commercial age without making ends meet. The fact is that, after the 1860s, the cult of athleticism had convinced the majority of late-Victorians that cricket clubs were as vital to society as schools and churches.

Cricket associations thus flourished everywhere and were usually very efficiently organized at the local level. Within a radius of a few square miles several clubs would join together to play a series of regular weekend matches from May to September. The main focus of these associations was the big urban sprawl, like Birmingham and Manchester. The standard of cricket varied from poor to excellent and was dominated by amateurs both on and off the field. Club cricket was in many ways an escape from the tedium of the factory and the mine and was generally played without the fierce intensity which characterized Association football. Village cricket, as Gerald Howat and others have shown, was also played in rural and remote areas.

Slightly more serious was league cricket which emerged in the urban centres of the Midlands and the north. Most of the cricket clubs involved in league competition hired professionals, charged admission fees and aimed at making a profit. This kind of cricket began with the Heavy Woollen District Cup which was first contested at Batley, Yorkshire, in 1883.[8] Of the professional leagues, the most successful was the Lancashire Cricket League, founded in 1890. It was originally called the North-East Lancashire Cricket League, but adopted the better known title in 1892. From the start it attracted as many as 14 clubs representing a 20-mile radius of east Lancashire: Accrington, Bacup, Burnley, Church, Colne, East Lancs, Enfield, Haslingden, Lowerhouse, Nelson, Ramsbottom, Rawtenstall, Rishton and Todmorden. These clubs became symbols around which the local folk rallied and their supporters displayed the same partisanship and parochialism that had become so pronounced a feature of Victorian soccer.[9]

The Central Lancashire League, founded in 1893, was the direct offspring of the South-East Lancashire Cricket League which had first appeared in 1892. Its founding president was the Rev. John Russell Napier who had captained Marlborough in 1878 and had appeared occasionally for Cambridge University before playing for Lancashire in the 1880s. He is another example of those Victorian clergymen whose commitment to muscular Christianity led them to promote all types of cricket. The Central Lancashire League included teams from Bury, Crompton, Darwen, Dukinfield, Glossop, Heywood, Littleborough, Longsight, Middleton, Milnrow, Moorside, Oldham, Radcliffe, Rochdale, Royton, Stalybridge and Walsden.[10]

The Lancashire and Central leagues were by far the biggest in that county, but they were by no means the only ones. Several smaller leagues arose, including the Ribblesdale Cricket League, founded in 1893 and catering to Blackburn and Clitheroe, and the Saddleworth and District Cricket League which was established in 1898. Thus, by the end of the century, more than 50 professional cricket clubs were operating in the county of Lancashire alone.[11]

In the Midlands the two dominant cricket leagues at the turn of the century were the North Staffordshire and District League, formed in 1889, and the Birmingham and District League, established in 1893. In the northeast, the two major leagues were the North Yorkshire and South Durham League, founded in 1893, and the Huddersfield League, which first appeared in 1892. In short, throughout the counties of Durham, Lancashire, Staffordshire, Warwickshire, Worcestershire and Yorkshire, professional cricket clubs sprang up during the late-Victorian period and doggedly stayed alive, even when they were not altogether successful in a financial sense.[12]

To sustain themselves, however, the Victorian cricket clubs needed money. They could not pretend therefore to be totally disinterested in profit-making. Indeed, they used a number of devices to raise funds. On the whole, their revenues were mainly derived from gate-money receipts and membership subscriptions. Sometimes they augmented their income by renting their grounds for other sporting events like athletics, cycling and soccer. Notwithstanding these strategies, however, the majority of Victorian cricket clubs did not prove themselves economically viable. It came as something of a surprise, for instance, when the Holbeck club announced a net profit of £9 from its fixtures in 1876. More normal was the experience of the Longsight club which had to appeal for local subscriptions in 1889, just as the Bolton club had been compelled to do in the previous year. In 1892, it took a serious fundraising campaign at the local level for the Longsight cricketers to muster the necessary £1,500 they required for new grounds and facilities. It is not surprising that they succeeded, for their club had long been considered a community enterprise. The local folk took fierce pride in their cricket heroes who, in the 23 years of the club's existence up to 1892, had themselves contributed no less than £1,200 to Manchester charities. A similar appeal to local generosity, however, did not save the Stavely club (which had produced the mighty Barlow) from sudden and unceremonious extinction in 1900.[13]

In 1886, after a series of deficits, the Wakefield club reported that it was in debt to the tune of almost £200. This was viewed with equanimity by the *Athletic News*, whose editor remarked rather snidely that 'It would be difficult, however, to point to a cricket club which did not get into debt. It is one of their brightest privileges.'[14] Even the Dorking club, a mainly middle-class institution in the south, failed consistently to balance its budget in the 1880s. Its deficit stood at £55 in 1887. It managed to make ends meet during the 1890s only by staging concerts and renting its ground to cyclists and footballers.[15]

As a rule, it was football which paid cricket's debts in dual clubs such as Bolton, Darwen, Halifax and Sheffield United. In Darwen, for example, it was the annual loss of £60 by the cricket club which prevented Tom Hindle from balancing the accounts. When that club's finances showed a marked improvement in 1889, the *Athletic News* was quick to point out that 'this is what comes of success, for the Darwen cricketers have performed extremely well of late'.[16] In 1879, when the Halifax club found itself with a net profit of £384, it proceeded to clear the debts incurred by the cricketers in order to leave the whole club solvent. It was also from their football profits that the Halifax cricketers were able to build a new pavilion in 1886.[17] As for Sheffield United, the *Athletic Chat* was able to report in 1900 that the football club realized a profit of £1,755 while the cricket club showed a net loss of £521.[18] In 1888 the cricket gates produced only £6 for the Sunderland Cricket and Rugby Football Club while £102 came from rugby.[19] It came therefore as a great surprise when Read showed a profit of £25 for its cricket club in 1887 while its football club lost £9. As the *Athletic News* observed, 'in 99 cases out of 100 it is the other way about – football helps cricket over the stile of financial embarrassment'.[20]

That is not to say that all English cricket clubs were forever in debt during the Victorian age. Many of them experienced normal ups and downs in accordance with fluctuations in the local climate and economy. Some of them incurred financial deficits by also embarking on ambitious projects of rebuilding and renovation. The Bromley Cricket Club, for example, purchased a new ground in 1886 and erected a new pavilion at a cost of £690 in 1901. It was not therefore until 1908 that its debts were paid off in full.[21] Harrogate, one of the most prosperous clubs in Yorkshire, also made a number of improvements at the end of the century, including building a new and spacious grandstand in 1896. By 1900, it had wiped out much of its capital debt thanks to generous subscriptions and successful bazaars.[22]

Some Victorian cricket clubs actually did very well. Liverpool, for instance, boasted more than 500 members in 1894, not counting schoolboys and ladies at reduced subscriptions. Hence it could show a healthy profit of £282 despite expenditures in excess of £1,500, including nearly £500 for groundsmen and professionals.[23] The wealthy Wimbledon club was able to purchase its own ground in 1889 for £3,612 and to improve its facilities there in the 1890s without going into debt.[24] Membership dues and subscriptions were sufficiently productive to keep the Liverpool and Wimbledon cricket clubs financially stable independently of gate receipts. This was the good fortune also of the bourgeois Hampstead Cricket Club, whose annual membership fee in the 1880s amounted to two guineas, higher than that of most county cricket clubs.[25]

More dependent on their gate receipts were the league cricket clubs whose membership dues were considerably lower. Some of them, however, did fairly well too. Waverley, for example, could boast a credit balance of £11 in 1880 and was still reporting a 'goodly balance in hand' one year later, with receipts of nearly £100.[26] Halifax finally rivalled its soccer brethren in the late 1890s by signing Cyril Bland, a young professional qualifying for Sussex, and J.T. Brown, an old Yorkshire county hero.[27] Enfield also prospered towards the end of the century when huge crowds came out to watch its matches against arch rivals like Accrington and Church.[28] Some cricket clubs also made ends meet by holding prize draws, as did Bury in 1887; or arranging a bazaar, as Bingley did so successfully in 1889. The former cleared all its debts with an unexpected windfall of £100; while the latter realized £300 from its bazaar, paid off its £200 deficit and improved its cricket ground.[29]

Some league clubs did well enough to hire professionals. In Bradford, for example, the Church Hill club was able to engage two professionals – W. Binns and J. Blamires – as early as 1880.[30] Some clubs hired as many as three or four professionals in the 1890s, and it was reported in 1893 that almost every village cricket club in Yorkshire had at least one professional.[31] Still, unlike their soccer counterparts, the league cricket clubs could never afford to hire more than a few professionals in any one year. In fact, in many of the leagues, clubs were expressly forbidden to employ more than two in any one game. Hence, even in the so-called professional leagues, the majority of the players were actually amateurs. This might perhaps explain why none of the cricket clubs could quite match the extraordinary growth of soccer and rugby clubs; the receipts of Warrington Football Club, for instance, rose from £134 in 1882–83 to £669 in 1885–86 and to £1,234 in 1886–87.[32]

These developments in league and club cricket had their parallels at the county level, where the number of teams and matches increased substantially even while the county clubs were experiencing financial difficulties. The vast bulk of first-class cricket during 1845–70 had been provided by the great All England and United professional touring teams, led by William Clarke, George Parr, the Lillywhites and John Wisden, who popularized cricket by taking it virtually to every nook and cranny of the kingdom. Clarke, a bricklayer by profession, was the moving force behind the formation of the first All England XI (AEE) in 1846. He persuaded Alfred Mynn and V.S.C. Smith, two of the best amateurs of their day, to join the squad, but its real strength lay in the nine veteran professionals whom Clarke gathered around him. The team included such famous early Victorian cricket professionals as James Dean, James Guy, William Martingell, Fuller Pilch and W.R. Hillyer. Beginning with a brief slate of games in its first two years, the AEE was participating in as many as 24 by the summer of 1850. After Clarke's death in 1856, the team continued to function mainly under the guidance of George Parr, and by the 1860s was playing virtually anywhere on almost every day of the summer.[33]

For many years, the AEE was in great demand, even in small villages, although it soon found competition from other professional touring teams, some of whose members had objected to Clarke's autocratic brand of leadership. While the AEE eventually represented the north of England in the main, the United All England XI (UAEE), founded in 1852, catered largely to the needs of southern professionals before collapsing altogether in 1869. The UAEE, which had itself been an offshoot of the AEE, now found too much competition from the United South of England XI (USEE), another splinter group, which W.G. Grace helped to keep alive during the 1870s. Despite the friction between these itinerant groups, it is clear that the professionals did much to inspire the growth of first-class cricket in England. They demonstrated that there was an almost insatiable demand for cricket of high quality and generally showed how that demand could be met. While it is partly true that the travelling teams hastened their own demise, it must also be said that they were the victims of steadily changing circumstances after 1850. As the county cricket clubs began to put themselves on a more structured basis and as a new county spirit gradually manifested itself, there seemed less and less need for travelling teams and local communities found it harder to identify with them.[34]

During the 1860s and 1870s, interest gradually shifted to the classic contests between Eton and Harrow, Oxford and Cambridge, the Gentlemen and the Players, and the North against the South. Such counties as Kent, Middlesex, Nottinghamshire, Surrey and Sussex began to play against each other more and more regularly and by the late 1860s had become accustomed to drawing up an annual schedule of about seven to ten matches each.

The county competition grew in a rather haphazard fashion. Each committee had to arrange its own fixtures and there was no central body to coordinate the counties' plans. The MCC, which might have been expected to do so, remained for many years curiously reluctant to provide effective direction or leadership.[35] All kinds of administrative obstacles consequently appeared in the path of the county cricket competition up to the end of the nineteenth century. It is almost a miracle that the competition prospered eventually as it did. Some idea of the chaotic nature of county cricket in the early 1870s may be gathered from the fact that in 1873 Surrey played 14 first-class matches while Derbyshire played only two, Middlesex three and Kent four. This uneven distribution of matches was not altogether eliminated until the twentieth century.[36]

The nine counties which participated in the first-class competition in

1873 were Derbyshire, Gloucestershire, Kent, Lancashire, Middlesex, Nottinghamshire, Surrey, Sussex and Yorkshire. Between them they played 31 games. This number rose to 38 in 1876, 46 in 1880 and 58 in 1887, at which point Derbyshire withdrew. The remaining eight counties played 54 matches in 1890. Somerset was admitted to the competition in 1891, when 67 county games were contested at the first-class level. Then came the addition of five counties in 1895: Derbyshire, Essex, Hampshire, Leicestershire and Warwickshire. The 14 clubs then played 131 games. When Worcestershire was accorded first-class status in 1899, the county championship involved 149 matches. These figures clearly demonstrate how first-class cricket mushroomed during the last quarter of the nineteenth century. Yet the important question of county qualification was not settled until 1873; no recognizable system for determining the champion county was devised for several years; and the competition itself was not regularized until the last years of Queen Victoria's reign.[37]

The sporting press, in fact, played the leading role in determining the champion county. The system devised by the journalists in the 1870s was extremely simple: they considered the winner of the unofficial championship the county which had suffered the fewest losses. This method not only put an unfair premium on drawn or unfinished games, but it failed to take into account the vast disparity in the number of matches played by the counties. The absurdity of this device was fully exposed in 1886 when Nottinghamshire won seven and drew seven of their 14 fixtures, and thus won the title by avoiding defeat. Surrey, however, won 12 and lost only three of their 16 games and it seemed clear to many enthusiasts that their record was superior. Three years previously, Yorkshire, with nine wins and two losses from 16 matches had also unjustly lost to Nottinghamshire whose record was four wins, one defeat and seven draws. The stonewalling tactics of the Nottinghamshire professionals had produced few victories but had given their county a huge advantage by their ability to escape defeat.[38]

Even so, almost incredibly, the system used by the cricket reporters had worked well enough on the whole to remain intact until 1890. It was in that year that the county championship became officially recognized by the Cricket Council, which had been formed in 1887 by the county secretaries. The council ruled that the number of defeats should be deducted from the number of victories and the drawn games ignored. That the county championship itself should have been determined by the press for so long bears ample testimony to the refusal of the MCC to provide the necessary guidance during the critical period of first-class cricket expansion.

The excellence of the Graces gave Gloucestershire a decided advantage during the 1870s. But Lancashire and Nottinghamshire, with their powerful professional auxiliaries, were also highly competitive in the early years of the championship. Nottinghamshire, indeed, won or shared the title no fewer than nine times during 1873–86. Then came the magnificent Surrey dynasty, led by George Lohmann and Tom Richardson, two of the most feared bowlers of the late-Victorian age. As Surrey also included some of the finest batsmen of the period, such as Robert Abel, William Brockwell, Maurice Read, Walter Read and John Shuter, that county won six consecutive titles beginning in 1887. At the turn of the century, it was Yorkshire, ably led by Lord Hawke, which became dominant.[39]

The escalation of first-class cricket was the direct result of the marvellous growth of the game among the local clubs and the academic institutions. So much cricket was played in the 1890s, and so many good cricketers were then being produced, that England could well have staffed more than 15 first-class counties. The great public schools developed the skills of most of the amateurs, who mainly represented the southern counties, while the county clubs in the north drew heavily from local cricket clubs. In Yorkshire, for instance, Lascelles Hall Cricket Club, which dates back at least to 1825, became a famous nursery.[40] Surrey, floundering somewhat in the 1870s, decided to institute a local challenge cup 'with the view of promoting cricket, and, if possible, finding out young players of promise'.[41] This strategy quite clearly produced excellent results, although in the 1890s John Shuter, the Surrey captain, was complaining that there were too many cup matches at the local level where, in his opinion, the game had become too professional. He much regretted that the seriousness of the competition in second-class cricket had reduced the level of sportsmanship and put too much emphasis on winning, sometimes at any price.[42] If Surrey profited from the escalation of club cricket within the county, Somerset did not. As late as 1892 the Somerset county captain, Herbert T. Hewett, was regretting that his club still had to depend too much on public school alumni and university graduates. Even the recent triumphs of the county, in his view, had done too little to stimulate the growth of good cricket there. The game, of course, was played regularly in Hewett's county but the quality of its club cricketers was apparently lower than elsewhere. In any case, Somerset suffered from having to depend upon too narrow a population base.[43]

Difficulties sometimes arose between local clubs and county cricket committees. The Derbyshire committee, for instance, lamented in 1896 that some local clubs had occasionally refused to release their professionals to represent the county. League cricket was flourishing in Derbyshire at that time and the emphasis on winning in such competition sometimes made the local clubs reluctant to dispense with their best players.[44] When Yorkshire played against Gloucestershire at Sheffield in

1874 for Luke Greenwood's benefit, Tom Emmett's club refused to release him to play for the county. Reflecting bitterly on this matter a quarter of a century later, W.G. Grace considered such an action 'bad enough at any time, but, considering that this was a benefit match for one of Yorkshire's most valuable players, it was a discreditable proceeding'.[45] Some leagues and clubs, however, were conscious of the immense advantage that could be derived from county status. A first-class professional, absent on a given Saturday, was an immeasurably bigger attraction upon his return. This was fully recognized for many years in Lancashire, whose county captain, S.M. Crosfield, freely admitted in 1892 that most cricket clubs were so keen to help the county that they often sacrificed their own interests for the sake of Lancashire.[46]

County cricket on the whole profited greatly from the professional leagues which served as the best training ground for recruits. It also received a tremendous boost from international competition. Victorian cricket would never have flourished as it did had it not been for the Australians. The latter adopted the sport as their own national symbol and furiously tried to outshine the English on the cricket field. The quality of their play had not been good when the initial English teams visited them in the early 1860s. Yet, by 1878, they had become most competitive indeed. Their fielding and bowling had become superior to the English and they demonstrated, during their first English tour in 1878, how effectively they could exploit some of the helpful English pitches. George Giffen, one of the Australian all-rounders, observed that during the 1860s his countrymen were incapable of coping with James Southerton's fast bowling. They therefore deliberately developed speedsters of their own and, by the 1870s, could boast the 'Demon', F.R. Spofforth, and Harry Boyle, two of the fastest bowlers of any generation.[47] Boyle and Spofforth methodically ransacked a much vaunted MCC team at Lord's in May 1878, bowling them out twice for a meagre aggregate of 52 runs. This, in the considered judgment of the *Athletic News*, was 'the wonder of the cricket world'.[48]

The emergence of Australia as a great cricketing force was largely due to the coaching of English professionals in the 1860s. Charles Lawrence of Surrey was engaged by Australian cricket clubs after the tour of 1861–62. William Caffyn, another Surrey professional, coached the Melbourne club for seven years after the 1863–64 English tour of Australia. Jesse Hide also left his mark on Australian cricket after 1878 by teaching the colonists how to prepare better pitches.[49] The Australians learnt their lessons so well that by the 1880s they were ready to challenge their imperial masters. As the *Athletic Review* observed in April 1882, the question no longer was whether the Australians were progressing, but could they defeat England on even terms?[50] This question was answered resoundingly in the affirmative that summer, when the Australians won the only Test at the Oval.

Altogether the Australians made 11 tours to England between 1878 and 1902. They won the Test series on only three of these occasions, but they were competitive even in defeat, and it was largely the fear of losing to these colonials that kept the Victorian cricketers on their toes. Moreover, when playing at home, the Australians did more than just hold their own from 1876–77 onwards.

Club cricket, league cricket, village cricket, school cricket, university cricket and county cricket all combined to produce Test cricket at the end of the Victorian era. Cricket, however, failed to capture the imagination of people beyond the British empire in the way that soccer and athletics were shortly destined to do. Although the Dutch displayed a surprising enthusiasm for the game the Europeans as a whole steadfastly refused to be indoctrinated. The North Americans, after playing cricket reasonably well in the first two-thirds of the nineteenth century, apparently lost interest in it after their Civil War. The Canadians, who were the first to welcome an English touring team (in 1859), did not maintain the same keenness thereafter. The Indians adopted cricket with astonishing fervour in the nineteenth century but without the necessary skills to become an international threat until much later. The South Africans also lagged far behind before temporarily narrowing the gap during the Edwardian period. The West Indians, who are now such a dominant force in international cricket, were not accorded Test match status until 1928. Only the Australians, then, could pose a serious threat to English cricket supremacy during the late-Victorian age. But the quality of their play more than compensated for the paucity of challengers on the international stage.

Two other branches of cricket also bear witness to the great explosion. Cricket festivals became immensely popular and ice cricket, at least for a while, appealed to a sizeable minority. The oldest of the cricket festivals was the Canterbury Week which began in 1842 and attracted large crowds, even when the weather was dreary. By the 1870s, daily attendance in excess of 10 000 had become a regular feature. The great Hastings Festival, inaugurated in 1887, traditionally became the latest cricket carnival each season in the south. It was a financial success from the start, yielding a net profit in 1889, for instance, of £170.[51] The Cheltenham Festival was first staged in 1878. It survived despite the limitations imposed upon attendance by the physical dimensions of the ground. It was one of the most successful of the smaller festivals. By far the most famous of these affairs was the Scarborough Festival, established for the first time in 1876 by C.I. Thornton, who is still remembered today as one of the hardest hitters ever to have played cricket. The Scarborough Festival represented the grand finale each year to the cricket season in the north.

It consistently attracted all the more colourful players and long remained a great financial triumph. It began with gate receipts slightly in excess of £150 and very soon doubled its intake. It actually yielded £365 in 1885, and £475 in 1889. The Scarborough Cricket Club is also reported to have made about £500 from the festival in 1882.[52]

The Victorians played so much cricket at so many levels during the summer that it is incredible that some of them should still have been so eager to play the game on ice in winter too. The winter of 1878–79 was long and bitter, and it enabled more ice cricket to be played than ever before. *Wisden* actually carried reports of about a dozen games during that season. These were 'fun' events on skates, normally with compulsory retirement for each individual upon scoring 20 or 25 runs. Several first-class cricketers, such as Henry Charlwood, William Mycroft and Joseph Rowbotham, participated in some of these games.[53]

In January 1880, the Sheffield Skating Club arranged a 20-overs limit game at Sanbeck, 'the sylvan retreat of the Earl of Scarborough'. At least one observer considered both the cricket and the skating of high quality. He was much impressed, too, by the performance of R. Gillott when the club arranged another contest in the same week, this time on the Wentworth waters 'with the kind permission of Earl Fitzwilliam'.[54]

In January 1881, the members of the Sheffield club continued to play ice cricket. They played on the extensive lake at Welbeck on one occasion and on the River Tees, at Gainford, near Darlington, on another. The latter contest was 'witnessed by a large assemblage of spectators. The ice was good, and the players seemed at home on their skates, so that falls were not as numerous as expected.'[55] Ten years later, ice cricket was still being played at Sheffield Park, through the generosity of Lord Sheffield, and at Horsted Keynes, also in Sussex.[56]

There is, in short, some evidence to show that winter cricket was a fairly popular Victorian pastime. It was played mainly for amusement and was not taken half as seriously as the summer game. It was naturally promoted by skaters as well as cricketers, and received considerable encouragement (like normal cricket) from aristocratic families. The Duke of Devonshire, for example, was the moving force behind an ice cricket match on his Swiss Cottage pond on 17 December 1878. The Marquis of Abergavenny and the Earl of Scarborough were also keen ice cricket patrons.[57]

The devotion to ice cricket, which could not be commercialized by the Victorians, is most instructive. If that branch of the sport prospered without being an economic success, it did so in accordance with developments in cricket proper. Victorian cricket, in essence, transcended economics. It had become so much an integral element of their ritual, mores and tradition that they could never have viewed cricket, as occasionally they regarded soccer, as a business proposition first and foremost. Cricket to them was rather in the same category as music, literature and the arts. This approach to cricket does much to explain the economics of the game at that time.

As a profit-making enterprise, Victorian first-class cricket was a signal failure, especially when compared with the remarkable prosperity of first-division soccer. This was clearly understood by contemporaries, such as Arthur Wilson, a former secretary of the Derbyshire county club, who observed in 1894 that the 'County football club often takes more in one match than the Cricket Club during a whole season.'[58] During the Victorian age, many county clubs, even in the first-class competition, actually stayed alive only because of the generosity of their patrons. A careful examination of the finances of the county clubs shows how willing were late-Victorian philanthropists to regard the noble game of cricket as one of the most deserving of charitable causes.[59]

Perhaps the most generous of all Victorian cricket benefactors was Lord Sheffield, who spent a fortune trying to sustain the Sussex club. In the early 1880s, according to *Cricket*, he was annually donating £300 to the county club.[60] He personally engaged Alfred Shaw and William Mycroft, two veteran but excellent cricketers, to develop promising talent in Sussex. He also did the most to help the county open its £10,000 cricket ground near Brighton in 1887.[61] He was such an ardent cricket promoter that he took his own team to Australia in 1891–92, investing some £16,000 in that venture. He emerged from it with a net loss of £2,000 but still saw fit to donate a trophy to the Australians for the winner of their annual inter-state competition.[62]

The Derbyshire county club, founded, under the presidency of the Earl of Chesterfield in 1870, began its life in debt since the original subscription list was much too small. It accumulated an overall deficit of £1,000 by 1887. It took the generosity of Walter Boden and the Hon. William Monk Jervis (two wealthy industrialists) to liquidate that enormous debt.[63] Thereafter, the liberality of the Duke of Devonshire, G.H. Strutt and W.H. Worthington kept the county cricket club afloat. Strutt, who had donated £175 during the great crisis of 1886, continued to spend his own money on the club's business after his promotion to its presidency in 1887. His last gift to the club, just before his death in 1895, was a new scoring box. He also left it a legacy of £200 in his will. In spite of Strutt's efforts, however, the Derbyshire club remained in dire straits and avoided a huge debt in 1893 only through voluntary subscriptions amounting to £630.[64] The problem here, as Arthur Wilson explained in 1894, was three-fold. The membership of the county club remained so inadequate that annual subscriptions yielded less than £400. County cricket in Derbyshire had also drawn less than £300 in gate receipts each year on average during the past ten years. Moreover, the area was suffering from an acute and prolonged economic depression.[65] Wilson might also have added that Sam Richardson, who had been assistant secretary since 1880, embezzled around £1,000 from both the county cricket and football clubs and departed for Spain at the end of the 1889 season. As a result of all of these misfortunes, individual members were frequently urged by the county club committee to make generous and voluntary donations above and beyond their annual dues. They often responded with astonishing enthusiasm.[66]

The Essex county club for a long time fared no better than its counterpart in Derbyshire. At first it was much hamstrung by the small-ness of its ground at Brentwood. But its move to Leyton in 1886 involved huge debts which it could never have defrayed without the liberality of Lord Lyttelton and Charles E. Green. Its debts still stood close to £3,000 in 1889 and the club seemed on the verge of dissolution in 1893. From this calamity it was rescued by Green, the numerous Buxtons of Essex, and C.M. Tebbutt who, in 1895, actually came forward with an interest-free loan of £2,000. By the time of Tebbutt's death in 1898, the Essex club had finally turned the corner after depending for so long on local donations. The turning point came with its decision to enter the football business. Its finances also improved after the Great Eastern Railway Company agreed in 1898 to run an express train to Leyton on all county match days. Thus was the deficit of £850 in 1888 gradually transformed into a credit balance of £349 in 1901, when the county club's total receipts amounted to £4,637. Its membership had now risen to almost 2000, paying an annual fee of one guinea each.[67]

The Hampshire county club remained for several years in debt and actu-ally contemplated closure in 1904. Its progress had been much impeded at first by the inadequacy of its headquarters on the Old Antelope ground. But the move to Bannister Road in 1884 was costly, and even more so was the decision to invest almost £6,000 on a new ground in 1894 in anti-cipation of the club's promotion to first-class competition in the following year. Hampshire's receipts increased from £350 in 1884 to £1,055 in 1887, and £3,289 in 1899; but its expenses also increased proportionately. Its deficit stood at £319 in 1898. The annual fee remained fixed at one guinea, but (as in Derbyshire's case) the members consistently rescued the club from bankruptcy by making huge voluntary donations and conducting successful fundraising campaigns throughout the county.[68] This was especially true during the period 1898–1902 when Hampshire seemed particularly hard hit by the impact of the Boer War.[69]

The Leicestershire county club operated constantly at a loss in the 1880s, gradually worked its way up to a credit balance of £350 in 1896, only to fall again on hard times, reporting a deficit balance of £860 in 1901. The purchase of a new ground for more than £4,000 in 1899 aggravated Leicestershire's financial problems, rendered all the more serious by the loss of £500 on the 1900 season, but the club was bailed out in almost spectacular fashion by its local supporters. The Leicester *Daily Post* launched a shilling fund which yielded an incredible 15,000 shillings, and a bazaar organized by the county club produced a profit of £1,300. A sustained drive to increase the membership lifted the roll to almost 1700 by the end of 1901. By way of contrast, the number of members each paying one guinea per year had only been 412 in 1888 and 515 in 1889. After many lean years, the Leicestershire club could boast receipts of £4,467 at the end of the 1901 season and could look forward to the Edwardian age with buoyant optimism.[70]

The Somerset county club was not quite so fortunate. In 1893 it recorded its first ever credit balance, only to have it disappear at once. Its deficit stood at £140 in 1896, and the club was facing a severe financial crisis by 1900. The situation would have been altogether intolerable had the county not succeeded in arranging a fixture with the Australians in 1899. Very often during his long tenure, Somerset was saved by voluntary contributions from H.E. Murray-Anderdon, its honorary secretary from 1884 to 1910, who paid many of the club's bills out of his own pocket.[71]

The Warwickshire county club, which was destined to do so much better in the twentieth century, experienced perpetual penury during the late-Victorian age. For many years it failed to arouse much interest in the county and as late as 1883 could show only £77 from its subscription lists. The situation improved after the club moved its headquarters from Leamington to Edgbaston in 1885 and its membership increased from 51 to 782 within two years. But the move itself was costly (at least £1,250) and the club's finances remained most unstable throughout the 1890s. Its deficit stood at £1,150 in 1892 and had risen to £3,000 by the turn of the century. Thus, despite the generosity of such loyal patrons as C.B. Hollinsworth, the club had to appeal in 1902 for public support. The response was overwhelming. Some £3,561 was raised to put the county club on a financial footing for the first time.[72]

Lord Dudley did his best in the 1890s to make the Worcestershire county club a viable proposition, but notwithstanding his remarkable generosity, its deficit had climbed to £2,292 by 1901. Net losses in 1900 and 1901 amounted to £1,055 and £861 respectively. The bulk of this debt sprang from building and renovation costs, even though Lord Dudley had offered to foot the bill for enclosing the county ground in 1891. Worcestershire's gate receipts failed consistently to compensate for the inadequacy of the club's membership. As late as 1890 there were only 195 paying members. The roll jumped rapidly to 798 when Worcestershire was admitted into the first-class county championship and reached 1153 by 1902. But the debt still amounted to more than £780 in that year, and would have been considerably larger had it not been for the continuing support of Lord Dudley and Paul Foley, its honorary secretary from 1888 to 1908.[73]

If some of the first-class county clubs fared so poorly, it is not to be expected that the smaller counties performed any better. Berkshire, for example, announced a deficit of £940 in 1901 and had to admit that its immediate prospects were extremely bleak.[74] The Cheshire club seemed on the threshold of extinction in 1893.[75] Two years later, the Glamorgan club was seriously contemplating dissolution. Its financial woes continued into the twentieth century when it ended the 1900 season £150 in debt. It took a generous gift of £1,200 in 1901 from Sir John Llewellyn, one of its founders, and a visit from the Australians in 1902 for Glamorgan to achieve its first healthy credit balance of £273.[76] In Northamptonshire in the 1880s the county club resorted to balls, bazaars and whist drives, but could not prevent its deficit from climbing to £423 by 1890. Its overall debt stood at £1,050 in 1904 and the club was saved from bankruptcy only through a wonderful series of gifts, loans and donations from John Powys, the fifth Baron Lilford.[77] The Northumberland club's financial distress was such that it had been compelled to close its doors in 1894, but it was resuscitated early in the twentieth century in order to join the Minor Counties Competition.[78]

Considerably more successful in a financial sense were Gloucestershire and Kent. The former profited enormously from the popularity of the Graces, who played so magnificently during the 1870s and 1880s. Thus the club attracted many spectators even when it was winning less often on the field. In 1870 the Gloucestershire county committee established an annual membership fee of ten shillings per person and £1 per family. A life membership could also be purchased for a mere five guineas. These cheap rates attracted hundreds of subscribers and the club was consequently able to report a healthy credit balance on an annual basis. By 1897, its balance in hand was £2,300, and even after a particularly wet and disastrous summer in 1900, the Gloucestershire club could report a favourable balance of £2,127.[79]

Kent regularly boasted a credit balance also, even though that county club's membership roll was slim in comparison with others. There were only 475 members in 1888, 590 in 1889 and 689 in 1890. Yet its credit balance rose from £640 in 1886 to £1,114 in 1889. By 1905, thanks in large measure to the exertions of Lord Harris who served for several years as its captain and honorary secretary, membership had risen to 2805 and subscriptions totalled more than £2,000. In spite of costly renovations and improvements in the 1890s, Kent still reported a credit balance of £512 in 1893, £878 in 1895 and £842 in 1898. The county club not only drew large crowds to its regular matches but profited also from the Canterbury

Festival which consistently produced a surplus.[80]

The wealthiest county cricket clubs were those in Lancashire, Middlesex, Nottinghamshire, Surrey and Yorkshire. Middlesex and Surrey, of course, profited from their fortunate location in the lucrative London market. After moving its headquarters to Lord's in 1877, the Middlesex club steadily prospered to the point where it could claim a credit balance of £900 in 1892. This was a far cry from the 1860s when it depended for its very livelihood upon such benefactors as C. Gordon, G. Lee, William Nicholson and the veritable host of Walkers from Southgate. By the 1870s the club had paid off all its creditors with the sole exception of V.E. Walker who, in the end, accepted only half the amount due him when, in 1881, the club was willing and able to repay the entire loan.[81]

The Surrey club, with its headquarters at the spacious Kennington Oval, dwarfed all other county cricket clubs. As early as 1871, it was reporting a credit balance of £900, despite expenses in the region of £27,000. Constant improvements, purchases and renovations throughout the last quarter of the nineteenth century failed to upset its yearly budgets. Its credit balance in 1889 stood at £7,213. Five years later it proudly announced a credit balance of £9,537, while its receipts from cricket alone came to £13,593 in 1899.[82] Reflecting upon Surrey's affluence in 1894, the *Cricket Field* remarked that 'its receipts are so vast that they must make other county committees regret that they also cannot secure the presence of a London crowd'.[83]

The Surrey saga is a classic illustration of the Victorian cricket boom – even if, in a purely economic sense, its success was unique. In 1855 it catered to only about 230 members and its total income was below £500. By 1861 its membership had risen to almost 1000 and its revenues came close to £2,000. By 1885 nearly 1600 members had enrolled and this number exceeded 4000 by 1899. By the time of Queen Victoria's death, the Surrey CCC was thus almost as strong as the MCC itself in a numerical and financial sense.[84] Its success was due not only to its cricket but to its ability to rent the Oval for football and other purposes. Much of the credit for the rise of Surrey must therefore go to its diligent secretary, Charles Alcock, who was secretary also of the Football Association. The Surrey CCC could thus afford to treat its professionals as well as its amateurs more generously than other clubs. Its budgets in the 1890s reflected a degree of extravagance which envious counties must often have found extremely disconcerting.

If Middlesex and Surrey profited from the location of their headquarters in the prosperous southeast, the three northern counties owed their financial success to their subscription lists and to their fine tradition of excellence on the field, where they were consistently represented by native-born professionals who played good, 'hard' cricket. They were fortunate to have established themselves very early on such spacious grounds as Bramall Lane, Old Trafford and Trent Bridge. This put them in a much better position than county cricket clubs in Essex, Gloucestershire, Kent and Sussex – where the population was much less dense and the grounds were much smaller.

Lancashire was thus able to make consistent improvements to the Old Trafford ground after 1857 without going into serious debt. The club remained financially stable throughout the Victorian period. In 1885 its gate receipts produced over £3,300 while the stands yielded a further £343. Among its members 1641 subscribed one guinea each, 71 gave £2 each and two paid two guineas each. There were also 336 female members paying five shillings each. The club's credit balance in that year was £1,431. By 1890, the Lancashire CCC boasted 2,310 members, a credit balance of £2,082 and gross receipts in excess of £7,400. By the end of the century there were more than 3000 members in this club, whose net profit from the 1899 season alone was almost £2,000. It could therefore proceed without difficulty with the building of a new pavilion which was expected to cost approximately £20,000.[85]

Apart from a mild and brief slump both on and off the field in the mid-1890s, the Nottinghamshire county club enjoyed great financial success during the late-Victorian period. In 1872, while preparing to build a new pavilion at Trent Bridge, it reported a credit balance of £188. Despite a series of renovations and improvements, its credit balance rose to £438 by 1880. Although there were only 960 paying members in the Notts club by 1890, its receipts were still in excess of £3,200. These rose to more than £3,500 by 1895. The gate receipts consistently exceeded the annual subscriptions and this remained the county's major concern for many years.[86]

The most successful of the northern county cricket clubs was Yorkshire which grew so wealthy under Lord Hawke in the 1890s that it could afford to treat its professionals as generously as Surrey was then doing. By 1901 its receipts were exceeding £10,000 and its credit balance stood at £1,814. It was therefore in a position to celebrate its county championship by presenting its nine regular professionals each with a silver cup worth £10, in addition to a bonus of £20. The popularity of county cricket in Yorkshire was such that even when the team was not performing successfully on the field it still did consistently well at the gate. Its first actual net loss was not suffered until 1889, when its credit balance was reduced to £132. This unusual result was mainly due to a series of experimental Colts matches which cost in excess of £200. In any case, these losses were soon redeemed as the club showed a credit balance of £2,767 in 1895 and £4,233 in 1896. Yorkshire could therefore spend lavishly on buildings, improvements and renovations during the late 1890s.[87]

It seems clear, however, that even if the northern counties had failed to provide consistently successful cricket, they would still, like their southern brethren, have been sustained by their patrons. Keeping the county cricket club in motion was considered a vital community service in those days. It was not altogether necessary therefore for the county to strive for a credit balance as was the case with their counterparts in football. Moreover, soccer clubs knew only too well what it meant to be demoted: there was a vast difference between first and second division soccer. But there was never any such pressure on first-class county cricket clubs. Thus, while the majority of first division soccer clubs operated at a profit, and almost had no choice but to strive for excellence on the field, only a minority of county cricket clubs did. This perhaps was the fault neither of the committees nor the players – the explanation lies in the nature of Victorian cricket itself: county cricket was still too much a leisurely and protracted affair geared to meet the requirements of Georgian gentlemen-farmers.

Certainly no fault can be found with the legion of unpaid and voluntary administrators who ran the game at all levels during this age of unprecedented expansion. It was the various secretaries and treasurers of the clubs and associations, largely honorary officials, who organized Victorian cricket when it mushroomed almost to unwieldy proportions. All classes participated in this great enterprise: workers performed as players and groundsmen; wealthy families provided grounds and facilities; while mainly middle-class minds provided the necessary organizational skills.

It was, for instance, the county secretaries who did most of the hard work to keep their cricket clubs in operation and to set the county championship in motion. While all counties boasted aristocratic patrons and presidents, the secretaries were generally middle-class men and/or public school alumni and university graduates, such as Charles Alcock of Surrey and S.H. Swire of Lancashire. Middle-class families, such as the Graces of Gloucestershire, the Fosters of Worcestershire and the Walkers of Middlesex, provided the administrative expertise and enterprise. Some aristocratic personalities, such as Lord Harris in Kent, Lord Hawke in Yorkshire and Lord Sheffield in Sussex, also left an indelible impression upon their counties and on the sport itself.

Upper- and middle-class direction also kept the celebrated MCC afloat during the nineteenth century. Its membership remained aristocratic throughout the Victorian age. Midwinter estimated that, even in the 1880s when the MCC's roll already exceeded 2000, there was still an average of one titled member for about every seven.[88] Its long list of presidents is aristocratic, but the spade work was done by methodical secretaries, like Robert A. Fitzgerald and Henry Perkins, who took charge of all the minutiae of MCC administration for an aggregate of 35 years.

As spectacular as was the growth of Surrey and Yorkshire, none of the county cricket clubs could quite match the performance of the MCC, whose extraordinary growth was really one of the major features of the great cricket explosion. In 1835, the MCC had only about 250 members and this number grew to approximately 600 by 1860. During Fitzgerald's tenure as secretary, from 1863 to 1877, the club's membership rose from 651 to 2080. Thanks largely to his zeal and enterprise, the MCC by 1869 had achieved independent ownership of Lord's, a new pavilion, tavern, press box, tennis courts and a level cricket outfield at long last. During the 1860s, too, boundaries were established at Lord's, nets for practising also appeared and a cricket museum was started. In 1870, Guy's Garden and the Grand Stand were purchased for £3,490. Turnstiles were introduced in 1871 for the purpose of crowd assessment and control and the re-levelling of the Lord's pitch was completed by 1875.[89]

The MCC continued its steady growth under Fitzgerald's equally zealous successor, Henry Perkins, who served as secretary during 1877–98. MCC membership rose to 2579 in 1880; 3666 in 1890; and over 4700 by the turn of the century. Still thinking of itself as a private (rather than national) organization, the MCC then considered limiting its membership to 5000. That self-denying ordinance, however, proved impossible to enforce.[90]

The MCC's revenues and its reputation naturally reflected that physical growth. In 1873, for example, its receipts amounted to £3,012. They rose to £15,065 in 1884, and reached £21,632 by 1890. The club's total income in 1898 had risen to £82,565 – including £37,200 from life memberships, £4,680 from gates and a further £6,905 from the stands.[91] Thus was the MCC able to renovate its headquarters at Lord's without ever going into serious debt. In 1888, it elected 100 new life members at £100 each and raised its entrance fees to £5 for ordinary members in order to purchase Henderson's Nursery from the Clergy Orphan Corporation for £18,500, as well as freeholds of Nos 17 and 21 Elm Tree Road and the leasehold of No. 43 St. John's Wood Road. In 1899, when it was considering further expansion to its facilities, its executive committee decided to elect 200 new life members at £200 each. With this simple expedient, the cricket club raised £40,000 in one fell swoop. The magnitude of this achievement can best be understood when it is contrasted with the small four-digit budgets of most of the county cricket clubs, many of which were then operating at a loss.[92]

As the wealthiest cricket supporters and the most promising amateurs all gravitated towards the MCC, which then hired the best professionals in the country, it simply became the strongest cricket club in existence. Its fame rested squarely on its affluence, its longevity and its cricketing skills. From the outset, it managed to attract influential families and its membership roll included several aristocrats, politicians and businessmen. But, for many years, it looked upon itself as just another private club among a host of others. Early cricket historians, like Ashley Cooper and Harry Altham, regarded the MCC as at once a supreme court and an imperial parliament during the nineteenth century. The MCC never did arrogate to itself such power and authority, however, during the Victorian age. These were functions and responsibilities thrust upon it during the Edwardian era by the county committees who had long recognized the need for some centralized authority and had grown tired of its bashfulness.

When, during the Georgian period, the MCC had codified the laws, it had done so primarily for the benefit of its own members. Others chose to accept these regulations because they naturally superseded older, oral, and therefore less articulate, traditions. In 1835, it was the professionals who compelled the MCC to accept the legality of round-arm bowling. The MCC remained, like cricket itself, too true to its Georgian roots. It was spawned by a society which glorified private enterprise and supported the dictum that the government is best which governs least. *Laissez-faire* could well have been its motto.

It has long been assumed that the MCC, almost as soon as it was founded in 1787, established itself as the supreme authority in the world of cricket. In fact, however, the MCC's early growth was somewhat pedestrian and the club behaved for many years as a private institution, organizing only a handful of matches in and around London. During its first hundred years, the MCC played only a small part in cricket's evolution. All the important cricket traditions which developed during the nineteenth century had very little to do with MCC guidance or intervention. The growth, for instance, of the Eton–Harrow, Oxford–Cambridge and Players–Gentlemen rivalries was the direct result of individual initiatives rather than MCC prompting. The gradual establishment of the county championship also depended entirely on the hard work and determination of the secretaries of the leading county cricket clubs.

Such writers as Rowland Bowen, Christopher Brookes and Maurice Golesworthy have done much to revise the old image of an omnipotent MCC. But they themselves still thought too much in terms of confrontation between the MCC and other rivals both real and imaginary.[93] The MCC did occasionally revise the laws, and did, in 1873, vainly attempt to institute a county challenge cup. But, in the main, it was a diffident and passive body, in modern parlance, doing its own thing and expecting others to do theirs. It remained consistently reluctant to assume the leadership of the game. The county secretaries, in fact, often despaired of the MCC's caution and hesitancy. They eventually formed a county council in 1887 to deal with some of the more pressing problems facing county cricket. It was the secretaries, too, who had met in 1873 to discuss the thorny issue of county qualifications; and it was their initiative which resulted in the residence restrictions announced by the MCC that year. The leaders of county cricket, however, did not succeed in persuading the MCC to take charge of the county championship until 1894.[94]

The County Cricket Council did not regard itself (as some writers have hinted) as in any sense a rebellious body seeking emancipation from MCC domination. Too many members of this small caucus, after all, were members also of the MCC. They felt they could play an advisory role and hoped indeed to obtain MCC sanction for their major resolutions. In effect, they were anxious to force the MCC to assume a more positive stance and in this they eventually succeeded. Even after the council had formally dissolved itself in 1894, on the understanding that the MCC would thenceforth accept responsibility for administering first-class cricket in England, the county secretaries had to meet again to standardize the county schedule at long last.[95]

At the very end of the Victorian age, the MCC finally relented, long after it had become clear that some cricket parliament was necessary in a period of furious cricket expansion. Even the responsibility for selecting English teams was not accepted by that club until the turn of the century. Almost incredibly, the first full-fledged MCC team to Australia was that of 1903–04. And it was not before 1899 that the decision was finally made to establish a national selection committee for the purpose of choosing England's Test teams. Like most of the important resolutions reached in Victorian cricket, this idea came also from the county secretaries.[96]

It is thus clear that Victorian cricket was never governed by the MCC to the same extent that soccer fell under the control of the Football Association after 1863. The latter organization was the product of an urban and industrial civilization which put much greater store on centralized administration, efficiency and control. The Football Association was deliberately intended to coordinate all the multifarious activities of local clubs, leagues and associations. This it proceeded to do in the businesslike, methodical fashion that is so characteristic of industrial capitalism. This could certainly not have been said of the Victorian MCC.

The MCC, it is true, sanctioned rule changes periodically during the nineteenth century; but it did so very often after the changes had been recommended by the counties. It was indeed the conservative spirit of the MCC itself that kept the Georgian cricket laws more or less intact throughout the nineteenth century. Beyond the legalizing of overarm bowling in 1864, Victorian cricket legislation did not lead to any fundamental changes in the structure of the game. It required a long and furious agitation in the 1890s even to persuade the MCC to remove the outmoded restrictions governing declarations and the follow-on. It took a similar campaign by men such as Lord Harris and Sydney Pardon, the editor of *Wisden*, to compel the MCC to act on the delicate matter of throwing. And it was not until 1904 that the MCC finally agreed, at the request of the counties, to form an advisory county cricket committee to consider vital issues emanating from the organization of the county championship. The president of the MCC became the chairman of this committee, whose resolutions thereafter came to be submitted for MCC approval.[97]

Many suggestions were also made, especially about the injustice of the lbw law, which the MCC chose often to ignore. When, for example, the County Cricket Council voted on 8 February 1888 to recommend a change in the lbw law, all the MCC was prepared to do was to resolve, on 2 May 1888, 'That the practice of deliberately defending the wicket with the person instead of the bat is contrary to the spirit of the game, and inconsistent with strict fairness, and the MCC will discountenance and prevent this practice by every means in their power.' On that occasion, the MCC also requested a longer period of reflection before acting on the new recommendations with respect to five-ball overs and the important question of closures.[98] Twelve years later, the MCC finally relented, changing the lbw law to the bowler's benefit, introducing six-ball overs, and passing a follow-on rule which made it optional for a team, with a first innings lead of 150 runs or more (or 75 runs in a one-day match), to ask its opponents to bat again.[99]

It is therefore difficult to conclude that the MCC made a significant contribution to Victorian cricket. It seems likely that the game would have developed in the way that it did, even had the MCC been dissolved. The most that can be said is that it became a legendary Victorian institution because of its wealth and the social structure of its membership. It became easily the most prosperous cricket club in the world and its roll included some 300 members of the landed élite during the 1880s. The majority of its presidents during the nineteenth century were titled members of the aristocracy, of whom there were still about 450 among the MCC roll in 1915. It was also the strongest cricket club in the world, and as such, was relied upon heavily for leadership even when it was itself most reluctant to provide it. The MCC was most helpful to those professionals, whom it engaged on its ground staff to bowl against gentlemen-amateurs. It generally paid better fees than the counties and also established a benefit fund to assist its professionals in time of illness and injury. It sometimes arranged a second benefit match for professionals whose original benefit had failed. It was thus the dream of every young cricketer to be invited to Lord's. The MCC engaged 15 ground bowlers in 1867. This number rose to 25 in 1880, 30 in 1884, 45 in 1890, 50 in 1893 and 62 by 1900.[100]

It was, in the final analysis, the extraordinary growth of cricket which compelled the game, almost in spite of itself, to modernize its own structure. It was impossible for so many clubs, leagues, associations, counties and colonies to play the game in the same parochial, haphazard, informal and uncoordinated way in which the Georgians had played it. This was a truth which the MCC, steeped in its Georgian ideology, recognized only very late.

In retrospect, it seems hardly possible that cricket could indefinitely have escaped from the influences by which it was surrounded on so many sides. The Industrial Revolution had created so many social and economic problems that the central government could no longer pretend that old-fashioned local institutions were capable of solving them. The Victorians responded to the new circumstances by establishing, indeed, a host of authoritarian bodies to regulate interpersonal relationships. Hence the emergence of sports councils, trade unions, professional associations, and even temperance movements. In the field of sports, the Victorians expected to find leadership from such institutions as the Football Association, Hurlingham, the Jockey Club and Wimbledon. As the historian W.L. Burn has so perceptively observed, the MCC was but the cricketing equivalent to such Victorian artefacts as the Institution of Naval Architects and the Institute of Chartered Accountants. The attempts to exalt the MCC were entirely in keeping with contemporary norms.[101] Had the MCC not been founded in the eighteenth century, the Victorians would assuredly have had to invent it in the nineteenth.

Notes

1.   Brookes, *English Cricket*, 90, 136. Lemmon, *Middlesex County Cricket Club*, 24–26. Mandle, 'Games People Played', 511.
2.   Webber, *County Championship*.
3.   Golesworthy, *Encyclopaedia of Cricket*, 145.
4.   Brookes, 90. Haygarth, *Scores and Biographies*, VI: 395. *Wisden 1879*, 19. *Wisden 1901*, 272.
5.   W. Vamplew, *Pay Up and Play*, 51–53. See also *Midland Athlete*, 23 February 1881, 139–40.
6.   *Athletic News*, 17 May 1887, 1.
7.   *Cricket and Football Times*, 22 January 1880, 163.
8.   Golesworthy, 134.
9.   J. Kay, 'League Cricket', in Swanton, ed., *Barclays World of Cricket*, 571.
10. *Ibid.*, 572. See also Green, ed., *Wisden Obituaries*, 646.
11. Kay, 'League Cricket', 571–75.

12. *Ibid.*
13. *Athletic News*, 2 December 1876, 7; 20 March 1888, 1; 9 December 1889, 1; 18 July 1892, 1; and 7 January 1900, 1.
14. *Ibid.*, 20 April 1886, 1.
15. Cole, *Two Hundred Years of Dorking Cricket*, 42–49.
16. *Athletic News*, 11 October 1887, 1; and 9 September 1889, 1.
17. *Ibid.*, 7 May 1879, 6; and 3 August 1886, 1.
18. *Athletic Chat*, 6 June 1900, 6.
19. E.W. Moses, *To Ashbrooke And Beyond: The History of the Sunderland Cricket and Rugby Football Club 1808–1962* (London, 1963), 61.
20. *Athletic News*, 11 October 1887, 1.
21. Eames, *Bromley Cricket Club*, 16–28.
22. Greaves, *Over the Summers Again*, 43–45.
23. *Cricket Field*, 31 March 1894, 42.
24. Wakley, *History of the Wimbledon Cricket Club*, 38–39.
25. Monro, *History of the Hampstead Cricket Club*, 30.
26. *Cricket and Football Times*, 15 January 1880, 156; and 13 January 1881, 142.
27. *Athletic News*, 17 June 1895, 1.
28. *Sports Telegraph*, 4 June 1898; and 23 July 1898.
29. *Athletic News*, 1 March 1887, 1; and 15 July 1889, 1.
30. *Cricket and Football Times*, 22 January 1880, 168.
31. *Cricket Field*, 6 May 1893, 67.
32. *Athletic News*, 14 June 1887, 1.
33. G.D. West, *The Elevens of England* (London, 1988), 4–46.
34. *Ibid.*, *passim.* Lemmon, *Middlesex County Cricket Club*, 24–26. P. Roebuck, *The Official History of Somerset County Cricket Club* (London, 1991), 11. Sissons, *The Players*, 3–82.
35. Brookes, 68–128. Lewis, 133, 146.
36. Webber, 18.
37. *Ibid.*, 14–39.
38. *Ibid.*, 16–22.
39. Webber, 15, 24, 33.
40. D. Hodgson, *The Official History of Yorkshire County Cricket Club* (London, 1989), 20–21. Martineau, *They Made Cricket*, 150.
41. *Cricket and Football Times*, 26 February 1880, 227.
42. *Cricket Field*, 28 May 1892, 59–60.
43. *Ibid.*, 27 August 1892, 313. Roebuck, 9–11.
44. *Cricket*, 27 February 1896, 18.
45. Grace, *Reminiscences and Recollections*, 138.
46. *Cricket Field*, 20 August 1892, 292.
47. G. Giffen, *With Bat and Ball* (London, 1898), 5.
48. *Athletic News*, 29 May 1878, 4, 6.
49. Giffen, 11, 199. Midwinter, *Grace: Life*, 45.
50. *Athletic Review*, 5 April 1882, 17–18.
51. See, e.g., *Wisden 1875*, 71; *Wisden 1879*, 66; and *Wisden 1890*, 28.
52. *Athletic News*, 27 September 1882, 1. *Cricket Field*, 15 September 1894, 467. Leveson Gower, *Off and On the Field*, 221.
53. *Wisden 1880*, 17–21.
54. *Cricket and Football Times*, 5 February 1880, 188–89.
55. *Athletic News*, 26 January 1881, 8.

56. *Cricket*, 17 January 1891, 16.
57. *Wisden 1880*, 17–21.
58. *Cricket Field*, 28 July 1894, 325.
59. Sandiford and Vamplew, 'The Peculiar Economics of English Cricket Before 1914', 311–26.
60. *Cricket*, 25 October 1883, 423.
61. *Athletic News*, 28 July 1885, 1; and 17 May 1887, 1. *Cricket and Football Times*, 22 January 1880, 168. Mandle, 'The Professional Cricketer', 8.
62. Lee, *Sussex County Cricket Club*, 110. Midwinter, *Grace*, 104. *Wisden 1893*, 329.
63. W.T. Taylor, 'History of Derbyshire Cricket', *Wisden 1953*, 104.
64. *Cricket*, 9 September 1886, 406; 9 June 1887, 185; 18 April 1895, 72; and 2 May 1895, 102. *Cricket Field*, 29 October 1892, 396; 31 December 1892, 427; and 4 May 1895, 63.
65. *Cricket Field*, 28 July 1894, 325.
66. *Ibid.*, 25 February 1893, 19. *Cricket*, 16 April 1891, 59; 14 April 1898, 58; and 25 April 1901, 91. See also Shawcroft, *Derbyshire County Cricket Club* (London, 1989), 21, 52.
67. *Cricket*, 26 November 1885, 456; 3 May 1888, 100; 31 October 1889, 447; 9 May 1895, 123; 14 April 1898, 53; and 11 April 1901, 55. *Cricket Field*, 3 September 1892, 332; 28 January 1893, 3; and April 1893, 52. *Wisden 1899*, 1.
68. Altham *et al.*, *Hampshire County Cricket* (Sportsmans Book Club, 1958), 29–52. *Cricket*, 24 November 1887, 462; 21 December 1899, 474; and 20 December 1900, 472.
69. Wynne-Thomas, *Hampshire County Cricket Club*, 65.
70. *Cricket*, 15 April 1886, 52; 25 March 1897, 45; 27 April 1890, 53; 29 March 1900, 44; and 28 March 1901, 42. E.E. Snow, *A History of Leicestershire Cricket* (Leicester, 1949), 96–172.
71. *Cricket*, 24 November 1898, 465; 21 December 1899, 476; 20 December 1900, 472; and 28 November 1901, 460. *Cricket Field*, 25 November 1893, 487. Roebuck, *Somerset County Cricket Club*, 32–33, 44–45.
72. *Athletic News*, 5 December 1892, 1. *Cricket Field*, 6 April 1895, 47. Duckworth, *Story of Warwickshire Cricket*, 12–87.
73. *Cricket*, 26 March 1891, 45; 26 November 1891, 481; and 28 November 1901, 454. *Cricket Field*, 2 March 1895, 32. Lemmon, *Worcestershire County Cricket Club*, 41.
74. *Cricket*, 11 April 1901, 57.
75. *Cricket Field*, 15 November 1893, 487; and 8 December 1894, 499.
76. *Ibid.*, 5 January 1895, 4. Hignell, *Glamorgan County Cricket Club*, 40–42.
77. J.D. Coldham, *Northamptonshire Cricket: A History* (London, 1959), 35–56.
78. *Cricket Field*, 25 March 1893, 35; and 2 March 1895, 32.
79. *Athletic News*, 5 May 1885, 1; and 16 April 1900, 1. *Cricket*, 15 April 1886, 51; 14 April 1887, 52; 5 May 1898, 105; and 18 April 1901, 73. See also Midwinter, 38.
80. *Cricket*, 29 November 1888, 458; 27 February 1890, 28; 26 March 1891, 44; 26 March 1896, 38; 24 November 1898, 465; and 28 November 1901, 459. See also D. Moore, *Kent County Cricket Club*, 32.

81. W.J. Ford, *Middlesex County Cricket, 1864–1899* (London, 1900), 4–11. Lemmon, *Middlesex County Cricket Club*, 48, 53.
82. *Cricket*, 2 May 1889, 87; 26 April 1900, 92. *Wisden 1872*, 78.
83. *Cricket Field*, 28 April 1894, 51.
84. Lemmon, *Surrey County Cricket Club*, 46–48. G. Ross, *The Surrey Story* (London, 1957), 27.
85. *Athletic News*, 19 January 1886, 1. *Cricket*, 25 February 1886, 31; 26 February 1891, 18; 23 February 1899, 27; 21 December 1899, 476; and 20 December 1900, 472. *Cricket Field*, 25 February 1893, 19; 24 February 1894, 19; and 2 March 1895, 31. Wynne-Thomas, *Lancashire County Cricket Club*, 64, 80.
86. *Athletic News*, 2 February 1881, 8; and 27 January 1885, 6. *Cricket*, 26 January 1888, 11; 27 January 1890, 7; 30 January 1896, 13; and 31 January 1901, 11. *Wisden 1873*, 208.
87. *Athletic News*, 29 December 1880, 7; and 6 August 1900, 1. *Cricket*, 27 January 1890, 12; 26 March 1896, 39; 25 March 1897, 42; 21 December 1899, 474; and 19 December 1901, 468.
88. Midwinter, 78. Brookes, 134–35. Lewis, 20, 40, 152.
89. Bowen, *Cricket: A History of its Growth and Development*, 101. Grace, *Reminiscences and Recollections*, 22–27. Lewis, 131, 160. Marshall, *Lord's*, 34. *Wisden 1870*, 17–18; and *1871*, 18.
90. *Cricket*, 7 May 1891, 98; and 25 April 1901, 91. *Wisden 1882*, 18; *1900*, 316; and *1901*, 272. Lewis, 13.
91. *Cricket*, 8 May 1890, 106. *Wisden 1875*, 23; *1886*, 90; and *1900*, 315.
92. *Athletic News*, 29 April 1889, 1. *Cricket*, 4 May 1899, 108. *Wisden 1889*, 192; and *1900*, 314–16.
93. Bowen, 101–05, 136. Brookes, 90–100, 120. Golesworthy, 16.
94. *Cricket*, 24 November 1887, 454. *Cricket Field*, 5 January 1895, 3. *Wisden 1874*, 93–96; *1888*, 345–57. Lewis, 133.
95. *Cricket*, 24 November 1887, 454. *Cricket Field*, 5 January 1895, 3; and 11 May 1895, 83. *Wisden 1874*, 93–95; and *1888*, 345–53.
96. Gordon, *Background of Cricket*, 155–58. Leveson Gower, *Off and On the Field*, 119. Midwinter, 105–06.
97. *Cricket*, 29 March 1888, 42. *Cricket Field*, 6 May 1893, 66. *Wisden 1895*, li-lviii; *1897*, 216; *1898*, lvii-lviii; *1888*, 354–57; *1894*, xlvii-liv; *1895*, xvi; and *1901*, xvii-xix.
98. Lewis, 174–75. *Wisden 1889*, 344–46.
99. *Wisden 1890*, xxxvi; and *1901*, 272–73.
100. Brookes, 134–35. *Cricket*, 1 May 1884, 90; and 3 May 1900, 102. *Wisden 1882*, 20; and *1892*, 168.
101. W.L. Burn, *The Age of Equipoise: A Study of the Mid-Victorian Generation* (London, 1964), 270–94.

CHAPTER FIVE

Amateurs and Professionals

Betting, corruption and professionalism had been integral elements in Georgian cricket. The Victorians discarded the first two and kept the third, while for a long time trying to exclude all three from soccer. In the end they failed and had to accept professionalism in Association football in 1885. Curiously, none of this soul-searching occurred in cricket where professionalism was always quite simply regarded as a necessary evil. First-class cricket, in fact, sprang directly out of professionalism. It was the touring professionals who taught the Victorians how to play as well as sell the game. Without the work of the All England and United Elevens during the period 1845–70, county cricket might never have evolved as it did.

The professionals who played under Clarke, Parr and Wisden were skilled entrepreneurs who contracted to display and exploit their skills on their own terms. They were not hired hands, as so many of the Georgian professionals had been. Yet, when the Victorians accepted professionalism in cricket, they preserved the Georgian image of professionals as retainers and consistently treated their best cricketers as hired servants rather than skilled artisans. The MCC did much to keep alive this notion by regarding fast bowling as menial work and engaging professional bowlers to keep its batsmen in form. Thus was generally established in the public mind the idea that masters batted while servants bowled.

If professional cricket was part of the Georgian legacy, so too was the distinction between the amateur and the professional. The amateur was the gentleman with the bat, and the professional was the labourer with the ball. To keep alive this distinction, cricket clubs (including the MCC) had promoted a series of games between the Gentlemen and the Players. These contests in time became the traditional classics arranged at Lord's, the Oval and Prince's Ground, and the custom persisted from 1806 to 1962. It was not before the latter year that Englishmen could admit the absurdity of eighteenth-century distinctions based on snobbish ideas about class and status.

Class distinctions were so rigidly preserved by the Victorians that professionals and amateurs used different facilities, dressed in different pavilions, used different gates, travelled in different compartments on trains and generally maintained a discreet distance between themselves.[1] As late as the Edwardian age, the divisions between lower-class professional and upper-class amateur were deep enough to leave men like E.J. 'Tiger' Smith of Warwickshire with very bitter memories.[2] Even the stands were built with the idea of separating the élite from the multitude. There were members' pavilions, balconies, grandstands, and open areas – each denoting, through price and usage, a certain social status.[3]

This question of status was as important to Victorians as matters of law and propriety. It was a fundamental feature of their mores. Class lines were then so inflexibly drawn, in sport as elsewhere, that labourers and artisans were long debarred by the London Athletic Club from participating in its athletic meetings.[4] Victorian professional cricketers were not, therefore, being maltreated or degraded in an unusual way. The relationship between themselves and amateurs was essentially the same as that between servant and master. A professional was a menial, an amateur a gentleman. The one denoted lower-class status, the other bourgeois or higher status. Professionalism in cricket, as in soccer, was seen as the sporting equivalent to unionism in industry; and for a very long time few middle- and upper-class Victorians were willing to support such a principle. The same tensions which separated professionals from amateurs on the cricket field operated also in soccer and golf.[5]

Even after trade unionism had been legalized in British industry, professionalism in sport remained stigmatized; and to make matters worse, the professionals themselves denounced unionism. Although the Victorian age witnessed a few isolated attempts by a handful of professionals to withhold their services, there was never any concerted movement towards a players' association. Many journalists who had no objection to professionalism in cricket still regretted any threat of strikes or suspicion of unionism. Thus, when three Nottinghamshire professionals refused to play against the Australians for the regular match fee of £10, the editor of *Cricket* took exception. He criticized William Barnes, Wilfred Flowers and Arthur Shrewsbury on the curious ground that cricket was not a business. Cricketers could not expect the same rights as workers in an industry, because the sport was not a source of profit to those who were running the county clubs.[6] Cricket, in essence, was a community service and not a profit-making enterprise.

It was precisely this kind of thinking that lay behind the Victorian hostility towards professionalism in sport. Games were intended to be a source of recreation. Cricket was essentially play, as opposed to work. Professionalism tended to destroy the element of sportsmanship and to make the game too serious. This opinion was perhaps most articulately expressed by the *Athletic Chronicle* at the end of the century. Professionalism, it argued, is not sport and never can be. Professionals play only to win and augment their income. They will therefore play for the highest bidder and can never develop any sense of loyalty to a particular team.[7] This idea that the professional was too selfish and too mercenary was then very widely held. It did not matter that the majority of cricket professionals played for only one county club and were, in any case, much restricted in their movements by the qualifying clause of 1873. This regulation prevented cricketers from playing for more than one county in any one season and established a minimum period of two years' residence in a county before an individual could be selected to represent it. A player who chose to represent the county of his residence was also prohibited from playing against the county of his birth. The Victorians also failed to take fully into account the fact that the vast majority of professional cricketers became totally devoted to their adopted county.

Most middle-class Victorians, like Frederick Gale and Rev. James Pycroft, preferred to see cricket played by amateurs purely for its own sake and their personal enjoyment.[8] This attitude was constantly echoed in the press, most militantly so by the *Athletic Review* which announced, in its first issue in 1882, that it intended to deal exclusively with amateurs and amateur sports.[9] The *Athletic News*, more moderate than most, favoured professionalism in soccer mainly because it foresaw that the problem would thereby become easier for the Football Association to control.[10] Even W.G. Grace, the arch shamateur of the age, held opinions on this subject that can only be described as reactionary at best.[11] The fairly general notion then was that it was improper to play for pay, and no respectable gentleman would therefore do it. The result was that a certain stigma attached to professionalism in sport which became almost impossible to eradicate completely.

A few enlightened spirits in the nineteenth century did support the professional idea. The editor of the *Midland Athlete*, for instance, called for a programme which would upgrade local cricket skills to avoid the importation of professionals. He promoted the principle that professionals must always form the backbone of county teams and should therefore be homegrown.[12] Walter Long, a prominent Conservative politician, considered that the professionals had put a good deal more into the game than they were extracting from it. He thought (in 1900) that even the best county cricketers were underpaid. It is noteworthy, however, that he was averse to any kind of unionism in sport. 'Heaven save us,' he wrote, 'from strikes, lock-outs, and unions in cricket – where the only strike in the game should, and always must, come from the full face of the bat.'[13]

Victorian cricket professionals received constant support, too, from a certain Mr Willoughby, an eccentric member of the MCC, who regularly attended its annual meetings for the express purpose of criticizing its committee. Year after year, among his sundry criticisms, he persisted in recommending better treatment for the professionals on the ground staff at Lord's.[14] But perhaps the staunchest supporter of professionalism in cricket at that time was Lord Harris, one of the most famous personalities in the history of Kent county cricket. He assumed a much more liberal position on the professional question than the majority of his contemporaries and believed it was unfair to prevent professionals from selling their skills to any county of their choice. 'The professional,' he declared, 'is entitled to exchange his proficiency for the best engagement he can make wherever the offer may come from.' Lord Harris had long been trying to attract professional talent to Kent, and he may well have been envious of the northern counties with their apparently unlimited supply of native-born cricket stars. But at least he was consistent in his sympathetic approach to professionalism.[15]

On the whole, however, the Victorian attitude towards professionalism in cricket remained too negative. The professional's status was no higher than that of a labourer, so he received a wage rather than a salary. That was a very significant distinction in those days. An honorarium or a stipend for a secretary, who was a gentleman, had to be far more substantial than a fee for a professional, who, *ipso facto*, was not. Thus, the MCC could willingly pay Henry Perkins an average salary of £500 per annum for the 22 years he served as its secretary, and then offer him an annual pension of £400 and a life membership on his retirement in 1898. On the very same day, by a remarkable coincidence, the MCC also offered Thomas Hearne a pension of £30 a year for his long and faithful service to the club. Ill health had finally compelled Hearne to resign; he had been the head bowler and chief groundsman at Lord's for 26 years.[16]

It was this kind of snobbery, too, which contributed most to shamateurism in Victorian county cricket. Many gentlemen could not afford to play regularly without accepting match expenses and other rewards from county clubs. It was also beneath their dignity to play for wages, or to use the same facilities as the professionals. Some amateurs therefore accepted stipends, honoraria, testimonials, match expenses and sundry forms of money. They thus earned more than the professionals without losing their genteel status. Walter Read of Surrey, for example, received an annual gift of £100 from the county committee, above and beyond very generous match expenses, before being awarded a testimonial of £828 in 1896. That sum, ironically, was actually higher than the amount which the great Surrey professional, Bobby Abel, derived from his benefit match in 1895.[17]

Shamateurism was denounced by the cricket reporters even more violently than professionalism because it represented a double violation of the Victorian moral code. In addition to playing for money, it involved deception. The *Athletic News* spoke for the majority when, in 1879, it declared:

Both cricketers and the public have become tired of the abuse of terms which confers upon one man the title of gentleman and upon the other that of a professional, when the only difference between them is that the so-called gentleman takes money when he has no right to, and the professional who honestly calls himself such finds himself outbidden at his business by the mercenary amateur, who repudiates the title of professional whilst appropriating all the emoluments connected therewith.

This blast was aimed at the Graces of Gloucestershire who were notorious for claiming unusually high match expenses.[18] Two years later, the *Midland Athlete* expressed identical opinions on the same subject. It was much distressed to find that although Gloucestershire had employed only two professionals in 1880, the county yet spent almost £580 in 'expenses of players'. Clearly, only a very small fraction of that sum had actually gone to Billy Midwinter and William Woof. The latter, after all, had appeared in only eight games. The *Midland Athlete* agreed that the Graces 'are wonderful cricketers, and if they cannot give their services without remuneration, let them be remunerated openly and fairly and then take their true rank as professional players', as Richard Daft of Nottinghamshire had so manfully done.[19] This matter had earlier elicited a very tart comment from the *Sporting Clipper*: 'Mr Grace...receives a salary, and is yet allowed to call himself a 'gentleman player', to go into the gentlemen's tent, and to have wine with his lunch, while Daft sits with the professionals and has his beer.'[20]

It is not surprising that Grace should have attracted the most attention. Not only was he by far the greatest cricketer of his time, he was also by far the best paid. After graduating as a doctor in 1879, he set up his practice in Downend, near Bristol, and forced the Gloucestershire County Cricket Club to pay for his *locum* during the summer. Sometimes the committee even had to pay for two of them. W.G.'s own match stipend was around £50 per game, and in his later years he received £600 per season from the London County Cricket Club, after having left the Gloucestershire county team in a memorable huff. He received a marvellous testimonial in 1879, and an even more fabulous one in 1895. Together, they yielded in excess of £10,400. He cleared more than £2,000 from his tour to Australia in 1873–74, and even more than that when he was persuaded to undertake a second journey thither in 1891–92. Midwinter has estimated that, directly or indirectly, W.G. must have earned around £120,000 from cricket between 1870 and 1910.[21] None of the contemporary professionals even remotely approached that kind of financial performance.

Grace, however, was untypical. Notwithstanding the allegations of shamateurism on the part of Archie MacLaren, Andrew Stoddart and

Sammy Woods, among others, the majority of Victorian amateurs were not so blatantly mercenary. C.B. Fry, himself a brilliant cricketer of international renown, pointed out the difficulty of playing regularly for the county and thus undermining one's real profession. For many amateurs, county cricket became too expensive a pastime towards the end of the century. Fry therefore regarded match expenses as eminently reasonable for those amateurs who were not independently wealthy, and he gladly accepted a testimonial from Sussex in 1903. He had supported himself through Oxford University and beyond, by writing copious articles for a variety of magazines and newspapers and could not have represented Sussex as often as he did had he not received some financial assistance from the county.[22]

Many cricketers remained true to the amateur code and consequently played at the county level all too infrequently. Men like Stanley Jackson, A.P. Lucas, Gregor MacGregor, R.A.H. Mitchell, Ernest Smith and George Strachan, for example, refused to neglect their normal profession or to follow the Graces into shamateurism. Others, like Daft, E.J. Diver, William Gilbert, A.G. Paul and Albert Ward, temporarily abandoned their original professions to play cricket for a living. And George Thompson, still one of the greatest names in the history of Northamptonshire cricket, made himself infamous by becoming one of the first public school alumni to play cricket professionally.[23]

Most of the professional cricketers in the nineteenth century were working-class men who inevitably became victims of Victorian snobbery. The best they could hope for was to be hired on the MCC ground staff at Lord's for £2–3 per week during the summer. Most first-class counties also paid £5 for each county game at home, and £6 for a match on the road (when the professional paid for his own travel and accommodation). The social significance of these statistics can perhaps best be understood when compared to Home Gordon's fees as a cricket reporter in the Edwardian age. As a writer for the *Daily Express*, he received £20 for covering a first-class match in London, and £30 when he had to leave the capital. He also boasted that he seldom earned less than ten guineas for any of the articles he submitted to cricket journals.[24]

Victorian snobbery, however, was not the only factor which militated against the financial prosperity of cricket professionals. An equally vital role was played by basic economic realism. The fact is that, throughout the second half of the century, the job market for professional cricketers was glutted. In the wake of the great cotton slump of the 1860s and the prolonged agricultural depression after 1873, there were literally hundreds of competent cricketers, especially in the northern counties, who were seeking an escape from abject poverty. On average, a good county player in 1875 could look forward to an annual income of £100 and about

£250 by 1900. A labourer's wage, by comparison, increased only from
£80 to £100 over the same period.[25] As late as 1904, 'Tiger' Smith was
glad to escape from a factory job which had brought him only 16 shillings
weekly for 60 hours of hard labour.[26] It is thus clear why there was so
much keen competition for county contracts.

From first-class cricket, the best professionals could expect bonuses in
the form of talent money, collections and benefits. Talent money came
from good performances on the field, most notably with the bat, and was
paid by the county cricket club. Collections came from the spectators,
thrilled by some noteworthy performance, usually by a member of the
home team. Benefits were organized by the county club for veterans who
had served with distinction for many years. Players who were invited by
the MCC to compete against the Gentlemen, or were selected to represent
England against Australia, could expect £10 per match. The Test (that is,
international) match fee was raised to £20 in 1899. Some professionals
also made good money from winter tours to Australia.[27]

All of these terms and perquisites generally exceeded the lot of the local
club cricketer who could, on average, expect to do only half as well as his
counterpart in first-class cricket. The best professionals in the Lancashire
leagues, for instance, were reported to have received £4 weekly from their
clubs in the 1890s. Over a season of approximately 20 weeks, this meant
£80, buttressed by relatively small bonuses and collections. Professional
cricket at the local club level was not often regarded as a full-time
occupation and players were therefore expected to supplement their match
fees by seeking more normal forms of employment. In any case, most clubs
could not afford to pay generous wages. Even when the Haslingden club
was operating as a prominent member of the Lancashire League in the
1890s, its best paid professional was J.W. Parton, who received £3 a week
in 1890 and then had to settle for £2 10s. in 1891.[28] This, however, was
better than the fee then being paid to the regular cricket professional
engaged by the Sunderland Cricket and Rugby Football Club. It was not
before 1907 that A. Morris was able to make £2 10s. a week there.[29] When
the Harrogate club offered Tom Burgess £2 10s. per week in 1892, he was
expected to serve as the groundsman as well. In 1898, John Redfearn,
a famous Lascelles Hall man, was offered £3 weekly plus a benefit
to perform similar responsibilities.[30] In the 1870s, the South
Northumberland Cricket Club paid R. Proctor 35 shillings a week to
coach and play in all of its matches except those against Morpeth and
Benwell (which had remained rigidly amateur). And as late as 1897
Penrith could afford to pay Spencer Read only £20 for the whole season.[31]

While the club cricket professional could also look forward to talent
money and collections, these bonuses were relatively quite small. Ellis, of
Bolton, received a collection of just under £3, for example, for taking nine

wickets against Liverpool in June 1889; while Taylor, of Hunslet, earned himself a collection of £3 14s. 6d. plus ten shillings talent money for his splendid showing against Leeds Clarendon a few weeks later.[32] In June 1877 Robinson of Bacup received a new bat and a collection of £9 2s. for his excellent batting against Haslingden; and three years later a magnificent 50 at Bentgate by Lockwood of Haslingden against Bacup earned him 'between £4 and £5'.[33] But these collections could never compare with those in county cricket where, on average, a good performance generally produced close to £10.

There were, in fact, several good collections in first-class cricket during the last quarter of the nineteenth century. The most lucrative perhaps was that which brought Tom Hayward, of Surrey, £131 for scoring 137 runs against Australia in a Test at the Oval in 1899.[34] George Hearne received a collection of £81 during his own benefit match at Canterbury in 1890.[35] Alec Hearne found £50 in his 'hat' after scoring an undefeated century against Gloucestershire on Ladies' Day during the 1892 Canterbury Festival.[36] Edwin James Tyler, the Somerset spin bowler, who twice beat Surrey at Taunton in the 1890s, received £80 in two instalments from the crowd.[37] Bobby Abel, one of Surrey's most popular heroes, is also known to have received collections of more than £30 on at least three occasions.[38] John Painter, of Gloucestershire, collected close to £30 for his century against Lancashire in 1884. And Henry Pickett, of Essex, once was awarded £26 by the Leyton crowd for contributing to an upset victory over the powerful Surrey XI. His captain, Cyril Buxton, thereupon offered him an additional £5.[39] These, however, were exceptional cases. More normal was William Scotton's £7 for his great innings against the Australians at Huddersfield in July 1884.[40]

Benefit matches at the club level were more frequent than in first-class cricket but they were generally much less lucrative. In August 1889, the Longsight professional, Porter, was thought to have done well, for instance, with a gate of £26. Wardall, too, was most fortunate to have collected over £31 from his gate at Hilton in August 1898.[41] On the other hand, at the county level, benefit matches could make a considerable difference to the fortunes of professional cricketers who were on the verge of retirement.

The idea of the professional cricketer's benefit match developed during the nineteenth century; it took shape slowly because of the context in which it evolved. There was no tradition in Victorian England of a pension for the ordinary worker. Individuals from the working classes (from which the bulk of professional cricketers sprang) were expected to prepare for their own retirement without any help from the state. The best that anyone had been able to do before 1850 was to make small contributions to a Friendly Society fund in the hope of accumulating enough pennies to pay for a decent burial. To be buried indecently by the state was then regarded by the poor as a fate worse than death itself.[42]

It is not surprising, given these circumstances, that few people paid much attention to the plight of the professional cricketer after his playing days were over. He was, after all, a part-time professional in any case, as he often continued with his normal trade or occupation during the winter months. The parish workhouse or the municipal almshouse was thought to be adequate to meet the needs of the aged and the indigent. Indeed, as late as 1901, John 'Foghorn' Jackson, the famous fast bowler from Nottinghamshire, died penniless in the Liverpool workhouse infirmary at the age of 68. His old friends had to collect enough shillings among themselves to ensure a decent burial for him.[43]

The professional cricketer's plight was clearly serious since his career tended to be short and susceptible to the hazards of illness and injury. This was recognized as early as the 1840s when the nomadic cricket professionals, led by William Clarke, began to arrange benefit matches for themselves. One of the earliest of such games was staged in August 1843 on behalf of Edward Wenman, the veteran wicketkeeper from Kent, and the touring All England XI played several friendly matches later in that decade for the benefit of such professionals as Tom Barker, Sam Dakin, Francis Fenner and William Clarke himself. But these affairs were not lucrative enough, as the most successful of the early benefits produced only £165 for Joseph Guy when the AEE opposed 18 from the Nottingham Commercial Club at Trent Bridge in 1856.[44]

The benefit match nevertheless remained the most vital source of investment income for the Victorian professional cricketer in his retirement. By the time the county championship had become more formalized in the 1870s, it had become clear that he needed greater financial security than that provided by his match fees. There thus arose the tradition that a trusted professional deserved a handsome 'benefit' after having served his club faithfully and meritoriously for many years. The benefit match came to be one in which the beneficiary paid all the expenses and kept all the gate receipts; net profits from all play during that game accrued to him alone. But in keeping with the severity of Victorian laws, such benefits had to be earned by the sweat of the cricketer's brow. One of the very first benefits awarded by the MCC was arranged in 1853 on behalf of William Lillywhite, the Sussex professional who had helped to pioneer round-arm bowling. His was a special case. He had only been on the Lord's ground staff for nine or ten years, but he was already 61 and was destined to die one year later.[45] In 1896, Middlesex offered J.T. Rawlin a benefit after only seven years of service; but he was already 38 years old, having spent the first portion of his career (1880–85) on the Yorkshire staff. He eventually remained at Lord's until 1909.[46]

More normal was the experience of the professionals in Surrey, where the very first benefit was awarded to William Martingell in 1860 after he had already retired. The first active player to receive a benefit match from the Surrey CCC was Tom Lockyer in 1867 after he had served it for 18 years. Julius Caesar received the third benefit there in 1868 after 19 years' service. William Mortlock, even more unfortunate, had to wait for 22 years to get his; he had first represented Surrey in 1848 at the age of 16.[47] In Sussex, John Lillywhite finally received a benefit match in 1871 after playing there for 20 years. John Wheeler was 49 before he was awarded a benefit of any kind in 1893. He had played eight years for Nottinghamshire (1873–81) before serving Leicestershire and the MCC.[48] The Notts professional, Walter Price, worked on the Lord's ground staff for 19 years before being offered a benefit match by the MCC in 1887. John West served the MCC for 20 years before he was awarded a benefit match in 1889.[49] William Barnes had to wait for 19 years before receiving a benefit from Nottinghamshire at the age of 41 in 1894. William Attewell, the exceptionally accurate bowler for Nottinghamshire, had to play for 17 years before being offered half the proceeds of the Whitsun match against Surrey in 1898.[50]

It is obvious, then, that the original idea was to reward a faithful servant for more than 15 years of distinguished service at the county level. This placed the professional completely at the mercy of the county committee who could always use the threat of denying him his benefit. Several good professionals thus finished their careers without any benefit at all. Perhaps the most notable example in this regard was William Scotton, who played in 153 matches for Nottinghamshire from 1875 to 1890 and represented England in 15 Tests against Australia but was dropped from the county eleven before he had been offered a benefit. In desperate straits, he ultimately committed suicide during a fit of depression in 1893.[51] Even as late as 1898 only eight benefits were awarded altogether by the 14 county clubs then engaged in the cricket championship.[52] The Yorkshire CCC was one of the most generous in this matter of awarding benefits to faithful servants. It went so far as to stage a benefit in 1895 for George Anderson when he was almost 70 and had retired as long ago as 1869. Yet, incredibly, it arranged no more than 39 such matches altogether during the first one hundred years of its existence (that is, up to 1963).[53]

While club professionals seldom gleaned more than £20 from their benefits during the late nineteenth century, net profits from county cricket benefits rose from an average of approximately £200 in 1870 to more than £600 by 1900. Some benefits yielded more than £1,000, and George Hirst of Yorkshire set an enviable record when he received a net profit of more than £3,700 from his benefit match in 1904. Professionals like John

Thomas Brown, Arthur Mold, Bobby Peel, Richard Pilling, Maurice Read, Tom Richardson, Alec Watson and George Ulyett also did marvellously well.[54]

A distressingly large number of benefits were ruined by the weather, however, and some players, like the hapless Tom Soar of Hampshire in 1900, actually emerged with a net loss.[55] Many benefits were doubly hit by rain in that not only was the attendance sparse but the pitches were too difficult for the batsmen to survive long. Thus, Walter Price's benefit was 'finished off in a single afternoon' in May 1887, after his lengthy service at Lord's.[56] Edward Barratt's match, in August 1887, lasted only two days – thanks to the devastating form of Surrey's George Lohmann who, five years later, again did most to restrict George Burton's benefit to two days' play.[57] Even more unfortunate was Henry Baldwin of Hampshire in 1898. No play was possible on the first day, 26 May, at Southampton, then Yorkshire routed the Hampshire batsmen twice the next day on a wet pitch, to bring the sad affair to 'a summary conclusion'.[58]

Thus were benefits always at the mercy of the elements. They were also at the mercy of the bowlers who could sometimes restrict the game to a single day or two. James Southerton's match in 1879 was limited to two days by the skilful bowling of Fred Morley, Billy Bates and William Midwinter. The popular Johnny Briggs attracted some 15 000 to Old Trafford in May 1894. The Lancashire county cricket committee had taken great pains to protect the wicket from the elements, only to have the Yorkshire captain, Lord Hawke, object to playing on the covered strip. The game therefore had to be played on an under-prepared wicket, much to the disadvantage of the batsmen on both sides. Bobby Peel and George Hirst consequently bowled out Lancashire twice for paltry scores and Briggs's benefit ended early on the second day even though the rain had held up.[59]

Sometimes benefits failed even in good weather. In 1878, for example, despite perfect conditions, the gate receipts were most disappointing for Robert Thoms's benefit. This ought not to have been the case since the game involved Middlesex and Nottinghamshire at Lord's in mid-July. Thoms, however, was saved by a long and bountiful subscription list. James Lillywhite could attract only small crowds to his match at Chichester in early June 1889. George Howitt's experience at Lord's in 1877 had been similarly frustrating.[60]

Benefits, in a word, offered too little security. They could fail for a variety of reasons: bad weather, small crowds, disappointing subscription lists, unattractive matches, unfortunate timing, excellent bowling or the small size of the home ground. Benefits arranged too early or too late in the season were unlikely to be profitable. Hence John Wheeler's match failed because it had been arranged too early in 1893, and G.F. Hearne suffered from having his benefit played too late in 1894.[61] On the smaller grounds, at places like Clifton, Chichester and Leyton, county cricket professionals could hope only for modest gains. Thus, players in Derbyshire, Essex, Gloucestershire, Leicestershire and Sussex could not expect to reap mammoth rewards from their benefits. John Painter was considered fortunate to have derived £250–300 from his match at Clifton in 1894. Arthur Pougher of Leicestershire realized £228 from his benefit in 1900. In *Cricket*'s words, that was a 'somewhat striking contrast to the proceeds of benefits in Yorkshire'. In even smaller counties, of course, the professional was lucky to make any profit at all from his benefit. William Hearn, for instance, received about three or four pounds from the Hertfordshire gate and about £60 in subscriptions in 1894.[62]

Sometimes the county professional was saved from financial embarrassment by the offer of a second benefit after the failure of the first. George Pinder, for example, could hardly balance the accounts from his benefit in July 1880. The Yorkshire committee speedily arranged a second game on his behalf in early September. This match, fortunately for Pinder, proved far more fruitful.[63] But Alfred Shaw of Nottinghamshire had the unique experience of two disastrous benefits in a single year (1879), and three such frustrations altogether.[64] More tragic still was the case of John West, whose benefit was totally abandoned without a ball being bowled in 1889. The MCC arranged a second match for him in May 1890. In the interim, however, poor West died.[65]

By 1900, it was clear that the benefit system was much too unfair and unreliable. After the fiasco suffered that summer by Tom Soar of Hampshire, the *Athletic News* called unequivocally for a new system of benefits that would guarantee the professionals a reasonable return for their years of service. This was in keeping with several lamentations uttered by the sporting press, led by *Wisden*, invariably after a popular cricketer had come to grief at his benefit. Countless appeals were made, in fact, by cricketers and observers for a rational review of the benefit system as it then stood. Alfred Shaw, one of the greatest bowlers of the Victorian era, remained convinced that a superannuation scheme would be far superior to the benefit system. He also thought that it should be applied to umpires who had nothing to fall back on after they had retired from the active list. This view received warm support at the turn of the century from Walter Long who recommended that county professionals should be guaranteed a minimum bonus of £1,000 at the end of their career. Like so many others, he condemned the Victorian benefit system as totally inadequate.[66]

The system, however, remained stubbornly in place – thanks to the innate conservatism of the cricket administrators. The latter were not

unsympathetic to the cricketers; they even subscribed generously from
their own pockets and were willing to arrange supplementary matches
where possible. The gentlemen-amateurs were also the moving forces
behind such progressive organizations as the MCC Benefit Fund and the
Cricketers' Fund Friendly Society. Lord Harris, Lord Hawke and the
wealthy Walkers of Southgate were very generous in their treatment of
charitable causes and of professional cricketers in distress. Outstanding
amateur players, like Fry, Grace and Ranjitsinhji, also did their best to
ensure that benefit matches were as successful as possible in a financial
sense. But the amateurs and administrators were loth to interfere with
tradition. It was not until very recently that the professionals learnt to plan
properly for their own benefit and to employ a whole army of accountants, agents, lawyers, friends and professional fundraisers to ensure the
maximum profit from their matches. As late as 1937, Leslie Ames, the
great Kent wicketkeeper/batsman, received only £1,265 from his benefit
and Emrys Davies of Glamorgan had to be satisfied with a paltry £688 in
1938.[67]

The benefit system obviously marked an advance on the older Victorian
treatment of professional cricketers. Considering that the average annual
wages of a semi-skilled worker amounted to little more than £150 in 1914,
a tax-free benefit of £1,000 represented a major windfall indeed. But only
a relatively small number of professionals derived more than £800 from
their benefit match prior to the First World War. The benefit remained a
highly unsatisfactory and unreliable source of revenue until 1948 when
Cyril Washbrook of Lancashire finally taught his professional brothers
how to insure themselves against the misfortunes that had occurred to
men like Henry Baldwin, Henry Pickett and Thomas Soar.[68]

Just how unpredictable was a professional cricketer's benefit match as
a source of retirement funds up to 1914 and beyond can be clearly seen
from the following estimates presented in Table 5.1, collected from a careful study of the files of the contemporary sporting press. The numbers in
brackets represent the period of years served by the professional before
his benefit was granted; and the amount (in pounds) at the end of each
entry is the yearly average of the worth of the benefit over the professional's entire career. In each case, it is assumed that the cricketer was
active for the full season in both his first and final years. Thus, for instance,
George Hirst is credited with 39 years of service to Yorkshire. Where the
career, as in the case of William Lockwood's and J.T. Rawlin's, involved
more than one county, its full length is given.

Table 5.1   Results of benefits, 1856–1914

Player	County	Career	Reward (£)	Year (no.)	An. ave. (£)
George Hirst	Yorks	1891–1929	3,703	1904 (13)	94.94 x 39
John T. Tyldesley	Lancs	1895–1923	3,111	1906 (11)	107.27 x 29
John T. Brown	Yorks	1889–1904	2,282	1901 (12)	142.63 x 16
Wilfred Rhodes	Yorks	1898–1930	2,200	1911 (13)	66.67 x 33
Walter Lees	Surrey	1896–1911	2,120	1906 (10)	132.50 x 16
Schofield Haigh	Yorks	1895–1913	2,071	1910 (15)	109.00 x 19
Arthur Mold	Lancs	1889–1901	2,050	1900 (11)	157.69 x 13
Robert Peel	Yorks	1882–1899	2,000	1894 (12)	111.11 x 18
David Hunter	Yorks	1888–1909	1,950	1897 (9)	88.64 x 22
David Denton	Yorks	1894–1920	1,916	1907 (13)	70.96 x 27
George Baker	Lancs	1884–1899	1,900	1898 (14)	118.75 x 16
Edward Wainwright	Yorks	1888–1902	1,800	1898 (10)	120.00 x 15
John Tunnicliffe	Yorks	1891–1907	1,750	1903 (12)	102.94 x 17
Albert Ward	Lancs	1889–1904	1,700	1902 (13)	106.25 x 16
Richard Pilling	Lancs	1877–1889	1,600	1889 (12)	123.07 x 13
Colin Blythe	Kent	1899–1914	1,500	1909 (10)	93.75 x 16
Edward Humphreys	Kent	1899–1920	1,300	1913 (14)	55.09 x 22
Ernest Hayes	Surrey	1896–1919	1,264	1908 (12)	52.67 x 24
Herbert Strudwick	Surrey	1902–1927	1,216	1911 (9)	46.77 x 26
Fred Holland	Surrey	1894–1908	1,202	1907 (13)	80.13 x 15
Maurice Read	Surrey	1880–1895	1,200	1893 (13)	75.00 x 16
Arthur Fielder	Kent	1900–1914	1,170	1911 (11)	78.00 x 15
Alec Watson	Lancs	1871–1893	1,102	1885 (14)	47.91 x 23
Richard Barlow	Lancs	1871–1891	1,100	1886 (15)	52.38 x 21
George Ulyett	Yorks	1873–1893	1,100	1887 (14)	52.38 x 21
Fred Tate	Sussex	1887–1905	1,052	1900 (13)	55.37 x 19
Alex Hearne	Kent	1884–1906	1,014	1898 (14)	44.09 x 23
William McIntyre	Lancs	1869–1880	1,000	1881 (12)	83.33 x 12
George Lohmann	Surrey	1884–1896	1,000	1896 (12)	76.92 x 13
William Attewell	Notts	1881–1900	1,000	1898 (17)	50.00 x 20
Tom Richardson	Surrey	1892–1905	1,000	1899 (7)	71.43 x 14
John T. Hearne	Mdsex	1888–1923	1,000	1900 (12)	27.78 x 36
William Lockwood	Surrey	1886–1904	1,000	1901 (15)	52.63 x 19
Arthur Lilley	War	1888–1911	850	1901 (13)	35.42 x 24
Richard Daft	Notts	1860–1879	800	1876 (16)	40.00 x 20
Walter Mead	Essex	1892–1913	800	1900 (8)	36.36 x 22
Robert Henderson	Surrey	1883–1896	798	1897 (14)	57.00 x 14
Edgar Willsher	Kent	1850–1875	794	1872 (22)	30.54 x 26

Table 5.1 (continued)

Player	County	Career	Reward Year (no.) (£)	An. ave. (£)
Thomas Hayward	Surrey	1893–1914	750 1902 (9)	34.09 x 22
William Gunn	Notts	1880–1904	730 1897 (17)	29.20 x 25
William Bates	Yorks	1877–1887	700 1889 (11)	63.63 x 11
John Lillywhite	Sussex	1850–1869	700 1871 (20)	35.00 x 20
John T. Rawlin	Mdsex	1880–1909	653 1896 (16)	21.77 x 30
William Oscroft	Notts	1864–1882	622 1883 (19)	32.74 x 19
Robert Abel	Surrey	1881–1904	621 1895 (14)	25.88 x 24
Frank Field	War	1897–1920	620 1912 (15)	25.84 x 24
Thomas Emmett	Yorks	1866–1888	616 1879 (13)	26.78 x 23
George Pinder	Yorks	1867–1880	600 1880 (13)	42.86 x 14
Arthur Shrewsbury	Notts	1875–1902	600 1893 (18)	21.43 x 28
Louis Hall	Yorks	1873–1894	570 1890 (17)	25.91 x 22
Ephraim Lockwood	Yorks	1868–1884	500 1882 (14)	29.41 x 17
John Shilton	War	1883–1895	500 1895 (12)	38.46 x 13
Henry Pallett	War	1883–1898	500 1897 (14)	31.25 x 16
Fred Roberts	Glos	1887–1905	500 1897 (10)	26.32 x 19
Charles Llewellyn	Hants	1899–1910	500 1908 (9)	41.67 x 12
William Brockwell	Surrey	1886–1903	490 1900 (14)	27.22 x 18
Albert Knight	Leics	1895–1912	470 1906 (11)	26.11 x 18
Septimus Kinneir	War	1898–1914	467 1914 (16)	27.47 x 17
Wilfred Flowers	Notts	1877–1896	457 1895 (18)	22.85 x 20
Henry Jupp	Surrey	1862–1881	450 1881 (19)	22.50 x 20
Edward Pooley	Surrey	1861–1883	450 1883 (22)	19.57 x 23
Henry Wood	Surrey	1876–1900	450 1894 (18)	18.00 x 25
George Griffith	Surrey	1856–1872	445 1872 (16)	26.18 x 17
John Whiteside	Leics	1888–1906	430 1902 (14)	22.63 x 19
George Thompson	Nhant	1897–1922	410 1905 (8)	15.77 x 26
Edwin Tyler	Smset	1891–1907	400 1899 (8)	23.53 x 17
John Devey	War	1888–1907	400 1906 (18)	20.00 x 20
Sydney Santall	War	1892–1914	400 1908 (16)	17.39 x 23
William Quaife	War	1893–1928	400 1910 (17)	11.11 x 36
James Wootton	Kent	1880–1890	396 1894 (11)	36.00 x 11
Alfred Law	War	1885–1899	380 1899 (14)	25.33 x 15
Allen Hill	Yorks	1871–1883	377 1884 (13)	29.00 x 13
Thomas Jayes	Leics	1903–1911	370 1912 (8)	41.11 x 9
Jemmy Dean	MCC	1837–1861	350 1857 (20)	14.00 x 25
Thomas Hearne	Mdsex	1859–1876	350 1876 (17)	19.44 x 18
William Barnes	Notts	1875–1894	350 1894 (19)	17.50 x 20

Table 5.1   (concluded)

Player	County	Career	Reward (£)	Year (no.)	An. ave. (£)
John Thewlis	Yorks	1862–1875	325	1875 (13)	23.21 x 14
Thomas Humphrey	Surrey	1862–1876	305	1876 (14)	20.33 x 15
Luke Greenwood	Yorks	1861–1874	300	1874 (13)	21.43 x 14
George Parr	Notts	1844–1871	300	1878 (28)	10.71 x 28
Henry Phillips	Sussex	1868–1891	300	1886 (18)	12.50 x 24
George Jones	Surrey	1875–1890	300	1889 (14)	18.75 x 16
George Anderson	Yorks	1850–1869	300	1895 (20)	15.00 x 20
John Painter	Glos	1881–1897	275	1894 (13)	16.17 x 17
Fred Wild	Notts	1868–1881	270	1890 (14)	19.29 x 14
John Jackson	Notts	1855–1866	265	1874 (12)	22.08 x 12
Walter Sugg	Derby	1884–1902	264	1898 (14)	13.89 x 19
William Martingell	Surrey	1839–1859	260	1860 (21)	12.38 x 21
Walter Wright	Kent	1879–1899	253	1900 (21)	12.05 x 21
James C. Shaw	Notts	1864–1886	250	1884 (20)	10.87 x 23
Arthur Pougher	Leics	1886–1902	228	1900 (14)	13.41 x 17
George Davidson	Derby	1886–1898	200	1896 (10)	15.38 x 13
John Selby	Notts	1870–1887	184	1887 (17)	10.22 x 18
Joseph Guy	Notts	1837–1854	165	1856 (18)	9.17 x 18
Arthur Webb	Hants	1895–1912	150	1904 (9)	8.33 x 18
Alfred Shaw	Notts	1864–1897	130	1892 (28)	3.82 x 34
Arnold Rylott	Leics	1872–1888	125	1889 (17)	7.35 x 17
John Pentecost	Kent	1882–1890	120	1892 (9)	13.33 x 9
Walter Richards	War	1883–1896	102	1904 (14)	7.29 x 14
Stephen Whitehead	War	1886–1900	102	1904 (15)	6.80 x 15
Richard Humphrey	Surrey	1870–1881	81	1885 (12)	6.75 x 12
John Wheeler	Leics	1873–1902	25	1893 (20)	0.83 x 30
Mordecai Sherwin	Notts	1876–1896	0	1896 (20)	0.00 x 21
Arthur Woodcock	Leics	1889–1908	0	1903 (14)	0.00 x 20
Thomas Soar	Hants	1888–1904	–6	1900 (12)	–0.35 x 17

Some comments on these statistics must be offered. While they provide more empirical data on the important subject of benefits, and in fact represent the most comprehensive list yet published, they are tantalizingly incomplete. There are no concrete sums offered for some of the benefits reputed to have been highly successful. Not enough is known, for example, of the profits made by H.H. Stephenson (Surrey) in 1871, Roger Iddison (Yorkshire) in 1872, Joseph Rowbotham (Yorkshire) in 1873, Thomas Mycroft (MCC) in 1895 and Robert Moorhouse (Yorkshire) in

1900. In Moorhouse's case, the Yorkshire County Committee was determined to prevent any recurrence of the Louis Hall catastrophe, and therefore began the subscription list with a generous donation of £500 to ensure that at least a minimum of £1,000 was raised. There is no reason to believe that this target was not eventually reached.[69] In the case of W.G. Quaife, a second benefit was ultimately awarded in 1927 from which he derived £917. He appears to have been the only professional of this era to have received a second benefit from his county.[70] If some benefits appear to have been offered unusually early, there is often a simple explanation. A few of them were actually staged after the cricketer had retired prematurely because of serious illness or injury. This was the case, for example, with Billy Bates, John Jackson, John Pentecost and James Wootton. The benefit match between Warwickshire and Essex in June 1904 was intended to honour Walter Richards and Stephen James Whitehead who had already retired. Richards shared the proceeds with Whitehead's estate since that beneficiary suddenly died on the very day after the conclusion of the match.[71] In Tom Richardson's case, the Surrey CCC committee was so determined to prevent him from moving to another county as he had threatened to do, that it negotiated a special contract with him and offered a much earlier benefit than usual. The same was possibly true of the great wicketkeeper Herbert Strudwick who received his benefit much earlier than was normal for other Surrey professionals. Tom Hayward, too, was able to bargain with that county for a supplementary testimonial in 1909 (from which he made £383).[72]

Such relevant details are easily unearthed. But the larger problem is trying to distinguish between gross receipts and net profits. It is not always clear from the sources whether the beneficiary actually pocketed the sums that were published. In the interesting case of Richards and Whitehead in 1904, the actual receipts amounted to only £308 and expenses came to £105. This meant that the recipients had to share £203 between them. On this the club records are quite specific. But other cases are more difficult to analyse. It is known, for instance, that the receipts for Mold's benefit in 1900 far exceeded £2,000, but it is not altogether clear what his total expenses were.

Nor is there much accurate data on such known failed benefits as those staged for Thomas Hearne (Middlesex) in 1863, George Howitt (Middlesex) in 1877, Frank Farrand (MCC) and C.K. Pullin (Gloucestershire) in 1881, Edward Barratt (Surrey) and Walter Price (MCC) in 1887, Arnold Rylott (MCC) in 1891, George Burton (Middlesex) and Robert Clayton (MCC) in 1892, Johnny Briggs (Lancashire) in 1894, Henry Pickett (Essex) in 1897, and Henry Baldwin (Hampshire) and George Hearne (Middlesex and MCC) in 1898. In Thomas Hearne's case, however, it is known that a second benefit was arranged for him in 1876 with much improved results.[73]

But the statistics, such as they are, still have enormous value for the social historian. They show that too little is still known about the earliest benefits and we are thus left to depend on the general estimates offered by such Victorian commentators as Rev. R.S. Holmes and an 'Old Harrovian'.[74] It is clear, however, that the value of benefits gradually increased, and that the most lucrative ones occurred in those counties – such as Lancashire, Middlesex, Surrey and Yorkshire – endowed with the most spacious stands, the most populous and thriving urban centres and the wealthiest patrons. The greatest surprise and the most baffling phenomenon in this connection is the consistent failure of the early benefits in Nottinghamshire. Even Attewell's triumph there in 1898 was due almost entirely to the generosity of the subscribers. Details are known about 14 of this county's benefit matches during 1874–1900. The statistics reveal that they averaged only £425 and each of the beneficiaries had to wait for approximately 19 years.

This kind of performance was even more disappointing than Warwickshire's from 1895 to 1914. That county was a relatively minor one, reaching first-class status only in 1895. It awarded 11 benefits in the last 20 years before the First World War. On average, its professionals had to wait for 15 years before receiving about £429 each. Leicestershire, another minor county until 1895, awarded seven benefits on which information is available between 1889 and 1912. The beneficiaries waited on average for 14 years and were rewarded with approximately £235 each. This was much different from the case in Lancashire, where eight professionals, after roughly 13 years of service, shared almost £1,700 each between 1881 and 1906. Even in Kent, where the grounds were relatively small, five benefits offered there during 1896–1913 yielded each cricketer approximately £1,047 after roughly 14 years of service to the county.

The information on early benefits granted by Surrey and Yorkshire is much more extensive. Six Surrey benefits can be fully analysed for the period 1860–86. They yielded an average of £332 each after 17 years. During 1887–1900, the waiting period fell to 13 years and the rewards rose to £732 on average for the eight players. From 1901 to 1911, six more benefits produced an average of £1,259 each after 11 years of service. In Yorkshire, the average between 1874 and 1886 was £453 after 13 years for six professionals. It rose to £1,178 after 13 years during 1887–1900 for eight cricketers, including Moorhouse; and to £2,320 after 13 years during 1901–11 for six very fortunate individuals.

These statistics (involving 106 cases) confirm that professional cricketers were awarded their benefits much less grudgingly as the years passed. They show that the average qualifying period fell from 18 years during 1856–74 to 16 during 1875–86, to 14 during 1887–1900 and to

13 during 1901–14. They also reveal that the average return from known benefits rose from £410 during 1856–74 to £529 during 1875–86, to £692 during 1887–1900 and to £1,123 during 1901–14. Of some interest also is the fact that the average first-class career of the professionals in the sample remained at 19 years throughout the period 1856–1900 and rose to 21 during 1901–14.

The arithmetic, however, paints perhaps too rosy a picture of the professional cricketer's plight. Several benefits, about which the records remain obscure, are known to have led to substantial losses and many a cricketer had to be rescued from embarrassment by his county committee. The fear of unlimited losses, in fact, was sufficiently strong to deter many professionals, especially in the smaller counties, from seeking a benefit match in the nineteenth century. This largely explains why so few benefits were awarded by such counties as Derbyshire, Essex, Gloucestershire, Hampshire, Somerset and Sussex. It is also true, of course, that some of these counties, like Gloucestershire, Hampshire, Middlesex and Somerset, traditionally hired fewer professionals than the others and were mainly dependent on their amateurs. After 1875, county matches became increasingly expensive to stage. Players' wages, fees for gatemen and attendants, travel and policing costs steadily escalated. These had to be borne by the beneficiary, who could make huge gains only if the crowds were large on at least two of the three days for which county matches were scheduled. In 1904, when Hirst made his legendary fortune, the expenses for which he was responsible came to almost £1,200.[75] Had the weather been unkind, he would have done very poorly indeed. The benefit, in fact, had become more and more of a gamble. The MCC and the wealthier counties, like Lancashire, Surrey and Yorkshire, could afford to underwrite the player's expenses in case of failure. But most of the other clubs were operating on shoestring budgets and often were themselves at the mercy of generous patrons. The chronic shortage of funds prevented the majority of the counties from offering the most lucrative matches as benefits even to the most popular of their professional stars.

On the brighter side, subscription lists were invariably opened for the beneficiary and kept alive for some weeks; in this way, friends and fans as well as liberal opponents could make contributions. Additional testimonials were also arranged for veteran professionals who had served with distinction over unusually long periods. Some cricketers naturally preferred the testimonial because it entailed no risk or expenditure on the beneficiary's part. But these were mainly reserved, curiously enough, for extraordinary amateurs, like W.G. Grace and Walter Read. Archie MacLaren, Lancashire's captain, collected more than £1,000 from his testimonial in 1905, and A.O. Jones, the amateur who captained Nottinghamshire from 1900 to 1914, gained over £1,500 from his in 1907.[76]

The success of the early testimonials left useful lessons for the modern cricketers. If nothing else, they demonstrated that gifts were just as important as admission fees at the gate. By relieving the beneficiary of the prospect of crippling losses due to rain, they also pointed towards the notion of insuring the match against such a possibility. Insurance premiums, of course, represented additional expenditure. In 1904, for instance, they had cost Hirst £116. But they naturally reduced the risk of total loss; Len Braund, the excellent all-rounder from Somerset, was one player left to regret that he had failed to take such an elementary precaution when, in 1908, his benefit match was totally ruined by the weather.[77] The misfortunes of the early benefits left bitter but vital lessons. In time, the professional came to regard his benefit as no gamble at all; he aimed to make profits from several avenues all at once and to depend less and less on the gate receipts.

It was the failure of the early benefit matches to meet the needs of the professional cricketers which had prompted the establishment of the Cricketers' Fund Friendly Society (CFFS) in 1857. The birth of this organization was due in large measure to the perseverance of John Wisden, who is best remembered now for establishing in 1864 the famous *Cricketers' Almanack* which still bears his name. Wisden was himself a professional fast bowler from Sussex who played for the AEE under Clarke before seceding from that group in 1852 and creating the rival UEE. A man with unusual sagacity in addition to his cricketing skills, Wisden saw the need for some national type of fund to save professional cricketers from penury and destitution in their old age. He succeeded in impressing a number of influential amateurs and even prevailed upon Edmund Wilder to accept the first presidency of the CFFS. Col. Marshall served as vice-president, with Wisden himself as treasurer. The original trustees were the Hon. Frederick Ponsonby, James Henry Dark (the proprietor of Lord's) and Charles Hoare. Robert Grimston and William Nicholson, both wealthy cricketers as well as cricket fans, acted as the initial auditors, while Frederick Lillywhite served as the first honorary secretary.[78]

The CFFS was reorganized in 1864, with Wisden becoming its secretary at £20 per annum. Its avowed objective was to relieve professional cricketers from the perils of old age, illness, accident and/or infirmity, and to offer temporary assistance to their widows and orphans in case of death. Aimed directly at the professionals, it established an annual subscription of one guinea, payable each year on 1 June. Gentlemen were invited to become honorary members and to contribute voluntarily to the fund. Professionals over 38 years of age were required to pay an entrance fee of £2 10s., and those over 40 were charged an entrance fee of £5. For cricketers between 42 and 45, the admission fee was £10. No professional was eligible as a paying member beyond the age of 45. In return, the society offered its members £2 per week during the summer, and £1 weekly between October and April, should they become ill and/or incapacitated. After one year of such support, the professional had to be permanently disabled to receive additional benefits. For permanent disability, members were allowed a maximum of ten shillings per week – with the specific sum to be determined by the newly formed Committee of Management. In case of death, needy orphans and widows were to receive a maximum of £20 to defray the funeral expenses, with the committee again determining the specific benefit in each separate case. To guard against immediate bankruptcy, the society ruled that members could become eligible for relief only after paying annual dues for five years, and their family was entitled to death benefits only after the deceased had paid his premiums for a period of three years. The Committee of Management was to meet four times each year and special meetings could be convened at the request of any two members in good standing. This committee was originally composed of the leading professionals of the day and included Tom Box (chair), George Anderson, Julius Caesar, Alfred Diver, John Lillywhite, George Parr and Edgar Willsher. Later, such distinguished cricketers as Robert Carpenter, Richard Daft and H.H. Stephenson also served as members.[79]

Wisden continued to do his best to promote the interests of the fund. He offered it ample advertising space in his annual *Almanack*, and he also persuaded the two travelling professional teams to play special exhibition matches against each other for the society's express benefit. Each year, throughout the 1860s and the early 1870s, they met at Lord's for this particular purpose, raising an average of approximately £140 per year. By far the most successful of these games was one played in June 1865; it attracted a record number of spectators and yielded a profit in excess of £268.[80]

As the trustees and auditors were members also of the MCC, that club was easily persuaded to make voluntary contributions too. But the MCC, hoping to gain greater control over its ground staff at Lord's, established a separate benefit fund of its own in 1862. For many years thereafter, it devoted an annual match to raising funds for its own needy professionals, whose number gradually increased from about a dozen in the early 1860s to more than 60 by the end of the century. The most lucrative of such charity games occurred in September 1884. It featured Smokers vs Non-Smokers and raised over £560 for the cause.[81] It was zealously arranged and promoted by Vyell E. Walker, one of that huge progeny of wealthy Walkers of Southgate who did so much to keep the Middlesex CCC alive during its fledgling days.

Both the CFFS and the MCC Benefit Fund were supported wholeheartedly by some of the wealthiest cricketers and cricket administrators of the Victorian age. In addition to the Walkers, for instance, they received tangible assistance from Charles Ernest Green, another famous cricket philanthropist, whose liberality did more than any single factor to keep the Essex county club alive in the last quarter of the nineteenth century. Lord Harris of Kent was also one of their most vital supporters and it was he who actually succeeded Edmund Wilder as the president of the society in 1886. The Surrey CCC, too, was another significant benefactor. It voted in 1888 to allocate the proceeds of one game annually to the CFFS and the results were contributions of £71 from the Sussex–Surrey match of 1888 and £64 from another contest in 1889. But neither the MCC Benefit Fund nor the CFFS flourished even though they were staunchly supported by many of the gentlemen-amateurs of that day. In 1871, the MCC Benefit Fund contained less than £400, although its membership had increased from 650 in the early 1860s to about 1600 and the club was already employing 15 professionals and a full-time groundskeeper.[82]

The CFFS floundered for many years. Ric Sissons, in his otherwise excellent *The Players: A Social History of the Professional Cricketer* (London, 1988), maintains that it prospered during its infancy. In fact, however, its annual receipts amounted only to £98 in 1872 when only 26 professionals were subscribing to it. The nomadic elevens soon disbanded altogether and that source of annual revenue disappeared. The match between the AEE and the UEE was replaced by the annual North vs South match at Prince's, but even the Prince's Cricket Club itself fell upon hard times and perished before the end of the 1870s. Prince's was an aristocratic cricket club which gave staunch support to the CFFS. But during the seven summers (1873–79), when it sponsored the annual charity game, it collected no more than an aggregate of £724 – just over £103 per annum. It actually incurred losses from the North vs South games in 1876 and 1879 when the weather was most inclement.[83]

By 1888, the society could offer minimal help to only 14 of its most destitute members. Early in 1886, it found itself in such dire straits that it had to reduce all of its benefits to members. Sick relief was cut from £2 to 30 shillings per week during that summer and from £1 to 15 shillings in the winter of 1886–87. The fact is that the bulk of the professionals could not afford to pay the high premiums and entrance fees charged by the society, and there were consequently fewer than a hundred members altogether in 1886. There were also too many destitute applicants that year. A serious fundraising drive, led as always by *Wisden*, was undertaken in the late 1880s, and this is the one to which the Surrey CCC responded so positively. The MCC also donated almost £300 to the society in 1888.[84]

But the organization continued to languish nevertheless. Even as late as 1901, the best it could do to assist the ailing and penurious John Jackson was to offer him 5s. 6d. per week while he lay dying in the Liverpool workhouse infirmary. The society lasted, it is true, until the 1970s and was a durable legacy from the days of the touring English professional elevens, but it never really prospered. Too many professionals failed to subscribe to it. Even had they not considered the society's premiums too exorbitant, they might still have been too independent and individualistic to support it wholeheartedly. The English cricket professionals were a proud group who traditionally frowned on the idea of establishing a players' union.

Notwithstanding the unreliability of benefits and the general failure of the CFFS to prosper in the nineteenth century, the first-class professional cricketer did much better than most British workers at this time because of increased opportunities after 1850. In addition to his regular career, he could find employment as a private cricket tutor, as did G.R. Atkinson, for instance, who was engaged by the Vaughans of Middlesborough from 1863 to 1869. Several families hired professionals to coach their children. Sir Henry Leveson Gower recalled that, in his youth, he had been coached at home by Fred Tate and Valentine Titchmarsh, among others.[85] Some first-class amateur batsmen, like the Palairets and the Studds, also hired good professional bowlers to help them remain in fine batting form.[86] First-class cricketers were also in demand as coaches in the public schools and universities. Even some of the smaller academic institutions, like Elstree School in the 1890s, had two professionals in addition to their regular cricket masters.[87] Some players also finished up as umpires, groundsmen, scorers and pavilion clerks. That is to say, they managed to remain profitably employed in cricket for most of their lives.

The expansion of cricket beyond Britain also opened up avenues for enterprising professionals who were prepared to devote both winter and summer to the game. C. Mills of Surrey, for instance, coached both in South Africa and the United States in the 1890s. During that decade, too, James Phillips, the Middlesex professional, habitually spent his winters in his native Australia. William Brockwell and J.T. Hearne went frequently to India after 1894 to coach the offspring of the Maharaj of Patiala.[88] Charles Lawrence spent many years in Australia after participating in the first English tour to that country in 1861–62. Two years later, William Caffyn was enticed to remain in Australia by an offer of £300 per annum from the Melbourne Cricket Club.[89] Johnny Briggs was offered £300 to coach in South Africa during the 1889–90 season, and George Davidson enjoyed a highly successful season there in 1894–95.[90] English professionals were also well paid for touring with representative teams during the winter. Each player, for example, made £90 from the first tour to Canada and the United States in 1859; £150 from the first tour to Australia in 1861–62; and £170 from the Australian tour of 1891–92.[91]

As cricket was only a seasonal occupation, many professionals supplemented their earnings by playing soccer professionally in the winter as well. This group included H.B. Daft, John Devey, Billy George, John Goodall, William Gunn, Ernest Needham, John Sharp, Frank Sugg and Fred Wheldon.[92]

Cricket, however, was a demanding career. The competition for places was always keen, and failure meant the possibility of instant demotion. There was never any semblance of security and the pressure consequently was overwhelming. John William Sharpe, for example, tried so hard to bowl faster than he was physically capable of doing that his career ended after five short years. Len Braund, emerging at a time when Surrey was all-powerful, could not crack that county side and had to seek employment elsewhere.[93] The Yorkshire professional, Albert Cordingley, was a promising bowler who could not dislodge the mighty Wilfred Rhodes from the county team. He migrated to Sussex and soon descended into oblivion.[94] Frank Shacklock rendered himself unpopular at Lord's by allegedly bowling too fast at the elderly members in practice.[95] Many good professionals were also unfortunate in belonging to the wrong county. George Davidson and Arthur Pougher, two excellent all-rounders, would undoubtedly have gone much further had they played for different teams.

These stresses and strains all took their toll. A disconcertingly large number of Victorian professional cricketers died young – even for an age in which the average life span of an industrial worker was no more than 45. Many cricket professionals suffered also from nervous and mental disorder. This fate befell Billy Bates, Johnny Briggs, George Griffith, William Scotton and Arthur Shrewsbury, among others. Some of them, such as Griffith, Scotton, Shrewsbury, and Arthur Woodcock, the well-known Leicestershire fast bowler, actually committed suicide. Typhoid fever claimed the life of Thomas Barnes of Nottinghamshire when he was only 24 in 1873; and Fred Crabtree, a young Nelson professional, was only 26 when he died in 1893. The list of Victorian professional cricketers who died before the age of 40 included Fred Morley (30), George Tarrant (31), George Davidson (32), Joe Hunter (33), Samuel Biddulph (35), J.T. Brown (35), George Lohmann (36), Henry Pilling (36), Scotton (37), Victor Barton (39) and Briggs (39). Among others, Billy Buttress (41), Edwin Mills (42), John Painter (42), Tom Richardson (42), John Shilton (42), Tom Lockyer (43), Bates (44), Herbert Hearne (44), Edmund Peate (44), John West (44), Woodcock (44), Griffith (45), Henry Pickett (45), John Selby (45), Edward Barratt (46), George Porter (46), Fred Wild (46), George Ulyett (46), William Barnes (47), Julius Caesar (47), Arthur Shrewsbury (47), Henry Jupp (48), John Lillywhite (48), William McIntyre (48), William Draper (49), William Chatterton (49), John Platts (49) and J.C. Shaw (49) all failed to reach 50. Nor does this list include

such cricketers as William Cropper and George Summers, who died tragically young as a direct result of accidents in sports.[96]

Although professional cricketers did much better financially, on the
whole, than industrial workers in the Victorian age, very few of them
seemed eventually to have made much progress up the social ladder.
In fact, many of them died poor. This was true of such fine first-class
cricketers as Biddulph, Caesar, Dakin, Good, Grundy, Humphreys, Jupp,
Lockyer, Morley, Mudie, Webster and a host of others.[97]

Perhaps the saddest case is that of William Brockwell, who played
extremely well for Surrey and England, enjoyed a lucrative benefit and
coached for some years in Patiala for a good fee. He had been a well-
groomed writer, photographer and conversationalist, with a keen interest
in literature and theatre. As a player, Brockwell had been immensely
popular, yet his life turned sour after his retirement in 1903, and he died
in abject poverty. As an old man, he was found destitute in a roofless and
deserted shack near a country golf course.[98]

William 'Dick' Attewell, one of the most accurate bowlers in the
history of cricket, represented Nottinghamshire from 1881 to 1900. He
played on ten occasions for England, and made three profitable trips to
Australia. His benefit match against Surrey at Trent Bridge in 1898 yielded
£1,000 and in 1903 he was awarded a second benefit from the MCC, on
whose ground staff he had also rendered long and yeoman service. On
retiring from first-class cricket, he acted for many years as an umpire and
as a coach at Shrewsbury School. Yet he finished up (in the 1920s) as a
labourer in a factory, just as he had started. Somewhere during his
post-cricket career, Attewell's life had taken a sorry turn.[99]

George Davidson was a superb cricketer who represented Derbyshire
with much distinction in the 1890s. He also played briefly as a professional in South Africa. Most observers felt that he would assuredly have
been invited to play for England had he belonged to a more important
county. His career was thus hampered by the accident of geography, which
also meant that he could derive no more than a modest profit from his
benefit match. Davidson had begun as an unskilled labourer in the
Brimington iron works for a mere 10d. per day, before accepting his first
professional contract with the Keighley Cricket Club. He was struck down
by pneumonia on 10 February 1899 before he had reached his 33rd
birthday. 'Sad to say, he has left a wife and five young children, who, with
the exception of the £200 which he received from his benefit match, are
quite unprovided for.' The editor of *Cricket*, in making this announcement, hoped that energetic steps would be taken by the gentlemen of
Derbyshire to raise a fund on the family's behalf.[100]

John Jackson, the famous fast bowler from Nottinghamshire, did as
well as most professionals could then have expected to do. He established

a reputation as one of the most fearsome fast bowlers in England during the 1850s and 1860s. He played for the AEE and accompanied Fred Lillywhite's team to Canada and the United States in 1859. But a serious leg injury in 1866 proved the turning point in his career. For a while he served as groundsman and bowler for the Liverpool club, and then took a series of odd jobs to survive. A benefit held for him in 1874 yielded only £275. He wound up totally penniless in the Liverpool workhouse infirmary, and died there at 68 on 4 November 1901. He received a decent burial only through the generosity of his friends.[101]

If it was difficult for a county player, who eventually joined the MCC ground staff, played for England and coached after his retirement, to stay afloat, then it must have been doubly so for the club cricketer at the local level. It is true that during the Edwardian age the eccentric Sidney Barnes preferred to take his chances in league cricket, but his case quite obviously was most exceptional. The majority of professional cricketers in the nineteenth century failed to use cricket as an avenue of escape from poverty and/or lower-class status.

It is not easy to explain this phenomenon. It is likely that many cricketers were badly advised, and therefore invested their money foolishly. More likely still is it that many professionals were ill-used by importunate friends and relatives who took unfair advantage of their generosity. It is also a fact that although, as Haygarth has shown, most cricket professionals in the Victorian age were skilled or semi-skilled artisans, they were not well enough educated in an academic sense to carve out even a modest niche for themselves when their playing days were over. Many cricketers were also well known to have cultivated too strong a taste for drink, and alcoholism certainly took its toll when they reached the age of retirement from the game. William Barnes, J.T. Brown, Buttress, Tom Emmett, William Lockwood and Peel were among the more notorious alcoholics.[102]

Ironically, it was an aristocratic amateur, Lord Hawke, who most clearly identified the major reasons why professional cricketers relapsed into poverty and who tried hardest to save them from the normal pitfalls. When he was invited to lead the Yorkshire county club in 1883, he found, as he himself put it, 'ten drunks and a parson' representing the county. He did his best, albeit in an autocratic manner, to improve the image of Yorkshire professional cricketers by teaching them to have pride in themselves. He insisted on proper discipline, decent and tidy dress, punctuality and respectable demeanour at all times. He introduced a novel marking method to replace the unsatisfactory system of talents which had generally favoured the bat at the expense of bowling and fielding. He offered his professionals winter pay for the first time, and established a system of trusts to prevent them from squandering the fruits of their benefits.[103] Lord

Hawke, in short, was an interesting Victorian whose philosophy and morals were not unlike those of the majority of his aristocratic contemporaries. Their views on professional cricketers, as on industrial labour in general, reflected a very odd synthesis of old-fashioned snobbery and benevolent paternalism. David Roberts once argued that the early Victorians firmly believed in an authoritarian and hierarchical society in which the wealthy had vital functions and responsibilities as well as privileges.[104] He might well have made the same remarks about the generation which followed.

When pursuing a similar theme in soccer, Mason observed that only a minority of successful professionals managed to make any appreciable progress up the socio-economic scale.[105] The same holds true for Victorian professional cricketers. It is true that William Clarke, who organized the All England XIs in the mid-century, was a successful entrepreneur as well as a professional cricketer, but he was really a relic of the Georgian era, having been born in 1798. Originally a bricklayer from Nottingham, he made enough money from cricket to establish himself as a licensed victualler. After a fortunate marriage, he bought the Trent Bridge cricket ground in 1838, and eventually died a very wealthy man in 1856.[106] More closely attached to the Victorian age was George Freeman, who used his cricket earnings to found a successful auctioneering business which prospered so rapidly that he retired after a brief career in first-class cricket to devote his full attention to its management.[107] William Gunn of Nottinghamshire, who represented England both in cricket and soccer, established the thriving bat-making firm of Gunn and Moore. He eventually became a director of Notts County. After having begun with very little, when he died at 63 in 1921, he left an estate of £60,000.[108] Richard Daft, who began as an amateur, turned professional in 1859 and used his cricketing fame to establish a variety of business interests. Not only was he a partner in a brewery at Ratcliffe-on-Trent, he was also a tobacconist and cricket outfitter in Nottingham and ended his days in relative comfort.[109] And George Wootton eventually retired to his own farm at Clifton 'more happily than most of his contemporary professionals'.[110]

These success stories, however, are the exceptional cases. It is true that R.G. Barlow, William Caffyn, George Hirst, John Painter, George Parr, Maurice Read, Wilfred Rhodes, Alfred Shaw, Arthur Shrewsbury, James Southerton, H.H. Stephenson and Alec Watson as well as the Hearnes, Lillywhites, Suggs and Wisdens are also known to have been financially successful. But in relationship to the total number of professional cricketers, the list is still painfully short. Only a minority succeeded in breaking the class barrier, and there is a strong suspicion that some of the group listed here among the successes were not, in fact, altogether poor when they embarked on their professional careers. Parr, for example, was descended from a long line of gentlemen-farmers.[111] Shrewsbury, too, belonged to a respectable family whose members had for years been successful businessmen in Nottinghamshire. His father was the proprietor of Queen's Hotel in Nottingham, where young Arthur himself, in partnership with Shaw, established a prosperous general sports warehouse.[112] Stephenson came from a family sufficiently well-to-do to have hired servants in his youth; and Read, who 'ended in a trusted capacity at Tichborn Park', was actually Stephenson's nephew.[113]

If the opportunities for social advancement were limited in the Victorian age, they were to become even more so during the Edwardian era. As Midwinter has noticed, this was the period when amateurs brought cricket more completely under their control at the county and international levels. Thus, the families who had used cricket to upgrade themselves became even fewer in the first quarter of the twentieth century. At the very time when, as Martin-Jenkins thought, Maurice Read seemed to be representing 'a new "school" of professionals: well-groomed, well-mannered, articulate, sober and thrifty', that breed was beginning to do less well financially than its Victorian predecessors had done.[114]

The Victorian professional cricketers cannot be blamed for this development even though they failed to organize any kind of players' union at the time when the Association footballers were moving in that direction. The blame must rest squarely on the shoulders of cricket's administrators, who bluntly refused to alter its rules or tools and thus insisted on preserving Georgian cricket in a more or less mummified form. As a result, the game remained too eighteenth-century in its outlook and gradually failed to compete with soccer as a spectator sport.

The net result of cricket's failure in this regard was that the majority of the county clubs could not take proper care even of their best professionals. This meant, in effect, that there was never any possibility that good players like Davidson (Derbyshire), Pougher (Leicestershire) and Tyler (Somerset) could become rich on the strength of their cricket. Those professionals who wanted to escape from their initial poverty had to be lucky enough to play for Surrey and Yorkshire, the wealthiest and therefore the most generous of the county clubs.

In the final analysis, the relationships between amateurs and professionals in Victorian cricket were very complex. While the master–servant dichotomy served to sustain an obvious barrier between the players and the gentlemen throughout the period, there was nevertheless a considerable degree of cooperation on the field of play. During the game itself, the professionals seemed more conscious of belonging to a particular club or county and promoting that group's interests, than of representing a particular class. This *esprit de corps* proved to be the most effective force in mitigating the worst effects of what, for the want of a better term, may be called the class struggle. If Victorian amateurs were often haughty and autocratic in their treatment of professionals, they were also often humane and benevolent. If, in relation to other Victorian sports, the cricket professional was underpaid, this was certainly not due to greed on the part of the amateurs who ran the cricket clubs. It had much more to do with the faulty economic structure of the sport itself. At the very time when most other aspects of Victorian life were becoming more effectively commercialized, cricket tried to adhere tenaciously to Georgian structures and forms because its administrators never considered it a commodity to be commercialized. The Victorians always felt that the professionalization of cricket, a veritable national symbol, would rob that sport of its very essence and meaning.

Notes

1. Brookes, *English Cricket*, 138.
2. P. Murphy, *E.J. 'Tiger' Smith of Warwickshire and England* (Newton Abbot, 1981), 4–13.
3. Midwinter, *Grace: Life*, 117.
4. See, e.g., an editorial in the *Athletic World*, 12 February 1879, calling for a liberal revision of the amateur clause which excluded artisans, mechanics and labourers (73).
5. Brookes, 117. Cousins, *Golf in Britain*, 32. Mandle, 'Professional Cricketer', 1; and 'Games People Played', 511–35. Mason, *Association Football*, 69–81. Walvin, *The People's Game*, 76–80.
6. *Cricket*, 31 July 1884, 253.
7. *Athletic Chronicle*, 31 October 1899, 1.
8. Gale, *Modern English Sports*, 28. Pycroft, *Oxford Memories*, 203.
9. *Athletic Review*, 29 March 1882, 1.
10. *Athletic News*, 12 November 1884, 1; 10 February 1885, 1; 7 April 1885, 4; and 28 July 1885, 4.
11. Midwinter, 120.
12. *Midland Athlete*, 19 January 1881, 41.
13. *Athletic Chat*, 6 June 1900, 5.
14. See, e.g., *Wisden 1876*, 20.
15. *Cricket Field*, 11 May 1895, 81–82. J.D. Coldham, *Lord Harris* (London, 1983), 77–78.
16. *Wisden 1899*, 231, 233.
17. See, e.g., *Cricket*, 21 June 1883, 190; 2 May 1889, 87; 30 April 1891, 87; and 30 April 1896, 107.
18. *Athletic News*, 15 January 1879, 4.
19. *Midland Athlete*, 4 May 1881, 390.
20. *Sporting Clipper*, 20 June 1874, 4.
21. Midwinter, 155–56. See also Sir C. MacKenzie, 'Shillings for W.G.: Looking Back Eighty Years', *Wisden 1973*, 103–07. H. Preston, 'W.G. Grace Centenary', *Wisden 1949*, 106.

22. *Athletic News*, 1 October 1900, 4. C. Ellis, *C.B.: The Life of Charles Burgess Fry* (London, 1984), 51, 72, 150–53. C.B. Fry, *Life Worth Living* (London, repr. 1986), 152.
23. Coldham, *Northamptonshire Cricket*, 40. Golesworthy, *Encyclopaedia of Cricket*, 90. Lemmon, *Surrey County Cricket*, 49–50.
24. *Athletic News*, 22 July 1895, 1. *Wisden 1872*, 18. Gordon, *Background of Cricket*, 36–39.
25. Midwinter, 118.
26. Murphy, 2.
27. *Athletic Chat*, 6 June 1900, 5. *Cricket*, 22 September 1887, 425–26. Grace, 261. Mandle, 'Professional Cricketer', 1–16.
28. *Athletic News*, 1892, 1. Aspin, *Gone Cricket Mad*, 44.
29. Moses, *To Ashbrooke and Beyond*, 30.
30. Greaves, *Over the Summers Again*, 41, 72.
31. Harbottle, *Century of Cricket in South Northumberland*, 22. Hurst, *Century of Penrith Cricket*, 29.
32. *Athletic News*, 10 June 1889, 1; and 1 July 1889, 1.
33. Aspin, 27, 31–32.
34. *Wisden 1900*, 298–99.
35. *Wisden 1891*, 51.
36. *Wisden 1893*, 138.
37. *Athletic News*, 22 August 1892, 1; and 26 August 1895, 1.
38. *Ibid.*, 3 August 1886, 1. *Cricket*, 17 August 1899, 348. *Wisden 1900*, 12.
39. *Cricket Field*, 4 August 1894, 347; and 20 July 1895, 308.
40. *Athletic News*, 9 July 1884, 1.
41. *Ibid.*, 9 September 1889, 1. *Sports Telegraph*, 6 August 1898.
42. J.A. Walvin, 'Dust to Dust: Celebrations of Death in Victorian England', *Historical Reflections* (Fall 1982), 9: 353–71.
43. R. Marlar, in an introduction to F. Lillywhite, *The English Cricketers' Trip to Canada and the United States* (London, 1860; repr. 1980).
44. Sissons, *Players*, 53–54.
45. Altham and Swanton, *History of Cricket*, 69.
46. Swanton, ed., *Barclays World of Cricket*, 433–34.
47. *Wisden 1870*, 65, 86; and *1898*, xlv–xlvi.
48. *Cricket Field*, 29 April 1893, 51. *Wisden 1872*, 133.
49. *Cricket*, 19 May 1887, 136; and 30 May 1889, 154.
50. *Cricket Field*, 25 November 1893, 487. *Wisden 1899*, 137.
51. P. Bailey, P. Thorn and P. Wynne-Thomas, *Who's Who of Cricketers* (London, 1984), 901. Sissons, 138.
52. *Cricket*, 14 April 1898, 58.
53. *Cricket Field*, 18 May 1895, 96. Swanton, ed., *World of Cricket*, 115.
54. *Cricket*, 25 October 1900, 439. Mandle, 'Professional Cricketer', 10–11. Swanton, ed., *World of Cricket*, 115–18.
55. Altham *et al.*, *Hampshire County Cricket*, 52.
56. *Wisden 1888*, 215.
57. *Wisden 1888*, 28–29; and *1893*, 98.
58. *Wisden 1899*, 195.
59. *Wisden 1880*, 156–57; and *1895*, 84.
60. *Wisden 1878*, 184–85; *1879*, 115; and *1890*, 271.
61. *Wisden 1894*, 232; and *1895*, 297–98.

62. *Cricket*, 28 March 1901, 42. *Cricket Field*, 10 November 1894, 483; and 18 May 1895, 97.
63. *Wisden 1881*, 198.
64. *Athletic News*, 12 May 1892, 1. *Wisden 1880*, 55–57, 82.
65. *Cricket*, 27 February 1890, 26. *Wisden 1891*, 203.
66. *Athletic Chat*, 6 June 1900, 5. *Athletic News*, 9 July 1900, 1. *Cricket*, 3 May 1900, 114.
67. M. Carey, 'Benefits', in Swanton, ed., *Barclays World of Cricket*, 395–96.
68. K.A.P. Sandiford, 'The Professionalization of Modern Cricket', *British Journal of Sports History* (December 1985), 2: 280–81.
69. *Athletic News*, 23 April 1900, 1.
70. Duckworth, *Warwickshire Cricket*, 675.
71. *Ibid.*, 93–94.
72. Sissons, 105–12.
73. Haygarth, *Scores and Biographies*, VI: 325. *Wisden 1878*, 184; *1882*, 32, 149; *1888*, 28–29, 215; *1892*, 171–72; *1893*, 98, 184; *1895*, 84; *1898*, 57; *1899*, 31, 195.
74. See an article by Rev. R.S. Holmes on the improving fortunes of professional cricketers in *Cricket*, 11 July 1895, 259 (which prompted a negative response from the editor of the *Athletic News* on 22 July 1895, 1); and another by 'An Old Harrovian' in *Cricket*, 25 October 1900, 438–39.
75. Sissons, 133.
76. *Ibid.*, 155–64.
77. *Ibid.*, 132–33.
78. *Wisden 1865*, 155–58.
79. *Ibid.*
80. Haygarth, *Scores and Biographies*, VI: 365–66; VII: 47; VIII: 288; and IX: 55–56.
81. *Wisden 1885*, 106.
82. *Cricket*, 2 May 1889, 87; and 1 May 1890, 85. *Wisden 1872*, 19; *1877*, 142; *1881*, 26; and *1887*, xix, 37. Vamplew, *Pay Up and Play*, 251.
83. Annual reports on the Prince's Cricket Club in *Wisden* during the 1870s. Vamplew, 251.
84. Vamplew, 251. *Wisden 1887*, xix; and *1889*, xxxix.
85. Haygarth, VI: 204. Leveson Gower, *Off and On the Field*, 18–19.
86. *Cricket Field*, 2 March 1895, 34. Warner, *Long Innings*, 35.
87. *Cricket Field*, 13 May 1893, 84.
88. *Cricket*, 24 November 1898, 466; and 26 October 1899, 446. *Cricket Field*, 28 May 1892, 52.
89. *Cricket Field*, 6 April 1895, 47. Midwinter, 45.
90. *Cricket*, 21 February 1889, 25; and 4 May 1895, 64.
91. Mandle, 'Professional Cricketer', 9. Midwinter, 44–45.
92. *Athletic News*, 2 July 1900, 1. Golesworthy, *Encyclopaedia*, 86–87.
93. Martin-Jenkins, *Who's Who*, 26, 130.
94. S. Rogerson, *Wilfred Rhodes* (London, 1960), 39–41. Thompson, *Hirst and Rhodes*, 103.
95. Gordon, 197.
96. Compiled from various obituary notices in *Wisden*.
97. Mandle, 'Professional Cricketer', 14–15.
98. Gibson, *Jackson's Year*, 8–9. Gordon, 117–18. Martin-Jenkins, 28–29.
99. Gibson, 9. Green, ed., *Wisden Obituaries*, 28–29.

100. *Cricket*, 23 February 1899, 17–18.
101. Altham and Swanton, *History of Cricket*, 98–99. Brookes, 118–19. Green, ed., *Wisden Obituaries*, 485–86. Marlar, introduction to F. Lillywhite, *English Cricketers' Trip*.
102. Altham and Swanton, 110. D. Hodgson, *Yorkshire County Cricket Club*, 58, 85. Martin-Jenkins, 17, 30, 115. Lemmon, *Surrey County Cricket Club*, 110.
103. Gordon, 115–18. Hodgson, 46–48. Kilburn, *History of Yorkshire Cricket*, 25–28. Warner, *Long Innings*, 42–43.
104. D. Roberts, *Paternalism in Early Victorian England* (New Jersey, 1979).
105. Mason, *Association Football*, 82–137.
106. Martineau, *They Made Cricket*, 108. Thompson, *Golden Ages*, 35–40; and *Odd Man In*, 20–22. Webber, *Phoenix History*, 25.
107. Altham and Swanton, 113.
108. Martin-Jenkins, 67.
109. Haygarth, VI; 87.
110. Altham and Swanton, 99.
111. Marlar, introduction to F. Lillywhite, *English Cricketers' Trip*.
112. *Cricket and Football Times*, 3 June 1880, 73.
113. *Cricket Field*, 1 June 1895, 141–42. Gordon, 266. Green, ed., *Wisden Obituaries*, 734. Martin-Jenkins, 121.
114. Martin-Jenkins, 121. Midwinter, 117.

CHAPTER SIX

Victorian Cricket Crowds

Attendance at cricket matches at all levels increased steadily during Queen Victoria's reign. County games, which had generally attracted around two or three thousand spectators in the 1840s, drew about 4000 on average in the 1860s. With the advent of W.G., the numbers doubled in the 1870s. By the 1880s, five digits on a daily basis were not uncommon – especially in the more popular contests, like Lancashire vs Yorkshire and Nottinghamshire vs Surrey. By the end of the century, between 15 000 and 20 000 spectators went to such matches. On special occasions, particularly the August Bank holiday, crowds in the 1890s sometimes exceeded 20 000. The Victorian record attendance for county cricket was set in 1892 when 63 763 people paid for admission over three days to watch Nottinghamshire vs Surrey at the Oval. The previous best had been 51 636 paying to watch the same two counties at the same venue in 1887. The total number of persons who actually saw the Notts–Surrey match in 1892, including members of the Surrey CCC, their guests, journalists and others, must surely have been close to 100 000.[1]

This trend was in keeping with other aspects of Victorian life. The gradual reduction of the working hours for middle- and lower-class Victorians and the steady increase of their per capita income allowed them to take a keener interest in mass leisure than perhaps any previous society. Increasingly large numbers of people assembled to watch brass band concerts, classical music festivals, athletic competitions and soccer matches.[2] It was really in soccer attendance that the crowd increase was most clearly marked. For whereas cricket had generally outdrawn soccer until the 1880s, the reverse gradually became true thereafter.

The urge to attend a sporting event in very large numbers was not a Victorian peculiarity. In 1791, when the MCC made its first trip north to play against Notts at Upper Meadow, some 10 000 were said to have watched the game. A similar number were reported present for the England vs Sussex cricket game at Brighton in July 1827. During Victorian times themselves there is evidence of an unusually large gathering for the famous cricket match at the Artillery Ground, Finsbury, on 11 July 1843. About 10 000 persons were estimated to be in attendance to watch the Three of Kent do battle with the Three of England on that occasion. The estimate of the crowd when the AEE played against Twenty of Sheffield at Hyde Park in 1846 was even placed as high as 16 000.[3] Considering what we know now about the difficulties of travel prior to the railway boom, and the condition of cricket grounds before 1850, it is safe to assume that these estimates were somewhat exaggerated. They do testify, however, to the increasing popularity of cricket in England.

For a long time, reporters covering cricket for *Bell's Life in London* or *The Times* made little comment about the crowd. When they did so, it was invariably to focus attention on the unique or the extraordinary. Thus, when *The Times* spoke of the aggregate total of 11 000 watching the charity game at Lord's on two days in late May 1863, it was marvelling at the unusual size of the attendance. The same is true of its report a few weeks later that as many as 6000 watched the annual Oxford vs Cambridge university classic on 22 June at Lord's.[4] Smaller crowds than usual also attracted comment. Hence *The Times* could blame inclement weather for the fact that only an estimated 4000 people watched the university match on 13 June 1864. It also expressed surprise at the attendance of 2000 spectators on 4 June 1863, despite competition with Ascot, when Surrey met Yorkshire at the Oval.[5]

It is from this kind of evidence that judgments must now be made about the average size of cricket crowds in the 1860s. The estimates for the popular matches during this decade were consistently placed between 4000 and 6000 by *Bell's Life in London* and *The Times*. It would seem therefore safe to conclude that the general average was slightly lower. It cannot, however, have been *substantially* lower than 4000 for county cricket at that time, since even a game between two physically handicapped sides in 1865 attracted an estimated 3000 spectators. On that occasion, in late August, the One-Arm team went down to defeat at the hands of the One-Leggers at the Oval.[6] Happily, however, with the introduction of turnstiles early in the 1870s, estimates became totally unnecessary. Cricket grounds began to publish official statistics on the precise number of customers who paid for admission. What these statistics clearly indicate is that attendance at cricket matches in England kept on rising very steadily until the end of the nineteenth century. But, in the decade immediately preceding the First World War, as Wray Vamplew has shown, the numbers tended to fluctuate in a more complex manner.[7]

It is very difficult, in analysing this socio-cultural phenomenon, to disentangle cause from effect. It can be said, for instance, that the transportation revolution emancipated the local cricket enthusiasts from their provincial chains by making it much easier for them to travel to the great cricketing headquarters in increasingly substantial numbers. Improved methods of travel also allowed them to move more freely and readily *within* the rapidly emerging industrial centres. But that in itself would have availed them naught had the great headquarters of the game

not also been transformed. The cricket crowds could not have mushroomed as they did if the Georgian grounds had not been expanded and
new facilities introduced. The famous MCC headquarters at Lord's, for
example, for a long time continued to allocate space for horses and
carriages, thus imposing a severe limitation on the number of spectators.
To cope with the increasing demand for spectator space, the MCC committee embarked on an ambitious programme of expansion, rebuilding
and renovation which occupied the last four decades of the nineteenth
century. The old pavilion was greatly enlarged in the 1860s; the new
grandstand was built from scratch; a third pavilion was opened in 1890;
and the Mound Stand was erected in 1898.[8] The Lord's of Edward VII's
reign was a far cry from the Lord's which his father, the Prince Consort,
had known.

It is almost amusing now to read the public announcement which R.A.
Fitzgerald, the MCC secretary, felt obliged to make in 1864:

> In consequence of the inconvenience experienced by the players in the
> School matches of the last two years, from the crowded state of Lord's
> ground, the Committee of the MCC have determined to place all the
> arrangements of the ground under the control of the metropolitan
> police...These regulations necessarily entail heavy expenses upon the
> club, the prices of admission will, therefore, be as follows on each
> day: Persons on foot, 1/-; on horseback, 2/6; carriages, two wheels,
> 5/-; carriages, four wheels, 10/-.[9]

There had been too much confusion in 1862 and 1863 when more than
7000 spectators had been admitted to the annual Eton vs Harrow game.
The old Lord's ground simply could not cope comfortably with so many.
By 1900, however, it could accommodate 30 000.

Similar expansion and renovation occurred at Kennington Oval, where
the Surrey CCC played its home games. By the 1890s, it could easily hold
in excess of 25 000. Lancashire's Old Trafford, by the end of the 1870s,
was already accommodating more than 15 000 spectators. So too could
Trent Bridge, the headquarters of the Nottinghamshire CCC. By the turn
of the century Lord Hawke was also able to claim that there were at least
three cricket grounds in Yorkshire capable of holding 20 000 to 30 000
spectators.[10]

Thus, in the populous north and prosperous southeast, county committees deliberately tried to meet the new demand by extending their
grounds and building modern pavilions. The other counties tried just as
hard, but were conspicuously less successful. Essex, for instance, eventually moved from Brentwood to Leyton, but the latter ground was still
not as spacious even as the Grace Road ground in Leicestershire which,
by the 1890s, was accommodating 11 000. Gloucestershire, Hampshire,
Kent and Sussex all continued to play on relatively small fields. There thus

remained a considerable disparity between the counties which was naturally reflected in the attendance and gate receipts. At all events, however, every county succeeded in building new pavilions, erecting scoreboards, and providing facilities for the customers and the press. By the end of the Victorian era, the first-class counties, then 16 in number, were playing before crowds varying approximately from 8 000 to 24 000 per day.[11]

Crowd attendance at that time depended upon exactly the same variables that are operative now: the weather, the size of the ground, the current form of the home team and the nature of the contest. The summer of 1879, for example, was miserably wet and most clubs therefore had cause to lament a pronounced decline in their revenues. The Nottinghamshire team was generally very popular during the last quarter of the nineteenth century, but a temporary slump on the field in the mid-1890s was reflected in their receipts. *Wisden* expressed the view that their stonewalling tactics and stodgy batting contributed also to their temporary eclipse.[12] There was a noticeable decline in the Kentish crowds, too, when that county was achieving only moderate success on the cricket field in the early 1890s.[13] On the other hand, the turning point for a struggling Lancashire CCC came in 1881 when it won the county championship outright for the very first time. Thousands began to flock to Old Trafford to see the champions play and that county club, playing consistently successful cricket for the next three decades, prospered greatly.[14] There were always certain types of games which proved far more popular than the normal county match. Of these, the chief were the annual university and public school contests at Lord's, games involving the charismatic W.G., those in which the Australians participated and the great festivals towards the end of the season.

Dr W.G. Grace was, for a period of 40 years, the most magnetic sports personality in Britain. Revered as a legend in his own time, he was lionized all across the kingdom.[15] Some county clubs capitalized on his magnetism by doubling the price of admission for matches in which he participated. Most professionals deliberately did the same by choosing the county game against Gloucestershire as their benefit match. To his everlasting credit, the Doctor seldom disappointed them. Several professionals, like John Lillywhite, Joseph Rowbotham, H.H. Stephenson and George Wootton, enjoyed enormously productive benefits because of W.G.'s participation.[16] When, in July 1885, Alec Watson's benefit yielded in excess of £1,200, *Wisden* sagely noted that 'Dr W.G. Grace's presence gave the fixture an importance and attraction unfortunately lacking in the North vs South contest for Richard Humphrey's benefit a fortnight previously at the Oval'.[17] On this occasion, the Doctor's magic drew some 30 000 fans through the turnstiles during the three days' play. In July 1873,

W.G. attracted an aggregate of 23 000 to Bramall Lane. The crowd of 12 000 on the 28th was then a record for that ground.[18] Four years later, he again drew well over 22 000 to the same ground, according to the estimate given by *Bell's Life in London*.[19] When the Champion made his first appearance at Old Trafford in late July 1878, between 15 000 and 20 000 people, according to the *Athletic News*, flocked thither on the Saturday. There was not enough space for all the customers, some of whom encroached upon the field of play and considerably reduced the distances from the boundary. The Manchester club had not anticipated such a throng and consequently failed to control the crowd; but its receipts easily exceeded £750.[20] It has been very well said indeed that 'half the bricks of the pavilions of the County Grounds around England belonged to W.G.'[21]

The Australians were always a source of considerable curiosity. They consistently attracted greater crowds than the normal county clubs. Their frequent visits after 1878 thus served not only as a stimulus to the sport but as a boon to the various county committees. Even lowly Leicestershire was able to boast of a new attendance record of 12 000 when the Australians invaded the Grace Road ground in July 1878. This record was destined to remain intact for 60 years before the Australians broke it again in Don Bradman's time.[22] So many spectators paid to watch the tourists at Old Trafford in August 1878 that the Lancashire CCC made a net profit of £730 from the match.[23] Some 20 000 are reported to have watched the Aussies play against England at the Oval on the first Monday in September 1880. Preparations for this game, in the words of the *Cricket and Football Times*, were 'totally inadequate to meet the requirements of the unprecedented attendance of spectators of both sexes and of all ages'.[24] The *Athletic News* considered that, at a modest estimate, close to 40 000 individuals must have paid for admission over three days to see the Australians vs Lancashire at Old Trafford in June 1884.[25] In 1886, on a dull and overcast Friday morning in mid-May, over 13 000 went out to see the tourists play against Lord Sheffield's XI at Sheffield Park in Sussex.[26] In the second Test match at Lord's in July 1886, there were over 33 000 paying customers, of whom 15 663 passed through the turnstiles on the 20th alone.[27] During the three days of the Lord's Test in July 1890, 30 279 spectators paid for admission. That number would doubtless have been much higher had the attendance not fallen rather noticeably on the third day, when the result was no longer in doubt and the match ended early in England's favour.[28] The Australians were still a huge attraction at the end of the century. They drew an estimated 28 000 to Old Trafford on the first day of their match against Lancashire in 1899.[29]

All of these statistics are better than the average county cricket attendance and attest eloquently to the popularity of W.G. and the Australians.

It is easy to understand why the late-Victorians flocked in such large numbers to watch Dr Grace play cricket. He, quite simply, played the game more proficiently than anybody else had ever done before. He was a very popular sports idol, in the same class as Donald Bradman and Garfield Sobers in the century which followed. Nor is it hard to see why the Victorians evinced such a keen interest in the Australians. The latter, after all, played extremely good cricket. Their bowling, as a rule, was tighter and more efficient than the English variety and their fielding was always brilliant. They also provided the extra dimension of international competition in an age when the English and the Scots were stridently nationalistic. Hence, even in a small park at Titwood in Scotland, the Australians could play against the Eighteen of Clydesdale in September 1880 before a crowd of approximately 7000.[30]

It is much more difficult to account for the Victorian approach to the Oxford–Cambridge and Eton–Harrow matches. Perhaps it is best to view this development as one of the natural consequences of the triumph of muscular Christianity. The widespread notion that sports encouraged the growth of superior attributes led to a remarkable cricketing craze in Victorian schools. The successful cricketer thus became the hero at Eton and Cambridge, while the frail scholar was despised. The public saw in these youthful cricketers the natural leaders of the future. It was this kind of attitude that helped substantially to create the climate of opinion in which Eton–Harrow and Oxford–Cambridge games, notwithstanding the mediocre quality of the cricket, could assume almost transcendental significance.

By the 1870s the annual classics between the academic institutions had already superseded in popularity and importance the old Gentlemen vs Players and North vs South confrontations. Even the contemporary press was occasionally puzzled by such a phenomenon. The *Athletic News*, operating as it was beyond the outskirts of the great metropolis, was once tempted to attribute it solely to that plague of idiosyncrasies by which Londoners were congenitally afflicted. Here was a bustling metropolitan complex with millions of inhabitants of whom only a measly dozen or two could bother with the Ten Miles Amateur Championship in athletics. Yet, tens of thousands of them were eager to get down to Lord's to watch juveniles play cricket, and not very well at that.[31] The editor of the *Athletic News*, who had long been a keen promoter of track and field, was also revealing his acute disappointment with the failure of the athletic championships in London in 1886.

In fact, by the 1860s, the great classics between the academic institutions at Lord's had already become more than cricket events. They were significant social occasions (in addition to fashion shows) which the wealthiest Victorian families were expected to attend. The great highlight of each summer was the Eton vs Harrow cricket match which attracted royalty as well as the nobility. The Prince and Princess of Wales often appeared and in 1876, for instance, were accompanied by the King of Greece and some 1200 carriages 'conveying the élite of English society'.[32] This annual encounter had apparently appealed to the proletariat as well, but the MCC thought it necessary to impose restrictions on them. In 1864 it brought in the metropolitan police. Ten years later, it raised the price of admission beyond the means of the lower-middle classes. The masses were blamed for the unruly behaviour that had occurred in 1863 and 1873 and were therefore deliberately excluded.[33]

In the first 17 games after the introduction of turnstiles at Lord's, the Oxford–Cambridge match attracted 377449 paying spectators during 1871–87. In 1892, over 52000 spectators came on the three days to watch the undergraduates. Between 1871 and 1886, about 244000 people paid for admission to 16 Eton–Harrow games.[34] As these statistics do not include the thousands of MCC members, relatives and guests, they are even more impressive than they seem on the surface. Such was the popularity of the Eton–Harrow fixture that over 40000 people altogether went to witness it in July 1873. A record number – 27082 – paid for admission that year. The crowd was obviously too large and it soon became unruly. The result was the celebrated MCC resolution in 1874:

> That it is desirable to make arrangements for diminishing the numbers of persons at the Eton and Harrow match, on July 10 and 11, and that, with that view, the price of admission on that occasion for each person on foot be raised from 1s. to 2s.6d.

This declaration only led to an increase in the applications for carriage spaces and one week before the game the secretary had to announce that all carriage spaces had already been disposed of.[35]

Fitzgerald expressed his total satisfaction with the results of the MCC resolution. He told the editor of *Bell's Life in London* that the 'increased tariff admission fulfilled the expectations of the Committee; it not only tended to check the attendance of several thousands, but it was especially conducive to the good order that prevailed'.[36] For the Eton–Harrow match of 1874, 15364 people paid for admission, whereas more than 27000 had done so in the previous two years. In 1871, almost 25000 had also gone through the turnstiles.[37] *Wisden*, however, felt that the MCC measures had been unavailing in 1874 and that 'for aught it would have affected the wonderful attraction of the match, the admission charge might as well have been raised to half a guinea as to half a crown'.[38] The annual Eton–Harrow game, in fact, remained very popular throughout the rest of the century. In 1898, for example, it was still producing a net profit of £442 at a time when most of the county matches were being played at a

1. *top: Alfred Mynn* (left) *and "Felix"* (Nicholas Wanostracht). Two famous Georgian cricketers. Mynn was a hard-hitting batsman and a very fast bowler. Felix was the finest amateur batsman of his time. He also invented tubular batting gloves and a bowling machine; *bottom: Gloucestershire XI, 1877.* Left to right, back row: W. O. Moberley, W. Fairbanks, G. F. Grace, F. G. Monkland, W. R. Gilbert, W. Midwinter. Front row: Capt. Kingscote, F. Townsend, R. F. Miles, W. G. Grace, E. M. Grace.

2.   top: *Fuller Pilch*. The most accomplished batsman before the advent of W.G., he was the pioneer of the drive off the front foot; *bottom: The first English touring team*. They made a highly successful trip to Canada and the United States in 1859.

3.   *top: Bats over time*. Five bats displayed at Lord's showing that
bats have changed very little since the eighteenth century. From left to
right: a curved bat of 1750, a straight bat of 1793, Fuller Pilch's bat,
W. G. Grace's bat, and Don Bradman's bat of 1948; *bottom: The
England XI which defeated Australia, 1882–3*. From left to right,
standing: W. Barnes, F. Morley, C. T. Studd, G. F. Vernon, C. F. H.
Leslie. Seated: G. B. Studd, E. F. S. Tylecote, Hon. Ivo Francis Bligh, A.
G. Steel, W. W. Read. Front row: R. G. Barlow, W. Bates.

4.   *top left: John McCarthy Blackham.* One of the greatest of all Australian wicket-keepers, and one of the inventors of modern wicket-keeping technique; *top right: George Giffen.* The leading Australian all-rounder during the 1890s; *bottom: John Shuter.* An outstanding captain of Surrey who led his team to many county championships during the 1890s.

5.   *top: W. G. Grace and Harry Jupp.* Two of the best batsmen in
England during the 1870s. W.G. established a host of incredible
records while Jupp scored the very first 50 for England in Test Cricket;
bottom: The English team to South Africa, 1898–9. From left to right,
standing: G. A. Lohmann (manager), W. R. Cuttell, F. Mitchell, F. W.
Milligan, A. G. Archer, A. A. White (umpire). Seated: S. Haigh, H. R.
Bromley-Davenport, Lord Hawke (captain), A. E. Trott, J. H. Board.
Front row: J. T. Tydesley, C. E. M. Wilson, P. F. Warner.

6. *top left: Bobby Peel.* A very successful all-round cricketer, whose career was abruptly terminated by Lord Hawke in 1897 when he turned up inebriated for an important Yorkshire county match; *top right: Andrew Stoddart.* One of the most accomplished of late Victorian batsmen, he nevertheless failed miserably in 1897 against the bowling of Clifford Goodman, the great Barbadian pioneer of the swerve; *bottom: George Lohmann.* One of the greatest bowlers in the history of cricket, he finished his first-class career with 112 wickets in 18 Tests at an average of 10.75 runs per wicket.

7.   *top left: William Brockwell.* A stylish opening batsman for Surrey and England, he fell upon hard times after his retirement and died in abject poverty; *top right: C. B. Fry.* A prolific scorer for Sussex, he began his career as a versatile athlete and ended it as a journalist, politician and cricket commentator; *bottom: Charles Kortright.* The fastest and the most famous of all the amateur fast bowlers in the late Victorian age.

8. *top left: William Scotton*. Famous for his stonewalling tactics and technique as a professional batsman for Nottinghamshire from 1870 to 1887; *top right: W. G. Grace in his MCC cap, 1890*. This is from a painting in oils by Archibald Stuart Wortley. W. G. was the greatest cricketer of his time and had the magnetism to attract huge crowds wherever he played; *bottom: Prince Kumar Shri Ranjitsinhji, Jam Sahib of Nawanagar, in his regal robes*. A truly great player for Sussex and England, Ranji demonstrated that cricket could be played brilliantly by Indians as well as Anglo-Saxons.

net loss.[39]

The university and the public school contests attracted a large number of alumni and their relatives, mainly because of the Victorian sentimental attachment to the *alma mater*. An old-Harrovian's loyalty to Harrow was as important to him as such basic virtues as parental affection and filial piety. The crowds were not always cricket enthusiasts; they were attending the game for the electrifying atmosphere rather than for the cricket itself. The truth of this was emphasized in a scathing editorial which appeared in *Cricket* in the early 1880s. 'It is not altogether a pleasant reflection,' the editor of that journal wrote, 'but a large proportion of the thousands, more especially of that part which occupies the front seats of the drags or carriages so closely investing quite one-half of the ground, do not go to Lord's to see the cricket.'[40] He also ruefully (but rightly) observed that the Eton–Harrow game had become a glorified fashion show.

Throughout the late-Victorian period there was a distinctive festive and carnival quality about the Eton–Harrow classics that rendered them far removed from the more serious business of county cricket. This may very well have sprung from the simple fact that the participants were all young gentlemen-amateurs whose livelihood did not depend upon their performance on the field. This is not to say that the competition was not keen. These rivalries, after all, stretched too far back into the past to have been otherwise. But the matches were essentially of the same genre as the great festivals which had sprung up during the Victorian age. They were, in effect, London's answer to the Canterbury, Hastings and Scarborough festivals which flourished at the time.

While statistics, however reliable, are available for the attendance at first-class cricket, it is much more difficult to judge the size of the crowds at the lower levels. There is enough evidence to suggest that a steady increase in attendance occurred at least up to the end of the century; that many of the clubs were successful enough to have improved their pavilions and other facilities after the manner of their soccer counterparts; and that crowds tended naturally to reflect the social structure of the locality in which the game was played. It is not surprising therefore that the majority of spectators who followed league cricket in the northern counties were industrial workers. Even so, as the *Athletic News* so often pointed out, cricket was not a financially viable proposition in the Victorian age. Most clubs had to play soccer in the winter in order to avoid financial embarrassment.

Some cricket clubs, however, like Burnley and Nelson in the Lancashire professional league, were reported to be playing before crowds of approximately 6000 in the early 1890s.[41] Enfield also occasionally drew a similar number towards the end of the century.[42] In fact, S.M. Crosfield, captain of the Lancashire CCC, was able to wax very enthusiastic in 1892 about the popularity of the sport within his county. 'It is not at all an uncommon thing,' he remarked, 'to find 5000 or 6000 spectators at a purely local match, and even at quite small villages there are often as many as a thousand.'[43] As early as the 1870s, Bacup and Haslingden were reporting in excess of 2000 fans in regular attendance.[44] A similar number also frequently attended purely local cricket matches in a small South Yorkshire village like Wombwell, whose total population at the end of the century was still only about 17000.[45]

Although by the time of Queen Victoria's death cricket attendance had grown far beyond the levels of 1870, the sport was by no means as healthy as a superficial reading of the scanty statistics might indicate. As a spectator sport in Britain, cricket had had no real rival – apart possibly from horse racing – when the F. A. Cup Final was first held in 1872. To that game, indeed, no more than 2000 spectators went.[46] The full significance of this statistic can best be appreciated when placed alongside the report of a local cricket match at Dorking in 1870 when, 'despite cold, showery weather...over 3000 attended'.[47] But in relation to other spectator sports, cricket steadily lost ground. This trend was very clearly perceived by the editor of the *Athletic News* as early as 1885. Much impressed by the enterprise and initiative being shown by the soccer organizations in Lancashire and Yorkshire, he foresaw the eclipse of cricket by soccer, as the more he observed 'of football crowds this winter, the stronger becomes my conviction that the game has not yet reached the height of its greatest prosperity'.[48] His prediction was based on the fact that the northern soccer clubs were directing their efforts increasingly towards working-class support and they were obviously succeeding.

In the long run, as Midwinter has pointed out, the post-Victorians would struggle to sustain 17 first-class county cricket clubs while almost 100 soccer clubs would be in effective operation. Already, by the end of the nineteenth century, there were at least ten professionals in soccer for every one in cricket.[49] To illustrate vividly the manner in which soccer had by this time superseded cricket, it is necessary to mention only one telling statistical item: the record attendance in 1901 for the F. A. Cup Final was almost 112000.[50] That, incredibly, was more than five times the normal size of good Test match cricket crowds at the turn of the century, even if, as Richard Binns recalled, a crowd 'variously estimated at between 35000 and 40000 persons' turned up at Leeds in June 1902 for the opening day of the match between the Australians and Yorkshire.[51]

Nor did the threat to cricket come only from soccer. In April 1880, approximately 15000 spectators were in attendance at the Northumberland Cricket Ground to watch a 100-mile cycling race, which was eventually won by the long-distance champion, G.W. Waller, in a record time of 6 hours, 22 minutes, 27 seconds.[52] This crowd would then have been considered an excellent one even for a Test match. Ominously, 'fully ten thousand' people were also reported in attendance at the Widnes Athletic Sports in late June 1880, just two days before about 5000 went in good weather to watch the MCC vs Cambridge University cricket match at Lord's.[53] By 1895, a critical commentator in the *Realm* was left to regret that cricket was then being followed only by old men who had played it in their youth, while the members of the younger generation were more interested in cycling, golf and soccer.[54] Even the mystique of the venerable Grace failed to make Crystal Palace a lucrative centre for the London County Club in the Edwardian age.[55]

Cricket's inability to compete with soccer as a money-making enterprise can be explained in a variety of ways. It can be argued, for instance, that, unlike soccer in the winter months, cricket had to contend in the summer with emerging rivals like athletics, golf, hockey, polo, rowing and swimming. There is also some validity in the claim that, with so many cricket clubs operating at so many levels all at once, cricket remained the great popular national pastime *par excellence* by attracting thousands of active participants rather than passive spectators.

The relative failure of cricket as a sporting spectacle in the later days of Queen Victoria's reign was variously explained by several men of the time. Somerset's captain, H.T. Hewett, for instance, expressed considerable regret that Taunton was so unfortunately placed. It was not as attractive as some of the cricket centres further west, and still it was too far from London for its own good. Hewett was prepared, in short, to blame geography for the failure of his county as a cricketing region during the 1890s.[56] In the same decade, the editor of the *Cricket Field* offered an even more intriguing explanation for the eclipse of Kent as a cricketing centre. He argued that the common people in that county were not as devoted to sports as their counterparts in the north, and even the Saturday half-holiday had not yet become a tradition there.[57] In 1894, Arthur Wilson, a former secretary of the Derbyshire CCC, stated his conviction that cricket had languished in his county during the past ten years for basically economic reasons. 'Trade,' he explained, 'has been very bad in Derby, and men cannot spare the time that is required to see cricket properly, whereas a football match only takes them away from work about a couple of hours.'[58]

These three commentators had thus emerged with different explanations for cricket's general malaise in three separate districts. But the problem lay much deeper than any of them perceived. The fundamental cause of cricket's relative decline as a sport spectacle in the late-Victorian age was the deliberate refusal of its administrators to modernize it. Cricket thus became a somewhat quaint and rustic anomaly in a highly urbanized age. It remained too much a leisurely and protracted affair geared to meet the needs of pre-industrial gentlemen-farmers.

This reactionary approach on the part of cricket's administrators was accompanied by an almost dogged refusal of the leading county club committees to sell the sport to the rising proletariat as aggressively and as effectively as the first division soccer clubs were then so brazenly doing. Some of the cricket clubs in the northern professional leagues tried to solve the problem by making the sport more attractive. They attempted to bring to cricket some of the explosive excitement which was soccer's major appeal. A league game, like a soccer match, was expected to be completed within a single Saturday afternoon. This placed a much higher premium on attacking strategies than a first-class match which was scheduled to last three days. But even the most successful of these competitors in league cricket could not come anywhere close to matching their counterparts in soccer.

It is tempting to attribute this partly to differences in ticket prices. In fact, however, it was generally more expensive to watch a good soccer match than a league cricket one. As Mason has shown, it cost between 3d. and 6d. to watch Association football during the 1870s and 1880s. No one could hope to see a good league game in the 1890s for less than 6d.[59] In cricket, meanwhile, the normal charge throughout this period remained between 2d. and 4d. for league matches. Even for the final in the Bolton and District Cup competition in 1889, the price of admission was no more than 3d.[60] Thus the charge of 3d. and 6d. by the Haslingden club in the 1860s was somewhat higher than the norm. Ladies, however, were admitted free.[61] Throughout the century the price of admission to the majority of county cricket grounds remained surprisingly fixed, like the laws of cricket in general, at 6d. – even at Lord's. This standard charge was doubled on special occasions, like a Test match against Australia or a visit by W.G. Surrey's charge of one shilling was therefore unusual, although there was a similar charge for admission to most of the great cricket festivals. The MCC also charged one shilling for admission to the university game, and (after 1873) 2s. 6d. to see the Eton–Harrow match. Towards the end of the century the various county committees catered to the Victorian obsession with order and status by segregating the classes. The modern cricket headquarters included members' pavilions, balconies, grandstands and open areas to accommodate different sections of society. Whether this kind of snobbery discouraged working-class attendance at county cricket is, of course, very difficult to determine. It certainly does not seem to have done so in soccer, where similar conditions prevailed. It is also arguable that such an arrangement increased attendance since classes tend to feel more comfortable in a segregated setting.

Crowd composition is much easier to judge. The Victorian reporters were so conscious of class distinctions that they seldom referred to attendance without also commenting on its social structure. It is therefore well known that the great festivals were monopolized by the cream of society. The *Sportsman* reported in August 1865, for example, that a very successful Canterbury Week had drawn 'full and fashionable audiences'.[62] The *Kent Herald*, in describing the aristocratic throng which assembled for the Canterbury Week in 1876, also thought it necessary to add that 'the effect of the charming costumes of the ladies made altogether a brilliant scene'.[63] Similar comments were invariably made about the university and public school classics. A typical example of such reporting was provided by the *Cricketers' and Sporting News*, when it remarked that the Eton–Harrow match in 1867 'was attended on both days by that great assemblage of the aristocracy that has for years made this match unique amongst the displays on this famous ground'.[64]

Contemporary journals also leave the impression that the northern counties enjoyed stronger working-class support than their counterparts in the south. That the standard admission fee of 6d. was not beyond the workers' means in Yorkshire is made clear by at least one serious complaint about the effect of important cricket engagements at Bramall Lane on the absenteeism of local workmen from their jobs.[65] In the south, the county cricket crowds would seem to have been largely middle and upper class. So many wealthy families belonged to the MCC, Middlesex CCC and Surrey CCC that the membership alone could often have accounted for a sizeable gathering.

Victorian cricket crowds behaved very well indeed. They were certainly less rowdy than contemporary gatherings at other sports. The newspapers found it necessary to comment on the behaviour of the cricket audience only when the local officials had failed to anticipate the numbers which eventually turned up, or when the crowd felt that some unjust or unsportsmanlike act had been committed by the players. Negative observations on crowd behaviour came mainly when more customers were admitted than the cricket ground could comfortably accommodate.

This was the case, for instance, on 17 June 1878, when too many people were admitted into Prince's Cricket Ground to watch the Australians. There was a resultant raid on the reserved seats which 'created great and general dissatisfaction'.[66] Similarly, the spectators proved rather unmanageable at Old Trafford in July 1878 when, as the *Athletic News* pointed out, the Manchester Cricket Club had not prepared adequately for the throng of almost 20000 who went to see the great W.G. *Wisden* noted that the attendance on that occasion was 'enormously large' and that 'at times the people so inconveniently encroached on the fielding ground as to stop the play'.[67] The same was the case with the overflow crowd at the Oval on the August Bank holiday in 1887 when 24450 customers paid to see Nottinghamshire vs Surrey. The security forces were too few and the boundaries were inevitably encroached upon.[68] When more than 15 000 customers went to Old Trafford on the opening day of the 'Roses Match' in 1883, the metropolitan police had to be brought in to control them.[69]

On a few rare occasions the Victorian cricket crowd drew attention to its conduct by heckling the players. This happened when the spectators were upset by what they regarded as improper cricket. Hence the general uproar on that day when E.M. Grace, the Champion's brother, dislodged a tenacious Henry Jupp with a high underhand full toss which sailed over the batsman's head and fell on the bails. The situation grew somewhat tense, as W.G. later recalled, because in the spectators' view E.M.'s tactic had all too literally been an underhand and ignoble one.[70] During the Scarborough Festival in 1895, one of the captains, H.T. Hewett, was blamed by the crowd for what it felt had been an unduly long delay for rain. So vigorously was he heckled that he withdrew peremptorily from the game and took no further part in it.[71] During the university match at Lord's in 1896, the Cambridge XI 'came in for a very hostile demonstration at the hands of the public', because their captain, Frank Mitchell, had instructed one of his bowlers to give up 12 byes to reduce their lead to 117. This tactic was intended to prevent Oxford from batting again immediately and was rendered necessary by the inflexibility of the old law governing the follow-on. As it was, the MCC shortly revised the law, but the spectators obviously felt that Mitchell's strategy was not in keeping with the spirit of the game.[72]

These, however, were isolated and irregular occurrences. There were far fewer complaints by the press and the public about the conduct of cricket spectators than there were about soccer crowds. The newspapers also complained much more frequently about rowdyism at the race track.[73] Wray Vamplew, in an interesting article on sports crowd disorder in late-Victorian and Edwardian Britain, suggested that large cricket audiences at that time were composed mainly of upper- and middle-class persons. He also concluded that they were better behaved than their soccer counterparts because, on the whole, there was much less drinking and gambling at cricket matches. Most of the cricket spectators remained seated and there was therefore less body contact among them than among those who normally watched soccer. All these factors, in Vamplew's opinion, conspired to make soccer crowds more disorderly. Soccer rowdyism, in his view, also sprang from the nature of the sport itself. It was much more explosive than cricket, which proceeded at too leisurely a pace to evoke emotional responses from the audience. Vamplew's conclusions are eminently sound. It is difficult, however, to accept his implied suggestion that cricket spectators were less frustrated, and therefore less prone to violence, because they represented as a rule the more socially respectable classes.[74] The Victorians who watched club and village cricket were less well-to-do than those who frequented Lord's and the Oval, but there is no evidence to show that they were any harder to control. If the *Bacup Times* once found it necessary to regret the 'deplorable ill spirit and ungovernable excitement on the part of the spectators' during the Bacup–Haslingden matches of the 1870s, it must also be said that, in the same decade, the MCC committee once had to appeal publicly to the alumni to set a better example during the Eton–Harrow game to prevent the recurrence of lawless conduct at Lord's.[75]

It is impossible not to detect that the late-Victorians treated cricket, cricketers and cricket crowds with much greater respect than they did other sports, sportsmen and spectators. This is perhaps because they too often supposed that cricket attracted the 'better sort' of people. This prejudice is reflected, for example, in the contemporary opinion of crowd disorder at the Oval in 1887. It was simply assumed that those who threw bottles onto the field were a holiday crowd rather than a cricket one.[76] When the Australians attracted 25 414 customers through the turnstiles at Lord's on 22 June 1896, the crowd overflowed the boundary and obstructed the view of other spectators. Their behaviour was therefore less becoming than was usual at Lord's. But *Wisden* reacted sympathetically. It regretted that the ground was too small, and concluded that 'under the circumstances it would hardly be fair to criticize the conduct of those present', even if 'there was certainly an absence of the quiet and decorum characteristic of the Lord's ground'.[77]

This kind of reporting is instructive. It not only helps to explain why cricket steadily ceased to be the major sports attraction in Victorian Britain, but it also leads to a better understanding of the difference between cricket and soccer crowds. Urban workers in an industrialized society do not generally go to a sports event for 'quiet and decorum'. Subconsciously or otherwise, they seek, through sport, an escape from the tedium of industrial labour. The sports event provides them with an opportunity to give vent to their emotions and to identify in an overt fashion with the local team or group. The stodgy atmosphere surrounding county cricket for so long must have served as a deterrent to a significant number of them. The soccer tradition was refreshingly different from the very beginning. No reporter has ever had occasion to refer to the quiet and decorum characteristic of Wembley Stadium.

Notes

1. *Wisden 1893*, liii. Ross, *Surrey Story*, 46, 56. Williams, ed., *Double Century*, 104.

2. Midwinter, *Grace: Life*, 58. Walvin, *Leisure and Society*, 98.
3. Golesworthy, *Encyclopaedia of Cricket*, 23. Lewis, *The Story of MCC and Cricket*, 35–36.
4. *The Times*, 26 May 1863, 14; 27 May 1863, 12; and 23 June 1863, 14.
5. *Ibid.*, 5 June 1863, 9; and 14 June 1864, 7.
6. *Sportsman*, 2 September 1865, 2.
7. Vamplew, *Pay Up and Play*, 59. See also Bearshaw, *From the Stretford End: The Official History of the Lancashire County Cricket Club* (London, 1990), 198, 202; and P. Wynne-Thomas, *Lancashire County Cricket Club* (London, 1989), 106–07.
8. Golesworthy, 138–89. Warner, *Lord's*, 90.
9. *The Times*, 25 June 1864, 14.
10. *Cricket*, 12 May 1898, 114.
11. Best on grounds are Marshall, *Lord's; Headingley*; and *Old Trafford*. I.A.R. Peebles, *The Watney Book of Test Match Grounds* (London, 1967). See also J.M. Kilburn, 'Test Match Grounds in England' in Swanton, ed., *Barclays World of Cricket*, 523–28.
12. *Wisden 1880*, passim; and *1895*, 116–17.
13. *Cricket Field*, 30 July 1892, 232.
14. Bearshaw, 71–97. Wynne-Thomas, *Lancashire County Cricket Club*, 43, 64, 80.
15. Mandle, 'Grace as Victorian Hero', 353–68.
16. Grace, *Reminiscences and Recollections*, 114–17. Martineau, *They Made Cricket*, 143.
17. *Wisden 1886*, 174.
18. *Wisden 1874*, 143–44.
19. *Wisden 1878*, 170.
20. *Athletic News*, 31 July 1878, 4. Bearshaw, 58. Marshall, *Old Trafford*, 22–23.
21. G. Parker, *Gloucestershire Road: A History of the Gloucestershire County Cricket Club* (London, 1983), 33.
22. B. Chapman, 'Following Leicestershire'. *Wisden 1964*, 152–53. Green, ed., *Wisden Anthology 1864–1900*, 664.
23. Bearshaw, 59.
24. *Cricket and Football Times*, 9 September 1880, 242.
25. *Athletic News*, 11 June 1884, 4.
26. *Wisden 1887*, 6.
27. *Ibid.*, 36.
28. *Wisden 1891*, 172.
29. Bearshaw, 150.
30. S. Courtney, *As Centuries Blend: One Hundred and Six Years of Clydesdale Cricket Club* (Glasgow, 1954), 35.
31. *Athletic News*, 13 July 1886, 1.
32. *Wisden 1877*, 72.
33. *The Times*, 25 June 1864, 14. *Wisden 1874*, 43; and *1875*, 53–54.
34. *Wisden 1887*, 98; and *1888*, 235.
35. *Wisden 1875*, 53–54.
36. *Bell's Life in London*, 25 July 1874.
37. *Wisden 1875*, 58.
38. *Ibid.*, 54.
39. *Cricket*, 4 May 1899, 106.

40. *Ibid.*, 20 July 1882, 164.
41. *Athletic News*, 6 June 1892, 1.
42. *Sports Telegraph*, 4 June 1898; and 23 July 1898.
43. *Cricket Field*, 20 August 1892, 292.
44. Aspin, *Gone Cricket Mad*, 28, 30, 32.
45. Woodhouse *et al.*, *Cricketers of Wombwell*, 1–2.
46. G. Green, *The Official History of the F.A. Cup* (Sportsmans Book Club, 1960), 20.
47. Cole, *Dorking Cricket*, 34.
48. *Athletic News*, 20 January 1885, 1.
49. Midwinter, 58–59.
50. P.M. Young, *A History of British Football* (Sportsmans Book Club, 1969), 142.
51. Binns, *Cricket in Firelight*, 9.
52. *Athletic World*, 16 April 1880, 234.
53. *Ibid.*, 25 June 1880, 388, 392.
54. *Cricket Field*, 22 June 1895, 211.
55. Midwinter, 136–44.
56. *Cricket Field*, 27 August 1892, 313.
57. *Ibid.*, 31 March 1894, 34.
58. *Ibid.*, 28 July 1894, 325.
59. Mason, *Association Football*, 150.
60. *Athletic News*, 19 August 1889, 1.
61. Aspin, 15.
62. *Sportsman*, 19 August 1865, 2.
63. Cited in *Wisden 1877*, 84.
64. *Cricketers' and Sporting News*, 16 July 1867, 2.
65. *Cricket Field*, 31 August 1895, 449.
66. *Wisden 1879*, 104.
67. *Ibid.*, 180. *Athletic News*, 31 July 1878, 4; and 14 August 1878, 4.
68. Ross, *Surrey Story*, 46–47.
69. Bearshaw, 95.
70. Grace, *Reminiscences and Recollections*, 29.
71. *Cricket Field*, 14 September 1895, 482. *Wisden 1896*, 67.
72. *Wisden 1897*, 282.
73. E.g., *Athletic News*, 2 June 1885, 1; 9 June 1885, 1; and 5 January 1886, 4. *Sporting Mirror*, 25 July 1892, 6. *The Times*, 3 May 1871, 12.
74. Vamplew, 'Sports Crowd Disorder', 5–20.
75. Aspin, 30. *Wisden 1875*, 25.
76. Ross, *Surrey Story*, 47.
77. *Wisden 1897*, 230.

CHAPTER SEVEN

Technique and Technology

During the nineteenth century aristocrats and wealthy patrons subsidized county cricket and presided over clubs and associations throughout the land. Amateur players and enthusiasts, springing chiefly from the middle classes, generally provided the administrative skills so necessary for the organization of Victorian cricket at all levels. But it was really the professionals, belonging mainly to the skilled and semi-skilled working classes, who made the major contributions to the technical advances within the game itself. They also transformed cricket into a truly national sport by popularizing it during the period 1845–70, when they played the game excellently against overwhelming odds all across the country.

Victorian cricket administrators and amateurs found the sport too well established to tamper with its rules and rituals. They preferred instead to preserve as many of its Georgian characteristics as they could. This inevitably meant that changes, even in cricket technique, were gradual and evolutionary; and the great industrial revolution was never allowed to alter the basic features of the sport to the same extent that it so drastically transformed almost everything else.

The Victorian cricket administrators, however, failed to shield their game altogether from the impact of industrial technology; and even more signally failed to prevent the professionals from making significant technical advances. It was the professional cricketers who developed round-arm – and later overarm – bowling, which gave the game its modern character. They had, of course, to wage a long and uphill struggle before they succeeded in compelling the amateurs to accept their newfangled notions about bowling. They experimented for some 30 years with the round-arm delivery before the MCC could be persuaded to sanction it in 1835. They then steadily raised their elbow above shoulder height and had to wait for almost another 30 years before that innovation too could be accepted by the reactionary amateur clubs. In the end, thanks to the perseverance of such men as John Lillywhite and Edgar Willsher, modern bowling was legalized by the MCC in 1864.[1]

The professionals also led the way in advancing the science of modern batsmanship during the nineteenth century. This is remarkably curious since it was the gentlemen-amateurs who traditionally posed as batsmen and hired proletarian bowlers to keep them in good form. It was the famous Kentish professional, Fuller Pilch, who perfected forward play in the art of batting during the 1840s. His new style of play was basically a response to the round-arm pattern of bowling which had become more or less the norm when Pilch was at his peak. He pioneered the drive, and his front foot strokes were universally admired. Reflecting in his old age on Pilch's abilities as a batsman, Fred Gale considered that if he were still alive and 'playing in these days, day after day, on a wicket like a billiard table, against bowling which he met match after match, as is now the case, he could do everything that any man I have ever seen, barring the Doctor, has done'.[2] When Pilch died in 1870, *Wisden* judged him '*the* great batsman of his time, and the finest forward player known'.[3]

Robert Carpenter, who played so brilliantly for Surrey in the 1860s, added a new dimension to batsmanship by introducing proper back-foot technique. He amazed his contemporaries by going on to his back foot to defend against the deadly shooters which fast bowlers then so often produced on badly prepared pitches.[4] It was Tom Hayward, one of Carpenter's colleagues on the Surrey team, who then combined the methods of Pilch and Carpenter to emerge with the 'graceful, half-cock sort of play, neither quite back nor forward'. He used this system quite effectively on defence, while also teaching contemporary batsmen the importance of nimble footwork on attack. He was among the first of modern cricketers to advance consistently down the pitch to counter balls of otherwise difficult length.[5] This is now a common technique.

While these professionals mainly earned their fame by inventing attacking strokes, it was Arthur Shrewsbury who, especially on bad or wet pitches, perfected the science of defensive batsmanship. He patterned his style on Carpenter's, but used a totally limp bat when he defended off the back foot. He thus developed the frustrating habit of playing the ball dead at his feet and often taking full advantage of the lbw law by using his pads as a second line of protection. He seemed able to play the ball later than most and was everywhere acknowledged, even at the age of 43 (in 1899), as the most difficult batsman in the world to dismiss.[6] He played with a tenacity that had become typical of Nottinghamshire professionals in the Victorian age and was often criticized for his extreme caution. Shrewsbury, William Gunn and Bill Scotton for a long time remained notorious for their stonewalling tactics. Another defensive specialist was Richard Gordon Barlow who represented Lancashire from 1871 to 1891. He elevated stonewalling to a science and carried his bat through no fewer than 12 completed innings for the county club, mainly on diabolic pitches.[7] If professionals at this time appeared to have been batting for the most part more defensively than amateurs this was due largely to two reasons. Careless play by professionals was not acceptable to the county committees or captains, who often advised them to perform the sheet anchor's role. Professionals also knew that their security of tenure on the county team depended entirely on their results. They were seldom allowed the amateur's freedom to play their strokes with gay abandon.

In perfecting such strokes as the drive, the cut and the pull during the nineteenth century, the batsmen were really reacting to the newer styles of bowling. They had to adapt to the faster pace and increasingly high bounce as the bowlers graduated from underarm to round-arm and to overarm deliveries. The techniques of 1835 could no longer have sufficed in 1870. Batsmanship in the later Victorian period had to cope with a wider variety of bowling styles, as the professionals continued to experiment with spin and flight, speed and swerve.

Notwithstanding their vital contributions to the development of modern batting, it was really in the areas of bowling and wicketkeeping that the professionals left an enduring legacy. During the Victorian period, fast bowling and wicketkeeping were commonly regarded as menial work beneath the dignity of gentlemen. Few Victorian amateurs therefore shone in these areas. It is true that such amateurs as Arthur Appleby (Lancashire), Walter Bradley (Kent), Charles Kortright (Essex), Robert Lipscomb (Kent), Rev. Edward Peake (Gloucestershire) and Sammy Woods (Somerset) were among the fastest bowlers in their time. Some excellent wicketkeeping standards were also achieved by such amateurs as Gregor MacGregor (Middlesex), A.E. Newton (Somerset), Rev. Charles Ridding (Hampshire), E.F.S. Tylecote (Kent) and Rev. A.P. Wickham (Somerset). But these were the outstanding exceptions to prove the general rule. That remarkable Indian prince, Kumar Ranjitsinhji, himself an amateur, called plaintively upon the gentlemen to pay more attention to their bowling skills as there were so few amateur bowlers available in 1897 to compete against the professionals.[8]

The one extraordinary amateur who left an everlasting imprint on Victorian cricket was, of course, the Doctor. W.G. Grace copied the better elements of aggressive stroke play and defensive technique that had previously been employed, and moulded them into an art form. It was Grace who first demonstrated the full potentialities of modern scientific batsmanship. He not only played all the orthodox strokes but taught later Victorians how to use them to the best advantage by steering them between the fielders. His approach to batting was pragmatic and utilitarian. He concentrated on the accumulation of runs and scored them in whatever manner the occasion demanded. His timing and hand–eye coordination were so well developed that almost single-handed he killed off a whole generation of fast bowlers and forced their successors to develop new and different skills. It was W.G. who compelled the professionals to work more diligently on flight and spin and to focus more sharply on breaking the ball rather than simply propelling it as vehemently as possible.[9] Charles Burgess Fry, himself a contemporary batsman of no mean repute, produced perhaps the best capsule summary of W.G.'s batting:

> There were no fireworks or extravagances. W.G. just stood at his crease to his full height (and everyone who wishes to play fast bowling well should so stand) and proceeded to lean against the ball in various directions and send it scudding along the turf between the fielders. No visible effort, no hurry; just a rough-hewn precision. He was not a graceful bat and he was not ungraceful; just powerfully efficient.[10]

Grace's batting technique did much to modernize cricket during the 1870s. He moulded the game into a form that is still recognizable now, and his successors have seemed almost reluctant to carry it further. By concentrating on runs rather than style, W.G. became a general stroke-player rather than a specialist, which had been the Georgian and early Victorian approach to batting. Before his time, despite the pioneering efforts of that great professional, George Parr, the general tendency was to ignore the leg side. Grace taught all cricketers the stupidity of such an attitude. In a much quoted phrase, he 'turned the old one-stringed instrument into a many-chorded lyre'.[11] All his contemporaries agreed that W.G. had done more to revolutionize cricket than any other individual. After the eclipse of the old travelling elevens, it was Grace who did most to transform Victorian cricket into a full-scale spectator entertainment. He dominated the pages of the sporting press and was idolized in a way in which none of his contemporaries were. He satisfied the nineteenth-century craving for a Carlylean form of hero worship.[12] W.G.'s mighty deeds with bat and ball were duly celebrated and unduly magnified. He was eminently successful in an age which put perhaps too high a premium on success and victory. Many Victorians were therefore willing to gloss over his blatant shama-teurism and his childish gamesmanship, which they felt were adequately redeemed by his 54 896 runs and his 2 876 wickets in first-class cricket. In all forms of cricket, Grace's achievements were absolutely staggering. He finished his playing days with 99 840 runs, 7 325 wickets and 1 512 catches as well as 54 stumpings.[13]

There is, nevertheless, something baffling about this Victorian colossus. The tendency to glorify results has concealed an important historical paradox. As a bowler, there is no special delivery which Grace invented by his own genius. He remained, to the end of his career, an old-fashioned, round-arm, slow to medium-paced trundler who broke the ball but slightly from the leg and depended for his success on steadiness of length, 'the curiously deceptive flight he imparted to the ball', and no small measure of trickery.[14] As a captain, W.G. is not especially remembered for any particular strategy or tactic, even in the vital sphere of field-placing. And as a batsman, even more astonishingly, there is no specific style or stroke that the great man pioneered. An imposing and extremely robust individual, who simply hit the ball very often and very hard, Grace could thus pose as the greatest muscular Christian of them all. His batting reputation, based essentially on brawn, could therefore dwarf that of Felix, Parr, Ranjitsinhji and Read, all of whom were immeasurably more stylish and more creative.

Nicholas Wanostrocht, better known as 'Felix', was a schoolmaster of Camberwell Green, who played for Surrey, Kent and the AEE during the 1830s and 1840s. His claim to fame rests chiefly on his invention of tubular batting gloves and the 'catapulta', a most ingenious bowling machine.[15] It was he who pioneered the modern square-cut, demonstrating to his contemporaries the inestimable value of nimble footwork. George Parr, that 'Lion of the North', was among the first batsmen to aim deliberately to score runs on the on-side of the wicket.[16] It was he who pioneered the modern sweep and the pull to leg during the 1840s and 1850s. Ranjitsinhji perfected the modern leg glance and the graceful glide, using perfect timing and deft flicks of the wrists to score countless runs in a manner that had never been witnessed before. With his oriental flair and matchless elegance, Ranji charmed spectators wherever he appeared during the 1890s. Like Grace, he had the ability to play all of the orthodox strokes and occasionally he manufactured a few of his own. From 1873 to 1897, Walter Read performed with much distinction for Surrey and England. His favourite stroke was the drive through the covers off the back foot, his special legacy to posterity.[17]

It can be said, perhaps, that Felix and Parr had fewer strokes in their repertoire than the Champion had in his. But this was clearly not the case with Abel, Ranjitsinhji and Read. What the Doctor had, in greater measure than any of his contemporaries, was a voracious appetite for runs. His phenomenal powers of concentration conspired with his extraordinary reserves of strength and stamina to make him the first run-scoring machine that the sport had ever known. At his peak, at the age of 28 in 1876, Grace scored 1278 runs in ten first-class innings in the month of August alone, against some of the best professional bowling then available. Against Nottinghamshire and Yorkshire, two of the most powerful counties, he scored 177 and 318 in the space of a few days, after having trounced a good Kent XI to the tune of 344 (then a world record) while playing for the MCC in the previous week.[18]

It was the immortal W.G. who struck fear into the hearts of all fast bowlers. Through him, there came a wide range of spin bowlers who tried to defeat the bat with guile rather than sheer speed. This important movement was led by professionals such as Briggs, Peate and Peel, who forced later Victorian batsmen to readjust their technique. Hence arose new batting styles as exemplified by Abel, Fry, MacLaren, Ranjitsinhji and Shrewsbury. By 1900, the bat seemed to have become superior to the ball.

Improved techniques accompanied by new methods of wicket preparation allowed batsmen in all grades of cricket to accumulate many more runs than they had ever been able to do before. Prior to the 1870s, any total score of about 250 was generally considered a good one. In the 1890s, teams were beginning to amass totals in the vicinity of 500.

To redress the balance, George Hirst, the great Yorkshire professional, began to concentrate on swerving the ball in the air by the clever use of the seam. This was as revolutionary a weapon as the more famous 'googly' which appeared in the Edwardian age. Before 1900, bowlers had generally depended on the state of the pitch for any unusual advantage. With Hirst's new invention, batsmen also had to beware the state of the atmosphere also. With any kind of headwind, he became almost unplayable. Other bowlers had tried to produce the swerve before Hirst. Clifford Goodman of Barbados, Barton King, the celebrated Philadelphian, Albert Trott, the Australian who migrated to Middlesex, and Walter Wright of Kent had all experimented with this kind of delivery. But it was Hirst who perfected it and therefore transformed the art and science of bowling by drawing attention to the advantage of the new ball.[19] Prior to 1900, spinners had in effect wasted the new ball at the beginning of each innings. It was Hirst who first emphasized the folly of such a stratagem. Ever since his time, all captains have sought to take full advantage of the original shine by encouraging their fastest bowlers to produce in- and out-swingers. It is now axiomatic that it is easier to cause the ball to swerve in the air when it is new than when it is old.

Shortly after the development of in-swingers and out-swingers by the faster men, the slow bowlers emerged with a destructive missile of their own. Led by B.J.T. Bosanquet of Eton, Oxford University, Middlesex and England, they finally discovered the dreaded googly – the art of turning the ball from the off-side while using an apparent leg-break action. Bosanquet is of special historical significance in that he is one of the few amateurs to have contributed to the technical progress made in bowling. Even here, some critics might argue that he was copying his googly from James Phillips, the Australian professional, who had migrated to Middlesex and established an enviable reputation as a fearless umpire. Phillips had been experimenting with the googly during the 1890s.[20]

All of these devices should have succeeded in bewildering the batsmen completely. But in the end the bat prevailed over the ball because of two major factors: the Victorian attitude towards batting, and the impact of industrial technology. The negative approach to bowling, fielding and wicketkeeping was accompanied by a widespread glorification of the batsman's role. Most Victorians and Edwardians wanted first and foremost to become famous hitters of the ball. The majority of cricketers therefore concentrated on this aspect of the game, often to the neglect of other areas. Precisely why this was so is very hard to determine. Perhaps the urge to become a great batsman reflected the deep-seated yearning to be regarded as a gentleman, as batsmanship then was so closely linked with gentility in the popular mind. Then, too, there has always been a certain manly assertiveness about striking the ball: the batsman can consider himself as subject and the ball and bowler alike as object. He is active; they are passive. In an age of aggressive militarism, nationalism, individualism and Social Darwinism, the defiant batsman could well be equated with the fittest survivor. Moreover, cricket has always been a game involving high numbers. The emphasis is on scoring, and the team with the most runs wins. This stands out in stark contrast, for instance, to baseball and soccer, where the team that restricts the enemy traditionally prevails. Soccer and baseball deal in single digits; hence the exaltation of the goalkeeper in Europe and the pitcher in the United States, where defence is far more crucial than attack. In baseball, a man plays as a specialist short-stop or third baseman. He is primarily a fielder, even though the consistent home-run hitter is universally feared. In cricket, a man who is not a bowler or a wicketkeeper plays essentially as a batsman.

This emphasis on batting, whatever its psychological basis, meant that Englishmen became better batsmen than bowlers or fielders. It certainly had economic roots also. Most clubs, at almost every level, encouraged batsmanship by offering greater monetary rewards for batting feats. Until Lord Hawke deliberately tried to improve the quality of Yorkshire's out-cricket, not much attention was paid to fielding and catching. Very few clubs offered talent money for catches, and a bowler had to perform a virtual miracle before the spectators considered him worthy of a collection. When Surrey defeated the Australians at the Oval in August 1886, for example, the spectators collected more than £68 among themselves for Bobby Abel and Maurice Read, who had both scored centuries. But not a penny was collected for Thomas Bowley and George Lohmann, whose magnificent bowling had made the victory possible.[21] It is also noteworthy that, with the solitary exception of New Zealand's Sir Richard Hadlee (in the 1980s), all the cricketers who have thus far been knighted for their services to the sport have either been efficient administrators, such as Sir Francis Lacey, Sir Henry Leveson Gower and Sir Frederick Toone, or brilliant batsmen such as Sir Donald Bradman, Sir Jack Hobbs, Sir Leonard Hutton, Sir Garfield Sobers and Sir Frank Worrell. There is thus a substantial element of truth in Fred Trueman's hackneyed quip that the 'last bloody bowler' to have been knighted was Sir Francis Drake in the time of Elizabeth I.[22]

Technological progress also militated against the success of the late-Victorian bowler. While mechanization produced faster and more even outfields, the lawn mower and the heavy roller led to the preparation of increasingly smooth pitches. During the Canterbury Festival in 1876, as the editor of *Wisden* observed, the pitch was 'rolled to unsurpassable smoothness by a steam roller'.[23] This was a far cry from the tedious and manual methods that had earlier been adopted. In fact, before the widespread use of the mower, horses and sheep had been put to graze in the outfield to control the growth of the grass and the shrubs.[24] Increasingly sophisticated gloves and pads had provided the batsmen with greater protection ever since Felix experimented with flimsy mittens and leg-guards.[25] The development of bowling machines, practice nets and indoor coconut matting pitches also gave them better opportunities to perfect their techniques. Moreover, the introduction of boundaries, in the interest of spectator safety as well as the maximization of space, gave the bat an incalculable advantage over the ball.[26]

But the impact of industrial technology on Victorian cricket technique was much less telling than it was on cycling, golf or field hockey because the basic implements of the game – bat, ball, stumps – remained incredibly true to the eighteenth-century models. Bats continued to be manufactured from willow, and balls from strips of leather. A more sophisticated seam in the ball, and a cane handle in the bat, represented the totality of technological interference with cricket's fundamental tools.[27] It is true that Duke & Son, the most famous of all cricket equipment manufacturers, filed a patent in 1897 for making the covers of cricket balls with 'chrome leather preferably made by treating the pelt with potassium bichromate or chromic acid, and then oxidising in a bath composed of hyposulphite of soda and hydrochloric acid'.[28] But the net result was not much different even then from the kind of cricket balls that Duke & Son had been manufacturing ever since the eighteenth century. As for the bat, the old-fashioned one-piece was finally destroyed after 1835 by the introduction of fast round-arm bowling. New methods of splicing and gluing the handle became common in the 1840s. In 1853, Thomas Nixon, a craftsman-cricketer who had already pioneered the use of leg-guards, invented the cane handle to make the bat more springy. In the 1860s, there gradually came the hump behind the bat to give the striker a slightly longer drive.[29]

If Victorian batsmen gained some slight advantage from the new handle and the hump in their bats, the bowlers also profited from the more pronounced seam in their ball which permitted them to break and swerve it more sharply. But these were minute changes when compared with the dramatic effects of industrial technology on other Victorian sports. Basketball, cycling, football, golf, ice hockey, rugby and tennis were completely revolutionized (or created from scratch) by new manufacturing techniques in the rubber and metal industries. New forms of synthetic and vulcanized rubber practically begat the majority of modern ball games. The invention of novel balls, clubs, irons and woods also made a mockery of ancient forms of golf.[30] To the late-Victorians, however, it simply was not cricket to introduce a vulcanized rubber ball which might have travelled much faster and further than the traditional implement made of cork, leather and twine. Nor would anyone then have been bold or futuristic enough to contemplate the use of an aluminium bat.

The full impact of industrial technology on Victorian cricket was felt in other ways. Railways and macadamized roads permitted cricketers and spectators to travel far more rapidly than ever before. Telegraphic services and newspapers could transmit cricket news much more readily. Telegraphic scoreboards, such as the one first introduced at Lord's in 1886, kept spectators increasingly well informed about the game they were watching.[31] Pavilions and grandstands were transformed by modern engineering, and the study of the science of groundskeeping was steadily perfected. By 1900, all the major cricket grounds in Britain and Australia had been levelled and resurfaced on modern lines. The pitch had been rendered almost as smooth as glass and was already being protected from the elements by the use of tarpaulins. The field was slanted in such a way as to allow excess water to drain away more rapidly after torrents of rain.[32]

The leading Victorian cricket scientists were, in fact, the groundsmen. This largely unsung army of crusaders, led by Sam Apted, Percy Pearce and a whole tribe of Hearnes, performed a series of miracles on late-Victorian cricket grounds. It was Pearce who went to Lord's in 1874 and diligently completed the task, begun in the late 1860s by his predecessor, David Jordan, which eventually made that ground deservedly famous for its playing surface as well as its heritage. Pearce had been a gardener and a keeper of lawns before he first made a name for himself as a cricket groundsman at Brighton. He was an expert in agriculture, horticulture and geology, although he had never pursued formal training in those disciplines. His careful and empirical study of soils, grasses and marls gradually produced a surface at Lord's that became the envy of every county club. He wrote many articles on the preparation of pitches and spent his last years laying down several cricket grounds across the country.[33] One of his contemporaries, George Street, also made himself famous by preparing such perfect batting strips at the Oval in the 1870s that the Surrey ground became known as a bowler's graveyard.[34] Jesse Hide, one of Pearce's disciples, exported his modern techniques to Australia where pitches shortly became even friendlier to the batsman than they had notoriously been in the past.[35] Sam Apted, the Surrey grounds-man from 1887 to 1911, left an enviable reputation for his uncanny ability to produce perfect strips.[36] The great Widdowson, serving his county cricket club for more than 40 years, made the Derby wicket one of the best batting pitches in England during 1889–1930.[37]

The focus on improving the playing surface during the 1870s was largely the offspring of a cricket tragedy which occurred at Lord's early in that decade. George Summers, a promising young Nottinghamshire professional, was struck a crippling blow, while batting against the MCC and Ground, by the fast bowler, John Platts. Within a week, poor Summers was dead.[38] It is ironic that this incident should have occurred after the MCC had already taken steps to improve the condition of the pitch at Lord's.[39] It was the type of unfortunate accident that could easily have occurred in the 1850s and 1860s when the wicket at Lord's had been a source of considerable dismay to batsmen. It was so bad indeed that, on two memorable occasions at least, the Sussex county team bluntly refused to play on it.[40] Surrey had complained bitterly about the state of the Lord's pitch in 1859, refusing to meet the MCC on it; and the travelling professional teams, arguing that 'so rough it was, that it was quite dangerous to play on', avoided the Lord's ground from 1859 to 1865.[41] Nor was Lord's by any means the worst offender in this regard. Even as late as 1881, in fact, a game between Oxford University and the Gentlemen of England had to be abandoned after an hour or so because the pitch on the Christ Church ground was too dangerous for the batsmen.[42]

In the days of underarm bowling, the Georgians had not been overly concerned about the state of the pitch. Round-arm bowling on under-prepared strips produced deliveries of uneven bounce and pace, and this was blithely accepted on all sides during the early Victorian age as one of the inherent challenges of the sport. But alternate shooters and bumpers, propelled from increasing heights and at increasing speeds, rendered batting very hazardous indeed. Players began to resort to the use of pads and gloves to protect themselves from serious injury. Even these aids occasionally proved unavailing against the pace of such men as John Jackson, George Tarrant and Edgar Willsher. After 1864, when overarm bowling was finally legalized, the problem of physical safety became even more critical. The urge to improve the playing surface in the 1870s sprang mainly from the fundamental need to preserve the batsmen's lives. The groundsmen succeeded beyond the batsmen's fondest dreams. By the 1880s it had already become axiomatic that a good batting team, winning the toss in excellent weather, had a glorious opportunity to accumulate a bushel of runs.

These were the circumstances which compelled professional bowlers to seek their own salvation through their wits and ingenuity. Some, such as Attewell and Shaw, took the line of least resistance and concentrated on defence. They focused exclusively on length and line and tested the batsman's patience. Shaw became so accurate indeed that he bowled an unconscionable number of maidens.[43] Many contemporaries feared that the game was heading towards a stalemate because of the evolution of increasingly defensive techniques on the part of both batsman and bowler. Gerald Brodribb, re-echoing these sentiments some 60 years later, felt that cricket had reached an impasse during the 1890s.[44] In that decade, when critics bewailed the abuse of Fabian tactics on the part of the batsmen, William Gunn and Arthur Shrewsbury countered with the suggestion that it was the bowlers, with their numerous 'off balls', who had brought the game to a standstill.[45] Shaw, meanwhile, came to the conclusion that slow play was the product of faulty footwork on the batsman's part.[46] Brodribb's thesis might well have been more sensationally obvious had Attewell, Gunn, Scotton (perhaps the most notorious stonewaller of them all), Shaw and Shrewsbury not all played for the same county!

As it was, the stalemate was avoided even before the advent of Hirst and Bosanquet by fast bowlers such as George Lohmann and Tom Richardson of Surrey who stressed the importance of relentless attack. In a similar vein, but totally different manner, 'lobsters' such as Walter Humphreys and D.L.A. Jephson resorted to offensive strategies by testing both the batsman's temperament and technique with very high flighted off-breaks.[47] The stalemate was also avoided by enterprising batsmen such as Gilbert Jessop and Charles Thornton who simply struck the ball with greater violence than anybody else.[48] The late-Victorian age also witnessed the emergence of a new breed of glorious stroke-players, led by Fry, Stanley Jackson, MacLaren and the inimitable Ranjitsinhji.

The most significant changes in Victorian cricket technique occurred in the area of wicketkeeping. So proficient did the wicketkeepers become that the long stop, an important fielding position in the Georgian era, gradually disappeared. It is true that, as the bowlers steadily became more accurate and the pitches became progressively more predictable, the wicketkeeper's job became less strenuous; but such men as John McCarthy Blackham of Australia, Tom Lockyer of Surrey and Richard Pilling of Lancashire showed how the fastest bowling could be handled even without standing too far behind the stumps. They cut down on the number of byes, and by the end of the century 'extras' yielded only negligible portions of the aggregate scores. All observers in the late-Victorian age considered this technical development worthy of special comment.[49] The wicketkeeping revolution really began in the 1850s with Lockyer. Until his time, it was customary for most wicketkeepers to ignore balls pitched outside the leg stump. Such deliveries were regarded as the long stop's responsibility. But Lockyer, displaying a wonderful agility, brought off several catches down the leg side, thereby introducing a new dimension to his craft.[50] Pilling became so good in the early 1880s that he was among the first to allow his captain to dispense altogether with the long stop. He also took the revolutionary step of standing up to Bill McIntyre and Jack

Crossland, then two of the fastest bowlers in England.[51] A classic example of how far the practice of wicketkeeping had advanced before the end of the century was provided by Rev. A.P. Wickham of Somerset who, in May 1895, conceded only four byes in Gloucestershire's total of 474 at Bristol.[52]

Fielding, however, was the one department in which the Victorians made only minimal progress. Too many amateurs treated it with the same contempt that they displayed towards manual labour, and even some of the professionals looked upon fielding as the least rewarding and the least glamorous of all their assignments. Contemporary critics certainly felt that Englishmen, except in Yorkshire, took fielding far too lightly. 'Livesflen', the cricket correspondent for the *Midland Athlete*, often regretted the undue emphasis on batting which had led to the sad neglect of fielding at all levels. 'Let batting,' he urged, 'be honoured, and cultivated in its highest form, but let it not monopolise an unfair degree of attention.'[53] The *Athletic News*, forever critical of the fielding at club cricket level, once scolded the Bolton players for having given 'a fine example of how not to field in their match at Lytham', in which they had missed too many chances.[54]

It was not only the club cricketers who fielded poorly. The *Athletic News* also lamented the decline of amateur fielding in first-class cricket where too much reliance was placed on the professionals for everything except batting. The net result was that, in the Middlesex XI, in which amateurs predominated, the fielding was often sloppy and only two of their players could bowl at all.[55] The paper often denounced the incompetence and sloth of K.J. Key on the field. He became a great Surrey captain and was a fine batsman, but the *Athletic News* felt that Key invariably conceded, through his feeble fielding, as many runs as he was likely to make with his bat.[56] As late as 1900, the *Athletic News* was still reporting that fielding was the 'one department of the game in which the Surrey team do not shine'.[57]

In the 1880s, *Cricket* also commented negatively on the quality of the fielding at the county level. It concluded that this was due to the lack of encouragement given to this branch of the game in preference to the others.[58] Much later, Sir Home Gordon was to marvel at Percy Perrin's 'remarkable incapacity for fielding'. Perrin was one of the finest batsmen of the late-Victorian era, but took no interest whatever in fielding. The result was that, although he scored many centuries for Essex, he was never invited to play for England.[59] C.I. Thornton, that renowned hitter of sixes, was also considered by Gordon to have been too ponderous in the field.[60] A far more sweeping condemnation of English fielding at all levels was issued by Ranjitsinhji in 1897. He bluntly declared that it was 'a department of the game much neglected at Public Schools, more at the

Universities, and more still in county cricket'.[61] He was convinced that faulty fielding was entirely responsible for the mammoth scores that were being achieved by batsmen during the 1890s.

A very critical article on fielding, by D.L.A. Jephson in *Wisden 1901*, aptly expressed the popular view of the time: first-class cricketers on the whole fielded very badly indeed. The northern counties, with their galaxy of professionals, were the only exceptions. Under Lord Hawke's guidance, the Yorkshire teams had established an enormous reputation for excellence in the field, and it was to their out-cricket that their success in the county championship had largely been due. Jephson admitted that there were some individuals who rose above the general average, and he was willing to concede that MacLaren was probably the greatest of all fielders in the history of the game. But, in his judgment, far too many county cricketers in 1900 were slow, cowardly and lethargic in the field. In the same issue of *Wisden*, the editor himself expressed the view that big scores were the direct result of incompetent fielding and catching rather than any inherent weakness in the game itself. 'If fieldsmen accepted a fair proportion of the chances offered them,' he wrote, 'we should hear very little about the necessity of altering the game of cricket.'[62]

Wisden's opinion was mightily reinforced by the magnificence of the Australian out-cricket. The colonists invariably displayed a great mobility and enthusiasm in the field, illustrating that many runs could be saved by alertness alone. This was one of the Australian contributions to Victorian cricket. They also pioneered more scientific field-placing.[63] As their pitches at home were generally easier for the batsmen than those in England, their bowlers learnt much sooner how to rely on variations of pace and flight. Almost all of the great English fast bowlers of the mid-Victorian period had depended on sheer speed. But the Australian bowlers, whatever their pace, knew that they had to concentrate on accuracy of length and line.

It was really the Australians who showed the English bowlers how to outthink their opponents. Whereas, on the bad pitches of the pre-Pearce years, the early Victorians only had to avoid half-volleys and full tosses to get good results, it was now necessary to do more than just bowl fast and straight. Harry Boyle and Fred Spofforth gave an unforgettable demonstration in 1878 of the value of controlled and scientific fast bowling. Later on, C.T.B. Turner and J.J. Ferris also showed the English bowlers how to take the maximum advantage of wet pitches.[64] These lessons were not wasted. Patterning his style on that of the great Australians, George Lohmann of Surrey emerged as one of the most devastating bowlers in the history of cricket. Despite persistent ill-health which culminated in his early death, Lohmann is still remembered as one of the game's most intelligent and versatile practitioners. Using the seam of the ball judiciously, he consistently produced good movement off the pitch. He also varied his pace so deceptively that in 18 Test matches for England, he captured 112 wickets at an average of only 10.75 runs each. This is still by far the best bowling average in international cricket competition.[65]

That the Victorians produced a more scientific brand of cricket than the type they inherited from the Georgians is beyond dispute. The sport they left behind after 1900 was much different from the one they had inherited at the end of the 1830s. In the final analysis, however, their refinements revolved mainly around the legalization of overarm bowling in 1864. By permitting this kind of attack, the MCC compelled batsmen to develop superior forms of defence. Overarm bowling on uneven surfaces presented such a palpable threat to the batsman's life and limb that steps had to be taken to improve the preparation of pitches. Industrial technology was thus allowed to transform the science of groundskeeping after 1870. Such was the demand for spectator space in the last quarter of the nineteenth century that industrial technology was also allowed to produce a new era of monumental cricket stadiums, pavilions and grandstands. By 1900, several county cricket clubs in England had acquired the necessary facilities to accommodate as many as 20 000 spectators.

Even so, any examination of cricket technique and industrial technology during the Victorian age must inevitably focus more sharply on technique, since the Victorians tried so desperately to preserve the nature and form of Georgian cricket. By refusing to apply the new technology to the manufacture of bats and balls, they managed to keep the Georgian game basically intact. It was not, in fact, until the 1930s that machine-stitched balls were manufactured in Britain. Incredibly, they had been laboriously and meticulously hand-stitched until the twentieth century.[66] Even as late as the 1920s, in the famous Gunn & Moore's cricket bat factory in Nottingham, traditional craftsmanship remained the order of the day. Modern machinery was put to only limited use.[67]

This is remarkably curious in view of the fact that the Victorians did not hesitate to employ the new technology in other sporting areas. A bouncing rubber ball, or a vulcanized one, for instance, would have revolutionized cricket in more obvious ways. This abiding reverence for the eighteenth-century products of Duke & Son tells us a great deal about the meaning of cricket to Victorian society. It was not a mere game, like golf, to be trifled with by industrial technocrats. Nor was it an ordinary sport, like soccer, to be treated mainly as a commercial enterprise. It was a valued and ancient institution, like the church and the Crown, which had at all costs to be buttressed and preserved in the face of rapid cultural and technological growth.

Notes

1. Altham and Swanton, *A History of Cricket*, 65–68, 131–32. T. Bailey, *A History of Cricket*, 14. Brookes, *English Cricket*, 93–96. T. Lewis, *Double Century: Story of MCC and Cricket*, 76–78.
2. *Cricket Field*, 25 March 1893, 46. Warner, *Lord's 1787–1945*, 38.
3. *Wisden 1871*, 113.
4. Lyttelton *et al.*, *Giants of the Game*, 16–17.
5. *Ibid.*, 18.
6. *Ibid.*, 64–67. Brodribb, *Next Man In*, 34. Warner, *Book of Cricket*, 160–61.
7. Green, ed., *Wisden Obituaries*, 45–47. J.D. Twigg, 'The Players of the Game: R.G. Barlow and the Stonewalling Tradition', *Journal of the Cricket Society* (Autumn 1987), 13: 6–10.
8. Ranjitsinhji, *Jubilee Book of Cricket*, 63–64.
9. Altham and Swanton, 133–34. Lyttelton *et al.*, 35–42. Warner, *Book of Cricket*, 116.
10. C.B. Fry, *Life Worth Living*, 214.
11. Ranjitsinhji's phrase, cited in Midwinter, 155. C.B. Fry, *Life Worth Living*, 214.
12. Mandle, 'W.G. Grace as a Victorian Hero', 353–68.
13. Midwinter, 150–68. *Wisden 1993*, 127.
14. Ranjitsinhji, 71.
15. Altham and Swanton, 81. A.A. Thomson, 'Lord's and the Early Champions, 1787–1865', in E.W. Swanton, ed., *Barclays World of Cricket*, 9.
16. Altham and Swanton, 90–91. Warner, *Lord's 1787–1845*, 45.
17. *Cricket*, 29 June 1888, 233. Brodribb, 33. Lyttelton *et al.*, 49–57. Ranji, 192. Ross, *Ranji: Prince of Cricketers* (London, 1983), 40, 133. Warner, *Book of Cricket*, 157–60.
18. Midwinter, 60–61.
19. Sewell, *Cricket under Fire*, 88–89. Thomson, *Hirst and Rhodes*, 37, 87–88. Warner, *Lord's*, 126. See also B. Hamilton, *Cricket in Barbados* (Bridgetown, 1947), 41–42; and Hodgson, *Yorkshire County Cricket*, 55.
20. Golesworthy, *Encyclopaedia of Cricket*, 45. Warner, *Book of Cricket*, 35–37.
21. *Athletic News*, 3 August 1886, 1. *Wisden 1887*, 41–42.
22. Swanton, ed., *World of Cricket*, 639.
23. *Wisden 1877*, 81.
24. Mandle, 'Games People Played', 517.
25. Arrowsmith, *County Cricket: Kent*, 51. Marshall, *Lord's*, 23.
26. Brodribb, *Next Man In*, 12–13. *Wisden 1892*, xlii-xlvii.
27. H. Barty-King, *Quilt Winders and Pod Shavers: The History of Cricket Bat and Ball Manufacture* (London, 1979), 19–127. Brodribb, 17–19, 42–43. Golesworthy, 32, 35. Swanton, ed., *World of Cricket*, 95, 101–02.
28. Barty-King, 63.
29. *Ibid.*, 107–10. Hodgson, *Yorkshire County Cricket Club*, 42. Lewis, 99, 131.
30. J.R. Betts, 'The Technological Revolution and the Rise of Sport, 1850–1900', in J.W. Loy and G.S. Kenyon, eds, *Sport, Culture and Society* (Toronto, 1969), 145–66.
31. Warner, *Lord's*, 86.

32. Swanton, ed., *Barclays World of Cricket*, 523–28, 538–47. Warner, *Lord's*, 123. *Wisden 1879*, 41.
33. *Cricket*, 6 May 1897, 113–14. W.H. Bowles, 'The Groundsman', in Swanton, ed., *Barclays World of Cricket*, 549–52. R.D.C. Evans, *Cricket Grounds: The Evolution, Maintenance and Construction of Natural Turf Cricket Tables and Outfields* (Bingley, 1991), 7–43. Martineau, *They Made Cricket*, 171–74.
34. *Wisden 1876*, 150.
35. Altham and Swanton, 143. Giffen, *With Bat and Ball*, 11.
36. Evans, 13. M. Williams, ed., *Double Century: 200 Years of Cricket in 'The Times'*, 119.
37. J. Shawcroft, *The History of Derbyshire County Cricket Club*, 52.
38. Grace, 108–09. Marshall, *Lord's*, 31. Shawcroft, *Derbyshire County Cricket Club*, 17–20.
39. Evans, 12. Lewis, 131.
40. Marshall, 21.
41. G.D. West, *The Elevens of England*, 86, 90.
42. Brodribb, 219.
43. Maidens are overs from which no runs have been scored. In his first-class career, Shaw bowled 16 922 maidens among his 24 700 overs, and conceded less than one run per over. This was a phenomenal performance.
44. Brodribb, 34. *Athletic News*, 11 June 1900, 1. *Cricket Field*, 25 June 1892, 130.
45. *Cricket Field*, 6 May 1893, 67.
46. *Cricket*, 10 May 1900, 114.
47. Brodribb, *Next Man In*, 76–77.
48. Brodribb, *Hit For Six*, 43–54, 72–86.
49. Brodribb, *Next Man In*, 89–91. *Cricket*, 25 October 1900, 439. *Wisden 1892*, xlvii.
50. Lemmon, *Surrey County Cricket Club*, 23–24.
51. B. Bearshaw, *Official History of Lancashire County Cricket Club*, 69.
52. Green, ed., *Wisden Obituaries*, 984.
53. *Midland Athlete*, 2 February 1881, 73.
54. *Athletic News*, 29 July 1889, 1.
55. *Ibid.*, 6 July 1886, 1; and 3 August 1886, 1.
56. *Ibid.*, 20 June 1892, 1.
57. *Ibid.*, 18 June 1900, 1; and 9 July 1900, 1.
58. *Cricket*, 7 June 1883, 152.
59. Gordon, *Background of Cricket*, 170–71. Altham and Swanton, 284–85.
60. Gordon, 220.
61. Ranjitsinhji, 7.
62. *Wisden 1901*, lxxvii–lxxxi, civ.
63. Altham and Swanton, 148. *Wisden 1887*, 5; and *1900*, 256–63.
64. Altham and Swanton, 147–48. Lyttelton *et al.*, 153–55, 165–68. Warner, *Book of Cricket*, 35. *Wisden 1892*, xlii–xlvii.
65. *Wisden 1993*, 151.
66. Barty-King, 128–47.
67. *Ibid.*, 176–83.

CHAPTER EIGHT

Cricket and Empire

The British empire expanded by leaps and bounds during the Victorian age. By the beginning of the twentieth century, it contained at least 660 million souls and was spread over more than 12 million square miles. It posed as an awesome force on the international stage and was by far the most enormous imperial system that the world had known. It occupied nearly one quarter of the world's area and included almost one quarter of its total population.[1] The Victorians were inordinately proud of this empire which they regarded as tangible proof of their racial and moral superiority.

The empire, of course, had much more to do with commercial and industrial expansion than with race or morality. Having industrialized before her rivals did, Britain was able to manufacture more goods than she could consume at home. Hence the frantic quest for overseas markets and raw materials which led, in one way and another, to the acquisition of colonies in Africa, southeast Asia, the South Pacific and the West Indies, without undue hindrance, until the other European nations also industrialized. Then, in the last quarter of the nineteenth century, the motivating impulse came as much from competition as from commerce. So fierce was this competition that the late-Victorians saw fit to acquire, much less absentmindedly than before, almost 5 million square miles of additional territory and about 88 million new subjects between 1870 and 1900.[2]

Victorian imperialism was more than just a matter of exporting goods and ideas. It also involved the transplantation of people. Millions departed the mother country in search of fame and opportunity. The great population explosion which the British Isles witnessed during 1750–1900 left them with a chronic sense of claustrophobia, for which mass emigration seemed the only cure. The result was that, by the time of Queen Victoria's death, there were about 100 million people of British stock occupying territories beyond the United Kingdom (despite the fact that the numbers within Britain itself had increased from approximately 24 million in 1831 to about 41 million in 1901). Several families established direct colonial links, as the exodus from Britain continued unabated during the nineteenth century.[3]

This large body of migrants included thousands of gentlemen who had been deliberately trained for imperial service by the universities and the emerging public schools. Whereas there had been a mere handful of public schools in Britain in 1840, the number rose beyond 100 by the start of the twentieth century.[4] There were therefore too many public school alumni and university graduates for the available jobs at home. The superfluous took their skills, such as they were, to Australia, Canada, India, New Zealand, South Africa, the West Indies and elsewhere. The Dominions, by one estimate, claimed some 45 000 British migrants of middle- or upper-class origin between 1875 and 1900.[5]

It was this segment of the Anglo-Saxon exodus which went forth with the idea that it could civilize the empire. As the late-Victorians equated civilization with the other three Cs – Cricket, Classics and Christianity – their aim was to promote these elements of culture in their far-flung dominions. The spread of the empire naturally meant therefore the spread of cricket. A migrant people, whether imperialist or imperialized, does not leave behind its cultural and intellectual luggage. The Victorians were determined to civilize the rest of the world, and an integral feature of that process as they understood it was to disseminate the gospel of athleticism which had triumphed so spectacularly at home in the third quarter of the nineteenth century.[6]

The British emigrants and imperialists carried their 'manly' recreations with them wherever they went. Indeed, from as early as the eighteenth century their armed forces had begun the dissemination of cricket. A young sailor writing from Quiberon Bay in 1760 was able to inform his family that he had had several opportunities to go ashore and play cricket.[7] The officers of the East India Company had also managed to establish the Calcutta Cricket Club as long ago as 1792.[8] The British army was most active in this matter of spreading the cricket gospel. It introduced the sport to so many foreign places that by the early nineteenth century cricket was regularly being played in Burma, Ceylon, Corfu, Egypt, Gibraltar, Hong Kong, Malta, Mauritius, Shanghai, Singapore, South Africa and Tasmania. In this connection, the military achieved their major triumphs in Australia and the Caribbean, where cricket had become securely entrenched before the end of the Georgian age.[9] There had, in fact, as Arthur Thomson shrewdly observed, always been a marked affinity between the good cricketer and the good soldier: 'Both need courage and endurance; both are skilled in adapting themselves without warning to various forms of sticky wicket, as in Burma or even Bradford Park Avenue.'[10]

Cricket, after all, had consistently been praised by British educators as one of the best practice nets for the Test match of actual warfare. It was no less important as a training ground for politics and diplomacy. As Bracebridge Hemyng had stated so clearly in the early 1870s, 'The playground shows what a man is capable of, and gives promise of what he can, may, and will do in the great world. The men who win boat-races and cricket matches are the men who win battles and change the fortunes of nations.'[11] As classical scholars who had also excelled at cricket, Lord Curzon and Lord Harris were considered the ideal colonial governors. They had just the right qualifications and connections to serve as British administrators in India during the 1890s. It did not matter, as the disgruntled S.H. Jeyes lamented (as late as 1897) that the products of the British élite education system were 'bright-eyed, clean limbed, high-minded, ready for anything, and fit for nothing'.[12] Both Curzon and Harris went confidently into that subcontinent with the complete assurance that their public school training had prepared them adequately to govern Hindus, Muslims, Parsees and Sikhs. If nothing else, their appointments ensured the strengthening of the cricket tradition in Calcutta and Bombay.

If Victorian cricket developed powerful links with the military, it did the same with religion also. At home, churches recommended the sport as a fine alternative to various forms of sin and missionaries also played a key role in the spread of cricket abroad, following the spectacular example of the so-called Cambridge Seven who marched boldly forth under the leadership of Charles Thomas Studd to introduce bat, ball and Bible to the natives of Africa, China and India.[13] Some natives, however, proved invincibly heretical. Buddhists, Hindus, Muslims, Parsees and Sikhs refused to exchange one God for another and remained quite jealous of their cultural heritage. But they instinctively recognized the practical value of British manufactured goods and the inherent virtues of British sports. Thus, even in those areas where the Evangelical missionaries signally failed to impress significant bodies of converts, they won over many millions of souls for the cricketing cult. If the Victorians could not always make Anglicans of natives, they frequently succeeded in otherwise anglicizing them.

This obsession with Anglo-Saxonism was partly inspired by – and partly reflected in – the extraordinary literature of the late-Victorian period. It was governed by the profound conviction that the progress of civilization depended entirely upon the advance of the British flag. Thus could Lord Curzon brazenly confess his opinion in 1894 that 'the British Empire is, under Providence, the greatest instrument for good that the world has seen'.[14] This was the kernel of the Anglo-Saxon gospel so persuasively preached by such authors as Charles Dilke, in his *Greater Britain* (1868); Sir John Seeley in *The Expansion of England* (1883); J.A. Froude in *Oceana* (1886); Benjamin Kidd in *Social Evolution* (1894); Rudyard Kipling in *The White Man's Burden* (1889), *Seven Seas* (1896) and *Recessional* (1897); and H. Rider Haggard in *Black Heart and White Heart and Other Stories* (1900). Poets such as Henry Newbolt, and novelists such as G.A. Henty and Robert Louis Stevenson, can also be numbered among the eloquent evangelists of imperial expansion.[15]

British migrants and colonial administrators thus convinced themselves that they were performing an essential service for all natives whom they introduced to Anglo-Saxon culture in its various forms. This deliberate indoctrination was undertaken by the academic institutions which the imperialists established throughout the colonies. Élite colonial schools were erected as far as humanly possible on the lines of Eton, Harrow, Rugby and Winchester. Curricula were slavishly borrowed from these public schools and the majority of the teachers were imported from Britain. Thus, for example, when the youthful Pelham Warner left Harrison College, Barbados, to attend Rugby in 1887, it did not require any considerable readjustment on his part.[16] Similarly, when young Ranjitsinhji transferred from Rajkumar College, Rajkot, to St Faith's, Cambridge, in 1888, the transition was relatively painless.[17]

It was quite natural for English public school Old Boys to recreate public schools wherever they went and to reproduce the norms and practices with which they had been familiar. Thus it was, for instance, that George A. Barber, the publisher of the *Toronto Herald*, came to introduce cricket into the Upper Canada College where he taught during the 1830s. He is still remembered as the father of Canadian cricket, having founded the Toronto Cricket Club in 1827. It was he who inaugurated in 1836 the historic series of matches between the Toronto club and Upper Canada College. It was also mainly due to his exertions that a memorable match was arranged between Toronto and Guelph in 1834.[18] Barber performed for Canada the same service that J.P. Firth tried to render New Zealand. As headmaster of Wellington College, Firth made the school famous for its cricket. He employed coaches and tried to popularize the game in the 1890s, but somehow it never quite captured the popular imagination until the 1930s.[19] Cricket developed very slowly in New Zealand and for many years the New Zealanders never quite managed to grasp its intricacies in the way in which they mastered rugby. Perhaps an explanation for this failure of civilization lies in the nature and/or the paucity of the public schools which came into being in New Zealand during the nineteenth century. Certainly there were demographic and geographical difficulties which compounded the problem.

It is true that cricket came to be regarded as the national sport of Canada by 1867, thanks largely to the efforts of men like Barber. By the 1840s it was being played in all those areas where the English had settled. As early as 1844, the ongoing series of contests between Canada and the United States was inaugurated and it is noteworthy that, in 1859, the first of all English touring teams chose to travel to the western hemisphere. By the 1890s, the Canada–U.S. confrontations were extremely popular. Large numbers of spectators were flocking to see the great Philadelphian, J.B. King, perform his mighty deeds with both bat and ball. In 1872

Canada also had an opportunity to witness firsthand the exploits of the immortal W.G., who struck a glorious 142 against Toronto. A strong Australian side visited Canada in 1878 and the Canadians themselves toured England, with chequered results, in 1880 and 1887.[20]

With cricket teams emerging in urban centres as far apart as Halifax, Winnipeg and Vancouver, it seemed as though Canada would soon become a major force in international cricket. By 1887, there were five or six cricket clubs in Toronto, eight in Montreal and three in Victoria. In the maritimes, similar clubs then existed in places like Antigonish, Fredericton, Saint John, Sydney and Truro. But the game failed to make much headway in the later Victorian age and gradually ceased to be an important sport in Canada. The key to an explanation of this phenomenon lies partly in the nature of Canadian immigration and partly in the performance of the newly created public schools. While increasing numbers of Britons journeyed to Canada from the 1840s onwards, they seemed to have been swamped by other European migrants. Hundreds of thousands of Jewish, Scandinavian and Ukrainian families moved into Canada during the last third of the nineteenth century. The Canadian culture which emerged from this melting pot was consequently much less Anglo-Saxon than it was destined to remain in places like Australia and New Zealand. Canadian culture also tended to be influenced significantly by developments in the United States. Thus, as American interest in cricket waned after their traumatic Civil War, so too did Canadian enthusiasm steadily decline.

In fact, in an age dominated by aggressive nationalism, both the United States and Canada began to search quite consciously for a national identity of their own, and ultimately settled upon baseball and lacrosse as their respective national sports. The British settlers did manage to establish the Winnipeg Cricket Club in 1878, but, during the last quarter of the century, the game became associated more and more with an older and more old-fashioned Anglo-Saxon élite. Thus curling, ice hockey and lacrosse gradually eclipsed cricket as the leading Canadian pastimes. Whereas by 1885 cricket was the third most popular sport in Canada, with 12 per cent of the sports coverage in the *Toronto Globe*, by 1915 it had declined all the way to 17th.[21]

It was the approach of the Canadian public schools which also seemed to presage the decline of cricket. Founded though they were by British public school alumni along British public school lines, the Canadian colleges refused to perpetuate the élitism of their prototypes or to preserve their outmoded curricula. Upper Canada College was opened in Toronto in 1829 and Bishop's College in 1836; they were the oldest and most conservative of the new Canadian schools. Those which came later, such as Trinity (1862), St John's (1866), Lakefield (1879) and Bishop Ridley

(1889), were equally respectable but more progressive. They kept alive the cult of athleticism but saw fit to promote a different brand of games.[22]

The behaviour of the late-Victorian colleges in Canada differed markedly from that of their counterparts in India and the West Indies. Rajkumar College, under the guidance of Chester Macnaghten, was very much like the host of Indian public schools founded after 1850 to cater to the sons of native princes and aristocrats. Macnaghten was a classics graduate from Cambridge who had been prevented by illness from attending Harrow in his youth. He systematically carved out an Indian Harrow in Rajkot, a central town in Saurasthra. There, dozens of young Indian princes were carefully anglicized by way of preparation for administrative and political tasks. Cricket, English, Greek and Latin were the principal ingredients of the curriculum.[23] The alumni then went forth upon matriculation to spread the gospel further. How well they did so is obvious from the history of Indian cricket. As an apostle of the games cult in India, Macnaghten was perhaps equalled only by the redoubtable Cecil Earle Tyndale-Briscoe, headmaster (1890–1947) of the Church Missionary School in Srinagar, Kashmir, who persuaded even the Hindus to play soccer.[24]

The long process of Indian anglicization had begun before the arrival there of Macnaghten and Lord Harris. They therefore found an unusually fertile soil in which, as it were, to sow more cricketing seeds. There is evidence, in fact, that cricket was played in India as long ago as 1721, and by the end of the Georgian age the game was regularly played in Bombay and Calcutta. The early teams in India were composed of Europeans but the Parsees established their own club in Bombay late in the eighteenth century. The Parsees toured England in 1877 and an English team visited India in 1889, but for a long time cricket on that subcontinent was largely restricted to European expatriates. The turning point came in the 1890s with Lord Harris's appointment as Governor of Bombay and Ranjitsinhji's selection to play for England. Lord Harris encouraged the natives to participate actively in the sport and Ranji's successes in England inspired the Indians to believe that cricket could be played most ably by non-Europeans. Lord Harris was instrumental in organizing Lord Hawke's tour to India in 1892–93. He also promoted the construction of cricket grounds for Hindus, Muslims and Parsees and thus transformed the sport into a truly Indian pastime. By the early twentieth century, Hindus as well as Muslims and Parsees had adopted the game as an Indian national symbol, and even the English became astonished by the depth of the religious fervour which the Indians brought (and still bring) to their cricket. There was no failure of the civilizing mission here.[25]

The Victorians succeeded in the Caribbean also. It was there, in fact, that the muscular Christians struck their most telling blows.[26] Throughout the West Indies, public schools were founded precisely upon the Victorian pattern. Queen's Royal College in Guyana (then known as Demerara), Jamaica College, Kingston College and St George's in Jamaica sprang up as so many Etons, Harrows and Winchesters in miniature. But the cream of the élite schools was Harrison College in Barbados, which emerged as one of the most famous secondary schools throughout the world during the administration (1872–1905) of Horace Deighton. Several Old Harrisonians distinguished themselves as classical scholars at Cambridge and Oxford. How successful Deighton was in propagating the doctrine of athleticism is manifest in the history of West Indian cricket. Not only did Harrison College produce many generations of brilliant scholar-cricketers but its alumni managed to convert the entire Barbadian society to the cricket cult before the century had ended. Several Old Harrisonians then became classics teachers and cricket masters in secondary schools throughout the English-speaking West Indies. They were the apostles who successfully disseminated the cricket gospel in such islands as Antigua, Dominica, Grenada, Jamaica, Tobago, Trinidad and St Vincent. During the late-Victorian age, cricket thus became a most significant feature of Caribbean life. It has remained so until this very day.[27]

Imperial administrators combined with anglicized West Indians to establish deep cricket roots during the nineteenth century. As early as 1806 the St Ann's Cricket Club was operating in Barbados. Cricket was so well organized in the region that intercolonial competition could commence in 1865, when Barbados met Demerara. By the end of the century, there were vibrant cricket clubs in Antigua, Grenada and St Vincent as well as in Barbados, British Guiana, Jamaica and Trinidad. Visits to the Caribbean by English teams in the 1890s did much to stimulate the growth of the sport there, and the West Indies undertook their first English tours in 1900 and 1906.[28]

The Australian experience was different from the others. Cricket there was not as dependent upon public schools, but profited from the fact that the white population tended to be more homogeneous than in Canada or South Africa. Cricket fanaticism began in Australia almost as soon as the initial British colonies were founded there and the game kept pace with the spread of colonization. From the beginning, the élite evinced a keen interest in sports and Governor Macquarie himself actually ordered the manufacture of bats and balls in government workshops when the first recorded match took place in Sydney between the military and the civilians in 1803.[29] By the 1830s the Hobart Cricket Club had emerged in Tasmania and the Melbourne club had been founded in Victoria. Australians were already familiar with intercolonial cricket before the end of the 1850s. The problems of distance, however, prevented the inter-colonial competition from reaching Queensland, Western Australia and

South Australia before the 1890s.[30]

But the transportation and communication difficulties which impeded the growth of imperial cricket elsewhere failed to check its inexorable advance in Australia. The Australians had the benefit of watching two teams of English professionals in the 1860s and a mixed but powerful group of players and gentlemen led by the legendary Grace in 1873–74. From these guests they learnt invaluable lessons, especially about the science of bowling. In 1861–62, during the first English tour of Australia, the local batsmen were bemused by James Southerton's pace and H.H. Stephenson's subtlety. These were the techniques which the colonials deliberately set out to master after the tourists had departed and in this they were much encouraged by Charles Lawrence, the English professional, who remained behind to take up a coaching appointment in New South Wales. William Caffyn of Surrey and All England also stayed on after the 1863–64 English tour to coach in Melbourne.[31]

Where the West Indians had had the benefit of muscular Christian educators, the Australians gained from copying the expertise of noted English professionals. Here, the influence of Caffyn, Lawrence and Jesse Hide was paramount. Hide was a Sussex player who taught the Australians a good deal not only about the art of bowling and batting but also about the science of wicket preparation. When Grace visited Australia in 1873, he was distressed by the quality of the pitches. When he returned in 1891, he was much impressed by the improvement that had taken place in all aspects of Australian cricket, including groundsmanship.[32]

By the late 1870s Australians were ready to challenge England's cricket supremacy. They defeated a strong English XI by 45 runs at Melbourne in March 1877, thanks to the magnificent batting of Charles Bannerman and the inspired bowling of Thomas Kendall. They enhanced their reputation by touring England triumphantly in 1878, when they humbled the mighty MCC at Lord's. In 1882, they went one stage further by becoming the first winner of the mythical 'Ashes' when they defeated England in the Test match at the Oval.[33] By the 1880s, Australia had superseded England in the arts of bowling, fielding, field-placing and wicketkeeping. The colonials were consequently able to hold their own despite the slightly inferior quality of their batsmanship. In the 1890s, however, they produced a fine array of brilliant batsmen, led by Joe Darling, Clem Hill, Monty Noble and Victor Trumper.[34]

Australian cricket thus came of age during the late-Victorian period, even though the country's population in the early 1890s stood at only around three million, then approximately but one tenth of the population in England and Wales.[35] Australia arrived at this happy situation because of the proud cricket tradition which had been established from the very beginning. The Australians have always played the game with the dogged determination and clinical proficiency of Yorkshire professionals, even though (until very recently) the majority of their players remained amateurs. They quickly adopted cricket as their national symbol and made every attempt to prove their equality with Anglo-Saxon imperialists by performing brilliantly on the cricket field. The doctrine of athleticism triumphed so completely in Australia that sports became the most important aspect of its culture. An event like the Melbourne Cup, for instance, could attract as many as 80 000 – fully one third of Melbourne's total population. Sport became the one colonial career open to all the talents. Australia copied the majority of British sporting models and stuck steadfastly to them. The only departure from this norm was the invention of Victorian rules football which enjoyed little popularity before the last few decades.[36] Anglo-Saxonism triumphed completely in Australia because the white population there remained largely Anglo-Saxon.

This was the essential difference between Australia and South Africa, where the white population not only formed a small minority but was divided between families of British and Dutch extraction. The Victorian imperialists consequently found South Africa a much more difficult nut to crack and cricket made only pedestrian progress in that country during the nineteenth century. The deliberate segregation of the races and the heterogeneous character of the white element hindered the growth of cricket at every turn. The millions of Blacks were not encouraged to play cricket and the Boers did not show much enthusiasm for the sport. British soldiers took cricket to the Cape during the Napoleonic Wars and by 1850 the game was well established at Cape Town, Pietermaritzburg and Port Elizabeth. The British also introduced cricket into Natal during the first half of the nineteenth century and into Transvaal during the early 1860s. In many parts of South Africa, too, new academic institutions such as the Diocesan College, the South African College and the Port Elizabeth Academy were playing the game with some enthusiasm during the 1850s.[37]

But South African cricket lagged behind the Australian and Canadian variety because it was mainly confined to small pockets of British expatriates in the major urban centres. Whereas English cricketers had been invited to tour Canada and the United States as early as 1859, no such invitation came from South Africa until 30 years later. Four English teams then travelled thither between 1888 and 1899, but – unlike the majority of the Australian expeditions – they were financial failures and the hosts provided very feeble opposition indeed.[38] Between 1888 and 1905, no English team ever lost a first-class cricket match in South Africa. Altogether they played 75 matches, including several against odds (and thus not officially recognized as first-class) and won as many as 49. Quite obviously, the South African level of play was hardly higher than New

Zealand's. Yet, incredibly, South Africa was awarded Test match status during the 1888–9 season.[39] The first real ray of hope occurred in 1889 when the Currie Cup competition was launched. This placed South African cricket on a more structured basis for the first time.[40]

On the other hand, India, New Zealand and the West Indies all had to wait until well into the twentieth century before achieving a similar status. The West Indian case is most peculiar. It was obvious from the first English tour to the Caribbean, which Slade Lucas led in 1894–95, that West Indian cricket had already reached a very creditable standard. Four competent English teams, during 1894–1902, played 37 first-class matches in the Caribbean, winning 18, losing 15 and drawing four. Yet, when the West Indies toured England in 1900, their matches were not officially considered first-class.[41]

This question of status in international cricket bears a suspicious correlation to varying colonial arrangements in the political arena. The so-called 'white' colonies were allowed considerable legislative autonomy in the nineteenth century, to participate with Britain in a sequence of Colonial Conferences after 1887 and eventually to attain dominion status before the Second World War. For the rest of the empire, a byzantine assortment of devices, ranging from indirect rule to Crown colony government, were left stubbornly in place. Racism was obviously a factor in such discrepancies. Blacks, Browns and Yellows had to endure a much longer and more painful period of probation. This was, of course, quite consistent with Victorian philosophy.

Racism was but a logical extension of the Victorian concept of order and degree. Their firm belief in the hierarchical ordering of society led them to the inevitable conclusion, based on selective reading of the Scriptures, that races were divinely classified in accordance with shades and colours. The same logic that dictated that amateur cricketers should have precedence over the professionals led the Victorians to conclude that Anglo-Saxons were ordained to have dominion over non-white peoples.[42]

Not surprisingly, then, racism was always a feature of imperialism and of cricket. Even the famous Ranjitsinhji, despite his obvious batting and fielding skills, had to wait for his final year at Cambridge before winning his coveted 'blue'. During the Australian tour to England in 1896, Lord Hawke was opposed to Ranji's selection to the English Test XI, although the Indian prince had long since satisfied the residence requirement.[43] Nor was this a peculiarly Victorian phenomenon. It was but a symptom of that universal bigotry that had persuaded American champion boxers, such as Jim Corbett and John L. Sullivan, to refuse for many years to fight against Peter Jackson, who was black.[44] It was in keeping, too, with the blunt refusal of the white South Africans to compete with or against Blacks. Hence the exclusion of the gifted Krom Hendriks from the cricket team

which toured England in 1894.[45] Racism was also an integral feature of
West Indian social life before the modern era of Independence. It was
reflected in the refusal of Barbados and Demerara to select black 'professionals' to represent them in the late-Victorian period. Racism and
snobbery eventually forced such capable cricketers as W.T. Burton, Archie
Cumberbatch, 'Fitz Lilly' Hinds, Oliver Layne and William Shepherd to
emigrate from Barbados altogether.[46]

Nor did the Aborigines fare much better in Australia. Thirteen of them
visited England, under Charles Lawrence in 1868, and performed cred-
itably enough, but were never taken seriously by their hosts. Faced with
an arduous schedule of 47 matches in 126 days in foreign conditions, they
avoided defeat on all but 14 occasions and won just as often as they lost
against cricketers who were far more experienced. Despite the evident
gifts of such Aboriginal stars as Cuzens and Mullagh, their games were
not considered first-class, and were ignored by the Australian media
altogether. The fact is that in England, too, their athletic exhibitions after
the matches were considered more significant than their actual cricket.
The white hosts regarded cricket as too serious a game to be mastered by
a race so lazy, flighty and irresponsible. This white image of the childish,
indolent native was kept alive long into the twentieth century. Frank
Gerald, a noted author-athlete, who played soccer for Wales and rugby
much later for New Zealand, could still describe the Aborigine in 1938
as 'always a child: he loves to play, he will play any game, however childish, all day long'.[47] C.B. Fry, another famous scholar-athlete, writing in
1939, was also able to declare that the Maoris in New Zealand were
'equally undevoted to work and to worry'.[48] The Aborigines had an
aptitude for cricket but it was gradually stifled after 1870 by the bigotry
of white Australians.[49]

If the racist stereotype killed Aboriginal (and perhaps Maori) cricket
in Australasia, it signally failed to destroy Hindu, Muslim and Parsee
cricket in India, where the imperialists were too completely outnumbered
by the natives. A long sequence of colonial administrators, in fact, felt that
cricket could serve as a civilizing force and encouraged the Indians to take
it up. It was still deemed improper for the races to intermingle and much
of the nineteenth-century cricket in India was characterized by segregation. These attitudes changed slowly after Lord Harris's tenure as
Governor of Bombay and after the great Ranji had amply shown that
Indians were much less effete and feeble than the Victorians had
assumed.[50] But, for all that, as late as 1921, in A Few Short Runs, Lord
Harris could still express the view that 'it is in the matter of patience that
the Indian will never be the equal to the Englishman'.[51] Nor was it until
1926 that the Europeans would condescend to play at the Poona Cricket
Club which belonged to Hindus.[52] This was the kind of racist mentality

that kept Indians out of Test cricket until 1932.

In the West Indies, meanwhile, the racial blows were mainly self-inflicted. Pelham Warner, a native of Trinidad, disagreed in the 1890s with the racist policy of Barbados and Demerara. He sincerely believed that the black professionals added a vital dimension, as the bowling of Cumberbatch and Woods for Trinidad had just shown. He thought that the West Indies should send a composite team to England soon, but bluntly added that if the black men were excluded 'it would be absurd to attempt to play the first class counties'. Warner was sure that a combination of nine white players and five Blacks could give the majority of English counties very stiff competition indeed.[53] This advice was only partially followed in 1900, when a few token Blacks were selected among the first West Indian cricketers to tour England. This gave the editor of the *Athletic News* a chance to observe that the 'men of colour' were hopelessly out of their element in a coldish summer, 'although it must be said that neither in the West Indies nor in England could this type of player ever hope to bring the same amount of intelligence to his game'.[54] This was the orthodoxy of that age which served to keep the West Indies out of Test cricket until 1928. It has to be admitted, however, that the sentiments expressed by the *Athletic News* coincided exactly with the prejudices of white West Indians who refused to appoint a black captain until after the Second World War.

Such biases on the part of local Whites represented a conscious desire to imitate the Anglo-Saxons at home. It was this transplanted Anglo-Saxonism that inspired the emergence of a vigorous and militant nationalism throughout the British empire. Cricket became, in effect, inextricably bound up with patriotic pride and national aspirations among the colonials from the start. As George Giffen readily admitted, it was the very height of patriotism to represent Australia on the cricket field.[55] Australian cricket captains did most to give their country an identity before the establishment of the federation, and the game itself undoubtedly contributed enormously to the development of an Australian sense of nationalism after the inauguration of the international series of Tests in 1877.[56] The jubilant *Bulletin* probably expressed this patriotic fervour most poignantly when, after Australian success in the 1897–98 Test series, it declared that 'This ruthless rout of English cricket will do – and has done – more to enhance the cause of Australian nationality than ever could be achieved by miles of erudite essays and impassioned appeal.'[57]

The editor of the Australian *Bulletin* was giving vent to the same kind of sentiment that had inspired a leading civil servant to declare Harry Trott 'a national institution' when that postman's colleagues complained about the inordinate amount of leave he was getting to play cricket. Trott, after all, was one of the most successful of Australian Test captains.[58] Another triumphant captain, William L. Murdoch, likened himself to General Wolseley, who had recently gone forth and crushed the insolent Arabi Pasha. He was proud of having just defeated his hosts, and thus could confess on 28 September 1882 that 'personally I have attained the height of my ambition, having captained a team which has beaten a representative Eleven of England'. Murdoch was particularly elated because 'the honour of Australia had been entrusted to our hands'.[59]

Such national fervour pervaded Indian and West Indian cricket, too. Both of these societies adopted cricket as their national sport and brought a religious devotion to it that has shocked many a visitor to those countries in the twentieth century. It is ironic that the Indians have been fiercely jealous of their heritage and have studiously resisted all forms of anglicization, yet they have developed a profound attachment to this most peculiarly English of all games. It was a baffling paradox which did not escape that shrewd Indian statesman, Sri C. Rajagopalachari, who once prophesied that the day might come when Indians would abandon English, but he could not imagine that they would ever give up cricket.[60] In the post-Victorian age, the Indians also looked upon their admission into the Imperial Cricket Council as one gigantic step towards political independence.

Imperialism is an almost inevitable offspring of aggressive nationalism. Patriotic fervour had much to do with the constant Victorian fawning over their colossal empire. Nationalism, however, also required them to demonstrate their supremacy over colonials, even though many of the latter were of British stock. At first, in the early 1880s, there was certainly a sense of mortification when Australian cricketers were defeating the best England elevens; and foreign scullers, like Ned Hanlan and Trickett, were making a mockery of England's finest oarsmen.[61] But gradually the late-Victorians resigned themselves to the fact of Australian cricket equality and took a certain vicarious pride in the achievements of transplanted Anglo-Saxons. Thus Fry, for instance, was able to soothe England's cricket wounds by reflecting that the Australian 'has rejuvenated the British race in a new world of his own without losing his attachment to the root qualities of the parent stock'.[62]

This attachment to Anglo-Saxon values was the ultimate triumph of Victorian imperialism. The cultural reproduction process did not affect only colonials of British stock. Both Blacks and Whites in the West Indies, for example, adhered doggedly to Victorian models long after they had been discarded by the British themselves. This was particularly true in Barbados (which has long been dubbed 'Little England')[63] but was also the case in Trinidad, as James demonstrated so clearly in his much acclaimed *Beyond a Boundary*. So anglicized had the Barbadians become that one black native, known to all as 'Britannia Bill', attended cricket matches against the English tourists in the 1890s waving a huge Union Jack and cheering mightily for the visitors.[64] He was not alone. Indeed, for many years there was a significant body of support among the locals throughout the Caribbean region for touring English cricket teams. Many Barbadians, including several cricketers, also joined a vigorous Volunteer Movement to assist the British against the Boers in the late 1890s. Sir Conrad Reeves, a brilliant mulatto lawyer, who had founded the Spartan Cricket Club for middle-class Blacks in 1893, expressed himself delighted to see so many Barbadians interested in defending the cause of liberty as well as their rights and possessions. Even though the colony had no military tradition, as Reeves himself acknowledged, he considered it the duty of all Barbadians to fight for their Queen and *their* empire.[65]

Reeves, the Barbadian jurist, was in exactly the same boat as Ranjitsinhji, the Hindu prince. Sir Conrad, who still ranks among the most famous of all West Indian Blacks, did not acknowledge that he was a colonial with the possibility of sharing common interests and aspirations with Boers or Bantus. Trained from birth to think in English ways, he instinctively sided with the metropolis. Ranjitsinhji did the same – as early as 1896 he was publicly calling for a perfect Anglo-Indian union that could safely confront all common foes.[66] Like Reeves, his admiration for English culture was lasting and profound, and he considered cricket one of England's most precious gifts to civilization. Like the vast majority of Anglo-Saxons of his generation, he was convinced that cricket had the magical power to bring all the polyglot peoples of the empire much closer together.[67] Sir Wilfred Laurier, a Francophone Canadian leader whom the Queen had knighted during her jubilee celebrations in 1897, remarked in the following year that Britain was, by almost every conceivable standard, the greatest of all colonizing powers in history.[68] Such was the awesome power of cultural imperialism. Laurier was not a cricketer but he had become almost as anglicized as Ranji and Reeves.

The deliberate pursuit of Anglo-Saxonism, which was often manifested in the cricket mania, provided perhaps the most effective imperial bond. The various tours undertaken after 1859 were consciously intended to act as a cementing link between colonies and metropolis. Consistently after the inauguration of the Colonial Conferences in the 1880s, the white colonies displayed a keen enthusiasm for the principle of imperial federation. No doubt this was calculated to win a greater share in the imperial decision-making process, but it was also inspired by the desire for closer ties with Britain especially in the wake of the German challenge. Cricket offered the easiest opportunity for such closer links and, by 1900, became many things to different imperialists as well as different colonists. It was at once a test of colonial progress and reinforcement of imperial standards as well as an imperial code of ethics.[69] Hence the Barbadian, Canadian and Australian responses to the Boer War.

It is ironic that the colonists should have shown more enthusiasm for that particular struggle than the majority of the British workers at home.[70] For the South Africans, in essence, were fighting for an extension of colonial rights. These curious attitudes and prejudices, however, demonstrate the extent to which, by spreading Anglo-Saxon culture abroad, the Victorians had succeeded in indoctrinating a variety of communities, both white and other. Cricket, it would appear, played at least as crucial a role in that victory as did commerce and Christianity. The colonists who aspired to administrative positions attended anglicized schools and absorbed Anglo-Saxon lessons. Their ability to play cricket and to speak English stood them in good stead. They, in turn, propagated the gospel of cricket and allowed it to prosper in many parts of the empire (and sometimes beyond).

Notes

1. R. Muir, *A Short History of the British Commonwealth* (London, 1962), 2: 637.
2. T. Lloyd, *The British Empire 1558–1983* (Oxford, 1984), 258.
3. B.R. Mitchell and P. Deane, *Abstracts of British Historical Statistics* (Cambridge, 1971), 8–9. L.C.B. Seaman, *Victorian England: Aspects of English and Imperial History 1837–1901* (London, 1973), 352.
4. B. Simon and I. Bradley, *The Victorian Public School* (London, 1975), 29.
5. P.A. Dunae, *Gentlemen Emigrants: From the British Public Schools to the Canadian Frontier* (Vancouver, 1981), 8.
6. J.A. Mangan, ed., *Pleasure, Profit, Proselytism: British Culture and Sport at Home and Abroad 1700–1914* (London, 1988), *passim*.
7. Ford, *Cricket: A Social History*, 44–45.
8. S. Sanyal, *40 Years of Test Cricket* (New Delhi, 1974), 1.
9. Swanton, ed., *Barclays World of Cricket* (London, 1986), 78–113.
10. Thomson, *Odd Men In*, 98.
11. B. Hemyng, *Jack Harkaway at Oxford* (London, 1872), 144.
12. S.H. Jeyes, 'Our Gentlemanly Failures', *Fortnightly Review* (1 March 1897), 61: 388.
13. J.A. Mangan, 'Christ and the Imperial Games Fields: Evangelical Athletes of the Empire', *British Journal of Sports History* (September 1984), 1: 184–201. Martin-Jenkins, *Who's Who*, 142. P. Scott, 'Cricket and the Religious World in the Victorian Period', 134–44.
14. G.N. Curzon, *Problems of the Far East* (London, 1894), v.
15. F. Bedarida, *A Social History of England 1851–1975*, translated by A.S. Foster (London, 1979), 145; J.B. Conacher, *Waterloo to the Common Market* (New York, 1975), 153. A.P. Thornton, *The Imperial Idea and Its Enemies* (London, 1959), 92–94.
16. Warner, *Long Innings*, 15–21.
17. A. Ross, *Ranji: Prince of Cricketers* (London, 1983), 27–40.
18. Swanton, ed., *Barclays World of Cricket*, 78.

19. *Ibid.*, 99.
20. K.R. Bullock, 'Canada', in E.W. Swanton, ed., *Barclays World of Cricket*, 78–79.
21. M. Mott, 'The British Protestant Pioneers and the Establishment of Manly Sports in Manitoba, 1870–1886', *Journal of Sport History* (Winter, 1980), 7: 25–36. See also A. Metcalfe, *Canada Learns to Play: The Emergence of Organized Sport, 1807–1914* (Toronto, 1987), 80–85.
22. Dunae, 231–32.
23. Ross, 28–34.
24. Mangan, 'Christ and the Imperial Games Fields', 193–94.
25. R. Cashman, *Patrons, Players and the Crowd: The Phenomenon of Indian Cricket* (New Delhi, 1980), 1–13. R. Holt, *Sport and the British: A Modern History* (Oxford, 1989), 214–16. R.A. Roberts and D.J. Rutnagur, 'India', in E.W. Swanton, ed., *Barclays World of Cricket*, 87–88.
26. B. Stoddart, 'Cricket and Colonialism in the English-Speaking Caribbean to 1914: Steps Towards a Cultural Analysis', in J.A. Mangan, ed., *Pleasure, Profit and Proselytism: British Culture and Sport at Home and Abroad, 1700–1914* (London, 1988), 231–57.
27. K.A.P. Sandiford, 'Cricket and the Barbadian Society', *Canadian Journal of History* (December 1986), 21: 353–70. K.A.P. Sandiford and B. Stoddart, 'The Elite Schools and Cricket in Barbados: A Study in Colonial Continuity', *International Journal of the History of Sports* (December 1987), 4: 333–50. B. Stoddart, 'Cricket, Social Formation and Cultural Continuity in Barbados: A Preliminary Ethnohistory', *Journal of Sport History* (Winter 1987), 14: 317–40.
28. Hamilton, *Cricket in Barbados*, 11. C.L.R. James and P.D.B. Short, 'West Indies', in E.W. Swanton, ed., *Barclays World of Cricket*, 130–31.
29. J.M. Kilburn and M. Coward, 'Australia', in E.W. Swanton, ed., *Barclays World of Cricket*, 61–62.
30. C. Harte, *The History of the Sheffield Shield* (Sydney, 1987), 1–12; and *A History of Australian Cricket* (London, 1993), 1–149. Golesworthy, *Encyclopaedia of Cricket*, 24.
31. Altham and Swanton, *A History of Cricket*, 107. Giffen, *With Bat and Ball*, 5. Holt, 229. R. Sissons, *The Players*, 42–49. P. Mullin and P. Derriman, eds, *Bat and Pad: Writings on Australian Cricket 1804–1984* (Oxford, 1984), 9–11. Webber, *Australians in England*, 9–10.
32. Altham and Swanton, 143. Giffen, 206–09. Grace, *Reminiscences and Recollections*, 104.
33. A. Wrigley, *The Book of Test Cricket* (London, 1965), 11, 19.
34. A.G. Moyes, *Australian Batsmen* (London, 1954), 44–61.
35. Mitchell and Deane, 9.
36. Midwinter, *Grace: Life*, 102.
37. Louis Duffus *et al.*, 'South Africa', in Swanton, ed., *Barclays World of Cricket*, 113.
38. P. Wynne-Thomas, *England on Tour* (London, 1982), 19–30, 33–34, 38–39, 45–46.
39. B. Frindall, ed., *The Wisden Book of Test Records* (London, 1986), 379.
40. Duffus *et al.*, 114.
41. Frindall, ed., 379.
42. C. Bolt, *Victorian Attitudes to Race* (London, 1971), 209–22. D.A. Lorimer, *Colour, Class and the Victorians* (Leicester, 1978), 133–48.

43. D. Birley, *The Willow Wand* (London, 1979), 96. Cashman, 11. Gibson, *Jackson's Year*, 14.
44. *Sporting Daily Mail*, 20 September 1892, 6.
45. C. Harte and W. Hadfield, *Cricket Rebels* (Sydney, 1985), 7–8. Andre Odendaal, 'South Africa's Black Victorians: Sport and Society in South Africa in the Nineteenth Century', in J.A. Mangan, ed., *Pleasure, Profit, Proselytism*, 203–04.
46. Stoddart, 'Cricket and Colonialism'.
47. Quoted in D.A. Allen, *Cricket on the Air* (London, 1985), 91.
48. Fry, *Life Worth Living*, 399–400.
49. 'Aboriginals at Cricket', *Australian Cricket Journal* (April 1987). Mullin and Derriman, 206–11.
50. R. Sissons and B. Stoddart, *Cricket and Empire* (Sydney, 1984), 29–33.
51. Quoted in Green, ed., *Cricket Addict's Archive*, 33.
52. Cashman, 2.
53. *Barbados Advocate*, 1 February 1898, 6–7.
54. *Athletic News*, 25 June 1900, 1.
55. Giffen, 53–54.
56. J.H. Fingleton, *The Immortal Victor Trumper* (Newton Abbot, 1979), 42. R. Robinson, *On Top Down Under* (Melbourne, 1975), 2.
57. Quoted in K.S. Inglis, 'Imperial Cricket: Test Matches between Australia and England 1877–1900', in R. Cashman and M. McKernan, eds, *Sport in History* (Queensland, 1979), 171.
58. Giffen, 54. Robinson, 64.
59. C. Harte, 'Mr. Murdoch's Speech', *Australian Cricket Journal* (April 1987).
60. Sanyal, ix.
61. See, e.g., *Athletic News* 16 February 1881, 4.
62. Fry, 382.
63. Sandiford and Stoddart, *passim*.
64. *Barbados Advocate*, 24 August 1898, 10.
65. *Ibid.*, 24 and 25 January 1900.
66. Ross, 75.
67. Birley, 13. Ranjitsinhji, *Jubilee Book*, 447–49.
68. Bedarida, 145–46.
69. Inglis, 173. Sissons and Stoddart, 29–47.
70. R. Price, *An Imperial War and the British Working Class: Working Class Attitudes and Reactions to the Boer War 1899–1902* (London, 1972), 233–42.

CHAPTER NINE

Close of Play

The Victorians revered cricket as an ancient institution because they sincerely believed that, like the church and the Crown, it had a very useful role to play in English life. The cultural and political leaders of the period looked upon cricket as having specific and vital functions to perform. It was in their view a safety valve for the excess energy of Victorian youth as well as those young men who, in a highly mechanized age, had become far more sedentary and physically inactive than their ancestors. The increasing use of industrial technology meant that more work could be done by fewer people in less time than ever before. Machines left British society with a surplus of energy. Hence the great athletic upheaval of the nineteenth century, of which the upsurge in cricket formed an important part.

Throughout the Victorian age, cricket was regarded by many educators as a great training ground for military and other purposes. At the end of the period Lord Harris was speaking for the vast majority of his contemporaries when he declared that 'Cricket is not only a game, but a school of the greatest social importance.'[1] Half a century earlier in 1841, the Duke of Wellington, as commander in chief of the British army, had issued an order that a cricket ground was to become an adjunct to every military barracks.[2] The Iron Duke obviously agreed with those early Victorians who firmly believed that cricket taught discipline, self-sacrifice and loyalty to team and country. The decree of 1841 ensured that cricket spread not only across the British Isles but to all of those colonies, ports and bases which comprised the expanding empire as well. Moreover, throughout the period 1864–1900, as Benny Green has shrewdly observed, 'cricket was for millions of Englishmen synonymous with Christianity'.[3] When writing about the late-Victorian era, English historian L.C.B. Seaman has also remarked that 'Cricket was associated with religion: just as freemasons referred to God as the Great Architect of the Universe, young cricketers were taught to think of Him as the One Great Scorer, and almost to regard a Straight Bat as second in religious symbolism only to the cross of Jesus.'[4] Indeed, the Victorians came to see cricket as the perfect medium through which could be taught a good deal about ethics, morals, justice, religion and life itself. As Corelli Barnett, the military historian, once remarked, 'Cricket's influence on the upper middle-class British mind, with its sense of orthodoxy and respect for the rules and laws and the impartial authority of umpires, can hardly be exaggerated.'[5]

The Victorians really attached too much significance to the fact that cricket involved a strict adherence to explicit rules and implicit conventions. To them, cricket meant accepting the umpire's verdict without question and thus developing a healthy stoicism. It meant contributing to a larger cause, that of the team, without focusing too narrowly on the self. It certainly could make brave men out of boys who were steeped in the practice of facing up manfully to the fastest bowling. None of these attributes, however, were peculiar to cricket. It took equal courage and self-sacrifice to participate in rugby and soccer, which are palpably more brutal contact sports. But the Victorians viewed the latter as modern and upstart recreations whose laws had only recently been codified. They also believed that rugby and soccer, perhaps because of their explosive nature, too often led to emotional excesses. Cricket boasted a much longer and richer history than most Victorian sports, but even on that score it was not superior to archery, athletics, bowls or golf. Golf, of course, suffered, like curling, from its having been invented by the lowly Scots. It would take England another generation or two to accept the respectability of golf and the English have still not yet managed to master the intricacies of curling.

There is, in the final analysis, no adequate explanation for the Victorian exaltation of cricket. The fact that it was considered an exclusively English invention helped its cause in an age of irrational xenophobia. Even so, soccer had also evolved in a uniquely English fashion – so much so, in fact, that when it spread to foreign lands its terminology was seldom translated into the local vernacular language. The same has also held true for rugby.

At all events, all classes were urged to play cricket for a variety of reasons, not the least of which was that many bourgeois leaders saw the sport as a useful instrument of socialization. The supreme irony here is that cricket signally failed to destroy class distinctions. The separation of the classes was deliberately preserved at all levels of the sport. At the street level, working-class boys played with rudimentary implements and were constantly at the mercy of the local police. There was no mingling of the classes here. At the village level, lower-middle-class players were encouraged by local teachers, priests and businessmen and there was considerable cooperation with working-class participants.[6] The Harrogate club, for instance, was ultimately sustained by the support of the northern proletariat although it was for a long time administered by its bourgeois founders.[7] In the 1880s, too, the Penrith club deliberately tried to encourage working-class participation by admitting 'workingmen, apprentices and youths' for five shillings a year, while gentlemen continued to pay 10s. 6d.[8] As Howat and others have shown, village cricket in the Victorian age was characterized by effective socialization and a noticeable degree of benevolent paternalism, especially on the part of the clergy. But even here, one is left with the impression that classes kept a rather discreet distance, even while playing together on the same sward.

The worst offenders in this regard were the club and county cricketers. Several exclusive cricket clubs flourished after 1850. The majority of them were created by Oxford and Cambridge graduates and the alumni of the famous public schools. Membership was usually by invitation only, and some of them were strictly confined to former students of specific schools. They played mostly among themselves and travelled all across the country to do so at their own expense. Such cricket clubs were non-profit organizations whose players remained amateurs in the truest sense. In essence, they reflected the desire of middle- and upper-class adolescents to continue playing among themselves in their adulthood. The various Blues, Ramblers, Rangers, Rovers and Wanderers, listed by the immortal Haygarth, were but the extensions of Eton, Harrow, Rugby, Uppingham and Winchester, where working-class boys had never been admitted.[9] In a thoughtful and intriguing doctoral thesis on the early years of Rugby Union football, James Martens (one of my own prize pupils) has shown that the middle classes in late-Victorian Britain were divided among themselves in a variety of ways. He detected a very definite split in their approaches to Rugby Union football between public school alumni and others, and between the metropolitan and provincial bourgeoisie. He saw the distinctions between north and south as being crucial to an understanding of the development of both rugby and soccer. Southern middle-class administrators and players were more committed to the amateur code and it was their northern counterparts who led the famous secession from the RFU in the 1890s.[10]

This study of cricket does not reveal any similar ideological differences between London-based bourgeois families and those in the provinces. The Victorian bourgeoisie seemed to approach cricket in essentially identical ways, taking the pragmatic rather than the doctrinaire line when faced with such delicate issues as the shamateurism of their brightest stars and/or the rebelliousness of their ablest professionals. Just as Gloucestershire made numerous concessions to such gentlemen as the Graces during the 1870s and 1880s, Surrey did the same in the 1890s to retain the matchless services of such professionals as Tom Hayward, George Lohmann and Tom Richardson.[11]

Martens marvelled at the ability of the same élite to agree so completely on professionalism in cricket while disagreeing on that issue in soccer and rugby. The fact, however, is that the Victorian bourgeoisie, monolithic or not, tended on the whole to be conservative. They did not think it proper to tamper with the traditional regulations which they found already established in such ancient sports as boxing, cricket and horse racing. So long as corruption, gambling and the more barbarous elements had been eliminated from these fields, the middle-class leaders were satisfied. In the newer sports, they recognized (and seized) the opportunity to play a more prominent role in their development. Hence the debates on such issues as professionalism and shamateurism which took place after 1880 in rugby and soccer. No such animated discussions took place in cricket at that time; such matters had already been decided upon in the pre-Victorian period.

In cricket, during the Victorian age, there were discussions with respect to residence qualifications and winter pay and, in the end, the amateurs succeeded in taking over complete control of the sport and treating the professionals more or less as they wished. As to differences between northern and southern amateurs, very few can be discerned. The most that can be said is that the northern counties traditionally depended mainly on their professionals, while the southern counties did not. Gloucestershire, Hampshire, Middlesex and Somerset fielded mainly amateur elevens throughout the period 1864–1900. For all of these teams, with the exception of Middlesex, the underlying cause was largely economic. These southern counties simply did not have the financial resources to hire several professionals and they were left at a considerable disadvantage by the operation of the residence qualification (which required outsiders to reside two years within the county before being eligible for selection).

Even if it can be argued that the behaviour of the Middlesex county committee reflected the ideology of the southern bourgeoisie which inspired all sports teams to remain more faithful to the amateur code, the Surrey experience would become much more difficult to explain. Profiting, like Middlesex, from its fortunate location in the bustling metropolis, the Surrey CCC was able to engage a large number of professionals and to play competitive cricket throughout the Victorian period. The only difference between Surrey and the northern counties came at the turn of the century when its new president, Sir Richard Webster, Viscount Alverstone, began to insist that as many amateurs as possible be included at all times. Alverstone apparently believed that the dramatic increase in the number of drawn games sprang entirely from the defensive strategies which the professionals were employing with both the bat and the ball. He therefore issued a stern directive to the county selectors in 1900:

> Desirable as it is that the county should always be at the front in county cricket, I certainly do not consider that the championship should be the only object. I should like, if possible, to arrange matters in the future so that at least three places in the eleven in all ordinary county matches should be filled by amateurs.[12]

All that Alverstone's meddling accomplished was the steady decline of Surrey. The county which had won nine titles between 1887 and 1899 was destined to win only one in the next 50 years. The search for young amateurs, which succeeded only in exasperating the veteran professionals, was not always fruitful in any case. In 1900, for instance, apart from D.L.A. Jephson, the captain, the only amateur who represented Surrey with any regularity was Vivian Crawford, who shortly departed to play for his native Leicestershire.[13]

The southern club which seemed most committed to the amateur ideal was the famous Prince's Cricket Club, founded in 1870, under the presidency of the Earl of Cadogan, expressly for the promotion of amateur and genteel cricket. Standing at the very top of the Victorian list of aristocratic cliques, however, it cannot be regarded as representative of the metropolitan bourgeoisie. It attracted some 700 nobles and gentry, prospered for a while, and then perished at the end of that same decade. The death of Prince's, reduced to a programme of 'unusual brevity' in 1878, was then thought to have been the work of 'those heartless foes to open spaces and Sports and Pastimes – the Improvement Mongers and Building Speculators'.[14] But, in fact, by 1880 there was no place in late-Victorian cricket for a club like Prince's. By this time, the county competition and the lower levels of club cricket had become regularized. Amateur cricket could still be played by Free Foresters, Harlequins, Quidnuncs and I Zingari, but the counties now dominated first-class cricket completely. The best amateurs preferred to represent their counties as regularly as they could. This spelt doom for Prince's.

After the fall of Prince's, Hampstead and Wimbledon emerged as the leading bourgeois cricket clubs in the south of England. They fiercely preserved their image of respectability by charging high membership fees. This relatively simple expedient allowed them to restrict their teams to upper- and middle-class players. There was no hint here either of professionalism or of cooperation between the classes.[15]

Victorian cricket clubs, in the final analysis, remained as much separated by class as by geography. The workers were debarred from the bourgeois and aristocratic teams and were reduced to playing among themselves. They seldom competed, for instance, with the more 'respectable' clubs founded by middle-class families like the Bakers in Canterbury, the Brenchleys in Gravesend and the Graces in Downend.[16] The majority of local cricket clubs, even when funded by publicans, priests and landlords, remained essentially working class in composition. There is nothing to suggest, for example, that the Starling Edge XI, so delightfully described by Richard Binns in his popular *Cricket in Firelight*, was untypical of the late-Victorian age.[17] The vast bulk of well-to-do players preferred to join the ranks of the nomadic teams who then roamed all over the kingdom after the manner of I Zingari.

There was thus a considerable degree of snobbery in the bourgeois and aristocratic approach to cricket throughout the Victorian age. Fortunately, however, this was tempered by an equal measure of benevolent paternalism. The wealthy Walkers of Southgate, for instance, gave enormous encouragement and support to the Cricketers' Fund Friendly Society;[18] and Lord Hawke, the famous captain of the Yorkshire CCC at the turn of the century, is well known to have taken a fatherly interest in the affairs of his professional players even though he was very much a martinet on the field.[19] It was this kind of paternalism which inspired wealthy landlords, successful businessmen and prosperous publicans to establish a host of cricket clubs during the nineteenth century.

Hundreds of cricket clubs thus appeared in Britain after 1850. They were conceived essentially as community enterprises supplying a proletarian need. In many villages, the cricket club became the focus of an intense loyalty and parochialism. Legends grew up around fast bowlers and big hitters in the district, and many a local blacksmith became more famous for his cricket than for his craft. No one can doubt that such clubs contributed to local feelings of solidarity and sometimes even stimulated the local economy. The Henfield Cricket Club, for example, became a village institution in Sussex, as did the Lascelles Hall club in Yorkshire.[20] Club cricket provided entertainment for local folk and gave exercise to hundreds of participants, for whom presumably the game served also as a release from the tedium of agricultural or industrial pursuits. If these are the functions of socialization, then the cultural leaders were eminently successful.

Club cricket, in short, had a function or series of functions and this was everywhere recognized. As early indeed as 1845, parliament had seen the need to legalize cricket, which usage had for centuries kept alive in defiance of the law.[21] It must surely also be significant that, in a public speech at Reading in 1891, George Palmer, the celebrated industrialist, found it necessary to argue that education was perhaps as important as cricket in the lives of the proletariat.[22] Another industrialist, Sir Titus Salt, did most in 1869 to establish the Saltaire Cricket Club which for a long time thereafter revolved directly around the Saltaire Mills.[23] As no one was prepared to question the value of club cricket, many teams were kept in operation by local capitalists on the ground that they were as important in a socio-cultural sense as literature, music and the arts.

If the cricket clubs were important to the social leaders, the sport was even more so to the participants. Many working-class players viewed cricket as more than just a game. It was a potential opportunity. If they could play it well enough they might attract sufficient attention to earn a professional contract. Many of them therefore took cricket very seriously indeed. This is very much in accordance with working-class norms both then and later. As Howard Slusher has observed, many workers have seen sport as capable of providing a dimension that permits them to find their own identity.[24] This is usually impossible for them to do in the workplace. The American psychologist, D.S. Butt, has also stressed the determination of underprivileged groups (especially Blacks in the United States) to use sports as a means of striking back at the social system.[25]

Victorian workers, in keeping with Butt's theories of ego-psychology, were all too conscious of their lowly socio-economic status and tried deliberately to overcome their basic feelings of insecurity by excelling on the playing field. It was really in the sporting arena that they often received their only chance. This was noticed at the turn of the century by C.E.B. Russell who, in a careful study of lads in Manchester, lamented the tendency of working-class boys to place too much emphasis on symbols, medals and trophies. They therefore showed none of the *esprit de corps* which so obviously flourished at the public schools. Russell felt that elementary schools should try harder to foster that spirit.[26] Nor was Russell the only critic of working-class attitudes towards sport. Many Victorian observers regretted that the proletariat had in effect transformed play into work. Cricket competition, especially in the north, had become too fierce and too much emphasis was now being put on winning. The critics feared that sportsmanship was departing from the sport when it came to be played in this serious spirit.

The proletarian approach here is most revealing. It provides a good example of cricket being much more than two teams having fun with bat and ball. Northern cricket, with all its seriousness, was really a mirror of northern life at that time. As A.A. Thomson has remarked, life itself was a very serious business in northern England in the wake of the great cotton slump of the 1860s, and the character of northern cricket (and indeed of northern soccer as well) was but a reflection of much harsher realities.[27] Many club cricketers were often underpaid and sometimes underemployed in the mines and the factories. Their ultimate dream was to escape from their poverty through professional cricket (or soccer) at the highest level. They knew that manifest excellence in the minor leagues could result in more lucrative contracts with a county club. That could also lead to invitations to join the ground staff at Lord's, or, better still, to travel with English teams abroad. For many workers, therefore, cricket had long ceased to be child's play. Not surprisingly, the northern counties produced the majority of first-class cricket professionals in the later Victorian period.

Professional cricket thus came to be regarded as a possible avenue of escape from the monotony and stigma of industrial labour. It allowed many workers to find and express their individuality more fully and freely than they could possibly have done otherwise. For the majority, as we have seen, it provided only temporary relief from pennilessness, but at least it permitted them to earn a living from what they could do best. If many of them failed to translate the cricketing opportunity into private fortunes in a financial sense, then it must also be remembered that the psychological and spiritual rewards from performing cricket miracles in public, and being exalted (albeit temporarily) by partisan spectators, cannot possibly be quantified.[28]

For a fortunate few, like George Freeman and William Gunn, professional cricket meant the opening of doors to business and industry that would most surely have otherwise remained closed forever. It must not be forgotten that men like Tom Emmett, George Hirst and Arthur Mold, who finished up far better off than when they started, had been desperately poor when they embarked on their first-class cricket careers. Emmett reported for his first professional engagement with his equipment wrapped in a copy of the local newspaper; he did not even own a suitcase. He had also walked to the cricket ground in clogs. He had no shoes and could afford no other means of transportation. Hirst was very similar, except that he had brought a cheap canvas bag in which to carry his paltry belongings. When Mold had his first trial with Lancashire, he bowled with his sweater on and could not remove it since he wore no shirt underneath.[29] Cricket gave men like these a chance to buy something as basic as clothing. It is not to be wondered at that they took the game so seriously.

It is far more difficult to explain why so many of them chose to remain in cricket after soccer had emerged as a more lucrative source of income. Only a small minority of professional cricketers also played soccer professionally in the winter. Soccer, however, was a simpler and cheaper sport in which to participate. A whole soccer team required only one ball, and even as late as 1900 soccer boots could be purchased at 9s. 6d. a pair. Workers could afford therefore to specialize in soccer. A complete cricketer's outfit, meanwhile, was much more expensive. It cost as least £2 10s. in 1881, which was then almost two weeks' wages for a non-skilled worker.[30] Apart from this, professionalism in cricket remained financially stagnant for almost a hundred years before it was rescued in the late 1970s by the infamous Packer Circus. Even when the counties began to open their doors in the late 1960s, to the great international stars like Gary Sobers, cricket professionals remained vastly underpaid in relationship to other sportsmen. It is also worthy of special comment that, from the very beginning, Australian 'amateur' cricketers have received better monetary rewards for their services than the English professionals.[31]

This was not due to greed or indifference on the part of the Victorian cricket clubs and county committees. Some county cricket clubs operated throughout the Victorian age in dire financial straits and even the more successful counties had no choice but to plough most of their profits back into the sport. Some clubs, operating in very small markets such as those in Derbyshire, Essex, Somerset, Sussex and Worcestershire, simply did not have the resources to offer generous contracts and substantial winter payments to their players.[32] The bald fact is that cricket was never a viable financial proposition. Had it not been for the steady transfusion of millions of pounds throughout its veins, by great tobacco firms such as Rothman's and Benson and Hedges, first-class cricket in England might well have perished after the Second World War.[33]

Mandle, Mason and others have rightly argued that professional sport in the Victorian age did not often lead to wealth and happiness. But it distorts Victorian social history to focus only on the professionals in this manner. To stress that many working-class men failed to escape, through cricket or soccer, from their original status might suggest that there was something innately wrong with the proletarian psyche and approach. We can disabuse ourselves of this idea by observing that Archie MacLaren, the great amateur who captained Lancashire and England, also failed signally in a series of business ventures. 'At various times,' we are told by his biographer, MacLaren

> obtained income from, among other ideas: journalism; radio broadcasting; advertising; hotel ownership; bloodstock agent; banking; cotton merchant; marketing of cricket equipment, including the invention of pneumatic pads and bats made from imported Spanish willow; whisky salesman; motor-car salesman; film extra in Hollywood; cricket magazine editor; cricket coach; lecturing; hiring out cricket films; manager of a private team; schoolmaster; personal secretary to Prince Ranjitsinhji; assistant secretary to Lancashire CCC.
>   It can honestly be said that not one of these ventures was ever remotely successful, but Archie never tired of trying to interest people in his latest idea.[34]

MacLaren's propensity for gambling made his situation much worse, and it is clear that had he sprung from working-class roots he would certainly have died in equally dire straits. By the beginning of the twentieth century, the county committees had established the principle of placing the professionals' benefit proceeds in a special fund to protect cricketers from the consequences of their own negligence and folly. When the Lancashire committee attempted to do the same for MacLaren, who earned in excess of £1,000 from his testimonial in 1905, he haughtily demurred. He promptly invested most of the proceeds in a new sports car, much to the annoyance of his benefactors.[35]

MacLaren was the second son of a successful cotton merchant and shipping agent based in Manchester. His family, though not wealthy, could help him to stay financially afloat in spite of himself. But much less fortunate was Robert Lipscomb, described by *Wisden* as 'one of the fastest and straightest amateur fast bowlers of his day'.[36] He left his widow and two daughters 'totally unprovided for' when he died in 1895.[37] No doubt there were other amateurs who fared no better at that time.

It is clear, then, that cricket failed during the Victorian age to bridge the gap between the classes, allowed only a select few from the professional ranks to rise beyond their initial state of poverty, and was itself conspicuously unprofitable as a commercial or financial proposition. Cricket nevertheless became a national symbol, perhaps because society did not really intend it to accomplish any of these miracles. If Victorian cricket failed in these respects, so too did the historic institutions like parliament, church and Crown. These institutions appealed to Englishmen more perhaps because of their peculiar Englishness than their ability to fulfil any specific functions. The Crown was revered in Victorian England primarily because it had been the first among all the great European monarchies to become constitutionalized. The Victorian parliament held a special place in all English hearts because it was the first legislative assembly throughout Europe to control the national purse and to dominate the public law. The Anglican Church represented the peculiar English compromise between Roman Catholicism and various European strands of Protestantism. There was no other Church quite like it, even though it had much in common with every other Christian sect. Cricket was in the same category. It represented an exclusively Anglo-Saxon contribution to civilization. It therefore stood as further evidence of English cultural supremacy, and if the Irish, Scots and Welsh played the game with far less enthusiasm or competence than they did soccer or rugby, that was rather a reflection on their philistinism than on any weakness inherent in cricket itself.

The cricketing cult prospered during the nineteenth century because it also formed part of the wider cult of athleticism which was then dominant. The Victorians were too much obsessed with the idea that a healthy mind depended upon the development of a robust body. Every good Christian therefore had to be strong and manly. This doctrine of muscular Christianity, supported by so many segments of Victorian society, certainly gave a stimulus to the sports explosion.

There was, of course, a religious base for this complex phenomenon. As R.C.K. Ensor has rightly emphasized, the Victorians were an intensely religious people.[38] Religion dominated their domestic politics to a remarkable degree. Factory acts, education bills, prison reforms and even Corn Law repeal were all treated in quasi-religious terms. But, as Bruce Haley has demonstrated, the Victorians were even more worried about their bodies than their souls. Good health was uppermost in their thoughts for the simple reason that it could never be taken for granted. The Victorians lived in mortal fear of typhoid, cholera, measles, influenza, pneumonia and an assortment of ailments which they lumped together under the general umbrella of 'gout'. No one can read the private correspondence of their political leaders without being struck by their constant preoccupation with the question of their own health. Physiology and religion became, indeed, the twin pillars of Victorianism. These were skilfully fused together in the philosophy of men as far apart temperamentally as the Arnolds, Carlyle, Hughes, Kingsley, Manning, Ruskin and Spencer.[39]

The result was a fetish for exercise. Kinetic activity was the instinctive Victorian response to the fear of death and disease. The Victorians came to see physical education as the most effective antidote to illness: exercise strengthened the physique and thereby immunized it from the majority of the common perils with which it then had to cope. Physical exercise did far more than just that – it also made men mentally alert and spiritually more adequate; for there was, in the Victorian mind, too close an interconnection between body and soul. The physique and the psyche were but opposite sides of the same coin. Cricket, like all sports in general, was in a very real sense a form of escape for the Victorians. It was an escape from death as well from the realities of life itself.

Notes

1. J.D. Coldham, *Lord Harris* (London, 1983), 109.
2. Swanton, ed., *World of Cricket*, 42. West, *Elevens of England*, 1.
3. B. Green, ed., *Wisden Anthology 1864–1900* (London, 1979), 4.
4. Cited in *ibid.*, 5.
5. Cited in *ibid.*, 6.
6. See, e.g., Greaves, *Over the Summers Again*. Harbottle, *Century of Cricket in South Northumberland*. Howat, *Village Cricket*. Hurst, *Century of Penrith Cricket*.
7. Greaves, *passim*.
8. Hurst, 26.
9. Haygarth, *Scores and Biographies*, VI: 395.
10. J.W. Martens, 'Rugby Union Football and English Society 1871–1914', PhD thesis submitted to the University of Manitoba, 1988.
11. Sissons, *Players*, 105–12.
12. Lemmon, *Surrey County Cricket Club*, 105–06.
13. *Ibid.*, 108. See also Webber, *County Championship*, 23–63.
14. *Wisden 1872*, 74–75; and *1879*, 101.
15. Monro, *History of Hampstead Cricket Club*. Wakley, *History of Wimbledon Cricket Club*.
16. Midwinter, *Grace: Life*, 11.
17. Binns, *Cricket in Firelight*, 39.
18. *Wisden 1885*, 106; and *1887*, xix.
19. Gordon, *Background of Cricket*, 115–18. Hodgson, *Yorkshire County*

Cricket Club, 47–48. Kilburn, History of Yorkshire Cricket, 25–28. Warner, Long Innings, 42–43.

20. Greaves, 70–72. Hodgson, 20–21. H.F. and A.P. Squire, Henfield Cricket and its Sussex Cradle, 74, 121–22.
21. Midwinter, 10.
22. S. Yeo, Religion and Voluntary Organizations in Crisis (London, 1976), 36.
23. Saltaire Cricket Club, Souvenir Centenary Booklet, 3.
24. H.S. Slusher, Man, Sport, and Existence: A Critical Analysis (Philadelphia, 1967), 12–25.
25. D.S. Butt, Psychology of Sport (New York, 1976), 4–10, 21–25.
26. C.E.B. Russell, Manchester Boys (Manchester, 1905), 82–87.
27. Thomson, Cricket: Wars of the Roses, 13.
28. See, e.g., D. Dougan and P.M. Young, On the Spot: Football as a Profession (Newton Abbot, 1975), 12–13.
29. Thomson, Hirst and Rhodes, 27–28.
30. J.I. Marder, 'Buying Back One's Past', Wisden 1975, 143–46.
31. See, e.g., Robinson, On Top Down Under, 11, 68.
32. Sandiford and Vamplew, 'The Peculiar Economics of English Cricket', passim.
33. K.A.P. Sandiford, 'The Professionalization of Modern Cricket', British Journal of Sports History (December 1985), 2: 270–89.
34. M. Down, Archie: A Biography of A.C. MacLaren (London, 1981), 5.
35. Ibid., 6, 111–12.
36. Quoted in B. Green, ed., Wisden Obituaries, 554.
37. Cricket Field, 2 March 1895, 31.
38. R.C.K. Ensor, England: 1870–1914 (Oxford, 1936), 137.
39. Haley, The Healthy Body. See also A.S. Wohl, Endangered Lives: Public Health in Victorian Britain (Harvard, 1983).

Bibliography

I. NEWSPAPERS AND PERIODICALS

All the Year Round
Athlete
Athletic Chat
Athletic Chronicle
Athletic News
Athletic Record
Athletic Review
Athletic Sports and Pastimes
Athletic Star
Athletic World
Australian Cricket Journal
Badminton Magazine of Sports and Pastimes
Baily's Monthly Magazine of Sports and Pastimes
Barbados Advocate
Barbados Agricultural Reporter
Bell's Life in London
Blackwood's Magazine
British Sport
C.B. Fry's Magazine
Cricket
Cricket and Football Times
Cricketer
Cricketers' and Sporting News
Cricketers' Herald
Cricket Field
Daily Telegraph
English Sports
Fortnightly Review
Frederick Lillywhite's Guide to Cricketers
Illustrated Sporting and Dramatic News
Illustrated Sporting and Theatrical News

Illustrated Sporting News
James Lillywhite's Cricketers' Annual
John Lillywhite's Cricketer's Companion
Listener
Midland Athlete
Midland Sporting News
News of the World
Pastime
Sporting Chronicle
Sporting Clipper
Sporting Daily Mail
Sporting Echo
Sporting Gazette
Sporting Life
Sporting Mirror
Sporting Opinion
Sporting Record
Sporting Review
Sporting World
Sportsman
Sports Telegraph
The Field
The Times
Wisden Cricketers' Almanack

II. OTHER SOURCES

Adamson, J.A. *Denstone Cricket 1874–1952* (London, 1954).
Ainger, A.C. *Memories of Eton Sixty Years Ago* (London, 1917).
Alcock, C.W. *Cricket* (London, 1882).
——— *Famous Cricketers and Cricket Grounds* (London, 1895).
——— *Cricket Stories Wise and Otherwise* (London, 1901).
Allen, D.R. *Cricket on the Air* (London, 1985).
Allison, L. 'Batsman and Bowler: The Key Relation of Victorian England',
    Journal of Sport History (Summer, 1980), 7: 5–20.
Altham, H.S. *A History of Cricket* (London, 1926).
——— and Swanton, E.W. *A History of Cricket* (London, 1948).
——— *et al.*, *Hampshire County Cricket* (London, 1958).
Altick, R.D. *Victorian People and Ideas* (New York, 1973).
Annan, N.G. *Leslie Stephen: His Thought and Character in Relation to
    His Time* (London, 1951).
——— *Roxburgh of Stowe* (London, 1965).

Anderson, W. *Selkirk Cricket Club Centenary 1851–1951* (Galashiels, 1956).

Arlott, J. *From Hambledon to Lord's* (London, 1948).

———— *The Middle Ages of Cricket* (London, 1949).

———— *Concerning Cricket* (London, 1949).

———— *Rothmans Jubilee History of Cricket 1890–1965* (London, 1965).

Armitage, J. *Man at Play: Nine Centuries of Pleasure Making* (London, 1977).

Arnold, M. *Culture and Anarchy* (London, 1869).

Arrowsmith, R.L. *A History of County Cricket: Kent* (Newton Abbot, 1972).

———— and Hill, B.J.W. *The History of I Zingari* (London, 1982).

Ashley Cooper, F.S. *Gentlemen vs Players* (Bristol, 1900).

———— *Chats on the Cricket Field* (London, 1910).

———— *Edward Grace Mills, Cricketer* (London, 1916).

———— *Eton vs Harrow at the Wicket* (London, 1922).

———— *Kent County Cricket* (London, 1923).

———— *Nottingham Cricket and Cricketers* (Nottingham, 1923).

———— *Derbyshire County Cricket* (London, 1924).

———— *Gloucestershire County Cricket* (London, 1924).

———— *Hampshire County Cricket* (London, 1924).

———— *The Hambledon Cricket Chronicle, 1772–96* (Nottingham, 1924).

———— *Cricket Highways and Byways* (London, 1927).

Aspin, C. *Gone Cricket Mad: The Haslingden Club in the Victorian Era* (Manchester, 1976).

Association of Cricket Statisticians, *Warwickshire Cricketers 1843–1973* (Nottingham, 1974).

———— *Worcestershire Cricketers 1899–1974* (Nottingham, 1975).

———— *Somersetshire Cricketers 1875–1974* (Nottingham, 1975).

———— *Middlesex Cricketers 1850–1976* (Nottingham, 1977).

———— *Leicestershire Cricketers 1879–1977* (Nottingham, 1978).

———— *Nottinghamshire Cricketers 1835–1978* (Nottingham, 1979).

———— *Surrey Cricketers 1839–1980* (Nottingham, 1980).

———— *Gloucestershire Cricketers 1870–1979* (Nottingham, 1980).

———— *Irish Cricketers 1855–1980* (Nottingham, 1981).

———— *Scottish Cricketers 1905–1980* (Nottingham, 1981).

———— *Derbyshire Cricketers 1871–1981* (Retford, 1982).

———— *Hampshire Cricketers 1800–1982* (Retford, 1983).

———— *Kent Cricketers 1834–1983* (Retford, 1983).

———— *Northamptonshire Cricketers 1905–1984* (Retford, 1984).

———— *Yorkshire Cricketers 1863–1985* (Retford, 1986).

———— *Essex Cricketers 1876–1986* (Retford, 1987).

———— *Glamorgan Cricketers 1888–1987* (Nottingham, 1988).

———— *Lancashire Cricketers 1865–1988* (Nottingham, 1989).

———— *Sussex Cricketers 1815–1990* (Nottingham, 1991).

———— *Barbados Cricketers 1865–1990* (Nottingham, 1991).

Bagshaw, H. and E. *Great Oakley Cricket: The History of a Village Club* (Northampton, 1964).

Bailey, P.C. 'A Mingled Mass of Perfectly Legitimate Pleasures: The Victorian Middle Class and the Problem of Leisure', *Victorian Studies* (Autumn, 1977), 21: 7–28.

———— *Leisure and Class in Victorian England: Rational Recreation and the Contest for Control, 1830–1885* (London, 1978).

Bailey, P.J. *et al.*, *Who's Who of Cricketers* (London, 1984).

Bailey, T.E. *A History of Cricket* (London, 1979).

Baker, W.J. 'The Leisure Revolution in Victorian England: A Review of Recent Literature', *Journal of Sport History* (1979), 6: 76–87.

———— *Sports in the Western World* (New Jersey, 1982).

———— 'The State of British Sport History', *Journal of Sport History* (Spring, 1983), 10: 53–66.

Bamford, T.W. *Thomas Arnold* (London, 1960).

———— *The Rise of the Public Schools* (London, 1967).

Barlow, R.G. *Forty Seasons of First-Class Cricket* (Manchester, 1908).

Barty-King, H. *Quilt Winders and Pod Shavers: The History of Cricket Bat and Ball Manufacture* (London, 1979).

Bearshaw, B. *From the Stretford End: The Official History of Lancashire County Cricket Club* (London, 1990).

Bedarida, F. *A Social History of England 1851–1975*, trans. A.S. Foster (London, 1979).

Beldham, G.W. and Fry, C.B. *Great Batsmen: Their Methods at a Glance* (London, 1905).

———— *Great Bowlers and Fielders: Their Methods at a Glance* (London, 1906).

Bennett, G. ed., *The Concept of Empire: Burke to Attlee 1774–1947* (London, 1953).

Benson, D.H. *Harborne Cricket Club 1868–1968* (Birmingham, 1969).

Berkeley, G.F.H. *My Recollections of Wellington College* (Newport, 1946).

Best, G.F.A. *Mid-Victorian Britain, 1851–75* (London, 1971).

Bettesworth, W.A. *The Walkers of Southgate* (London, 1900).

———— *Chats on the Cricket Field* (London, 1910).

Betts, J.R. 'The Technological Revolution and the Rise of Sport, 1850–1900', in J.W. Loy and G.S. Kenyon, eds, *Sport, Culture, and Society* (Toronto, 1969), 145–66.

Binfield, C. *George Williams and the YMCA* (London, 1973).

Binns, R. *Cricket in Firelight* (Sportsmans Book Club, 1955).

Birley, D. *The Willow Wand: Some Cricket Myths Explored* (London, 1979).

Blunden, E. *Cricket Country* (London, 1944).

Bolt, C. *Victorian Attitudes to Race* (London, 1971).

Bolton, G. *A History of the O.U.C.C.* (Oxford, 1962).

Bovill, E.W. *The England of Nimrod and Surtees 1815–54* (London, 1959).

———— *English Country Life 1780–1830* (London, 1962).

Bowen, D. *The Idea of the Victorian Church* (Montreal, 1968).

Bowen, R. *Cricket: A History of its Growth and Development Throughout the World* (London, 1970).

Box, C. *The English Game of Cricket* (London, 1877).

Boyd, A.K. *The History of Radley College, 1847–1947* (Oxford, 1948).

Bradfield, D. *A Century of Village Cricket* (London, 1946).

———— *A History of the Box Cricket Club* (London, 1970).

———— *The Lansdown Story* (London, 1971).

Bradley, A.G. *et al.*, *A History of Marlborough College* (London, 1923).

Britton, C.J. *G.L. Jessop* (London, 1935).

Brodribb, G. *All Round the Wicket* (London, 1951).

———— *Next Man In* (Sportsmans Book Club, 1953).

———— *The Book of Cricket Verse* (London, 1953).

———— *Hit For Six* (Sportsmans Book Club, 1961).

———— *Felix on the Bat* (London, 1962).

———— *The Croucher: A Biography of Gilbert Jessop* (London, 1974).

Brohm, J.M. *Sport: A Prison of Measured Time* (London, 1978).

Brooke, R. *John Edward Shilton's Book: Triumph and Disasters of a Warwickshire Cricketer* (Derby, 1984).

Brookes, C. *English Cricket: The Game and its Players Through the Ages* (Newton Abbot, 1978).

Brown, A. *The Pictorial History of Cricket* (London, 1988).

Brown, L.H. *Victor Trumper and the 1902 Australians* (London, 1981).

Brownlee, W. Methven *W.G. Grace: A Biography* (London, 1887).

Buckley, G.B. *Fresh Light on Eighteenth Century Cricket* (Birmingham, 1935).

———— *Fresh Light on Pre-Victorian Cricket* (Birmingham, 1937).

Burn, W.L. *The Age of Equipoise: A Study of the Mid-Victorian Generation, 1852–70* (London, 1964).

Burnell, R.D. *The Henley Regatta: A History* (London, 1957).

Burstyn, J. *Victorian Education and the Ideal of Womanhood* (London, 1980).

Burton, E. *The Early Victorians at Home* (Newton Abbot, 1973).

Butt, D.S. *The Psychology of Sport* (New York, 1976).

Caffyn, W. *Seventy-One Not Out* (London, 1899).

Canynge Caple, S. *England v India 1886–1959* (Worcester, 1959).

———— *Thornbury Cricket Club 1871–1971* (London, 1972).

Cardus, N. *A Cricketer's Book* (London, 1926).

———— *Cricket* (London, 1930).

———— *English Cricket* (London, 1945).

Carman, A.H. *Wellington Cricket Centenary 1875–1975* (New Zealand, 1975).

Cashman, R. *Patrons, Players and the Crowd: The Phenomenon of Indian Cricket* (New Delhi, 1980).

———— *'Ave a Go, Yer Mug! Australian Cricket Crowds from Larrikin to Ocker* (Sydney, 1984).

———— *The 'Demon' Spofforth* (New South Wales, 1990).

———— and McKernan, M. eds, *Sport in History* (Queensland, 1979).

———— *Sport: Money, Morality and the Media* (New South Wales, 1982).

Chandos, J. *Boys Together: English Public Schools, 1800–1864* (Oxford, 1984).

Chapman, B. 'Following Leicestershire', *Wisden 1964*, 152–53

Chester, G.J. *The Young Men at Rest and at Play* (London, 1860).

Chignell, W.R. *A History of the Worcestershire County Cricket Club 1844–1950* (Worcester, undated).

Clayre, A. *Work and Play: Ideas and Experience of Work and Leisure* (London, 1974).

Coldham, J.D. *Northamptonshire Cricket: A History* (London, 1959).

———— *William Brockwell: His Triumph and Tragedy* (London, 1970).

———— *Lord Harris* (London, 1983).

Cole, K.J. *Two Hundred Years of Dorking Cricket 1768–1968* (London, 1969).

Conacher, J.B. *Waterloo to the Common Market* (New York, 1975).

Constantine, L.N. *Cricket in the Sun* (London, undated).

Country Vicar, A. *Cricket Memories* (London, 1930).

———— *The Happy Cricketer* (London, 1946).

Courtney, S. *As Centuries Blend: One Hundred and Six Years of Clydesdale Cricket Club* (Glasgow, 1954).

Cousins, G. *Golf in Britain: A Social History* (London, 1975).

Cuming, E.D. ed., *Squire Osbaldeston: His Autobiography* (London, 1926).

Cunningham, H. *Leisure in the Industrial Revolution* (London, 1980).

Curzon, G.N. *Problems of the Far East* (London, 1894).

Cust, L.H. *A History of Eton College* (London, 1899).

Daft, R. *Kings of Cricket* (Bristol, 1893).

——— *A Cricketer's Yarns* (London, 1926).

Dalby, K. *Headingley Test Cricket 1899–1975* (Ilkley, 1976).

Dale, B. *The Influence of the Weather on the Wicket* (London, 1891).

Darwin, B. *W.G. Grace* (London, 1934).

Day, A. and Cox, D. *The History of Hornsey Cricket Club 1870–1970* (London, 1970).

Day, H. *Luck of the Toss* (Sportsmans Book Club, 1971).

De Grazia, S. *Of Time, Work, and Leisure* (New York, 1962).

Devereux, B. *A Century of Cricket: Nottingham Forest Amateur Cricket Club* (Nottingham, 1976).

Diggle, J.W. *Godliness and Manliness* (London, 1887).

Dobbs, B. *Edwardians at Play: Sport 1890–1914* (London, 1973).

Dougan, D. and Young, P.M. *On the Spot: Football as a Profession* (Newton Abbot, 1975).

Down, M. *Archie: A Biography of A.C. MacLaren* (London, 1981).

Duckworth, L. *S.F. Barnes: Master Bowler* (Sportsmans Book Club, 1968).

——— *The Story of Warwickshire Cricket* (London, 1974).

Dumazedier, J. *Sociology of Leisure* (Amsterdam, 1974).

Dunae, P. *Gentlemen Emigrants: From the British Public Schools to the Canadian Frontier* (Vancouver, 1981).

Dunning E. ed., *Sport: Readings from a Sociological Perspective* (Toronto, 1972).

——— and Sheard, K. *Barbarians, Gentlemen and Players: A Sociological Study of the Development of Rugby Football* (New York, 1979).

Dyos, H.J. and Wolff, M. eds, *The Victorian City: Images and Realities*. 2 vols (London, 1973).

Eames, G.L. *Bromley Cricket Club 1820–1970* (Bromley, 1970).

Edwards, H. *Sociology of Sport* (Illinois, 1973).

Ellis, C. *C.B.: The Life of Charles Burgess Fry* (London, 1984).

Ensor, R.C.K. *England 1870–1914* (Oxford, 1936).

Escott, T.H.S. *Social Transformations of the Victorian Age* (London, 1897).

Evans, R.D.C. *Cricket Grounds: The Evolution, Maintenance and Construction of Natural Turf Cricket Tables and Outfields* (Bingley, 1991).

Fingleton, J.H. *The Immortal Victor Trumper* (Newton Abbot, 1979).

Fitzgerald, R.A. *Wickets in the West* (London, 1873).

Fletcher, C.R.L. *Edmund Warre* (London, 1922).

Ford, J. *Cricket: A Social History, 1700–1835* (Newton Abbot, 1972).

Ford, W.J. ed., *Cricket* (London, 1897).
———— *Middlesex County Cricket Club, 1864–99* (London, 1900).
———— *A History of Cambridge University Cricket Club* (London, 1902).
Forrest, A.J. *Village Cricket* (London, 1957).
Foster, D. and Arnold, P. *A Hundred Years of Test Cricket: England vs Australia* (London, 1977).
Fraser, M.F.K. 'Warwickshire's Ups and Downs', *Wisden 1950*, 88–91.
Frewin, L. *The Boundary Book* (London, 1962).
———— *The Poetry of Cricket* (London, 1964).
———— *The Best of Cricket Fiction* (London, 1966).
Frindall, B. *The Wisden Book of County Cricket* (London, 1981).
———— *The Wisden Book of Test Cricket 1877–1984* (London, 1985).
———— *The Wisden Book of Cricket Records* (London, 1986).
———— *England Test Cricketers* (London, 1989).
Frith, D. *The Fast Men* (Newton Abbot, 1976).
———— *'My Dear Victorious Stod': A Biography of A.E. Stoddart* (London, 1977).
———— *The Golden Age of Cricket 1890–1914* (London, 1978).
———— *The Slow Men* (New South Wales, 1984).
Fry, C.B. *The Book of Cricket* (London, 1900).
———— *Life Worth Living* (London, 1939; repr. 1986).
Gale, F. *Public School Matches* (London, 1867).
———— *Modern English Sports: Their Use and Abuse* (London, 1885).
———— *Life of Hon. Robert Grimston* (London, 1885).
———— *The Game of Cricket* (London, 1887).
———— *Sports and Recreations in Town and Country* (London, 1888).
———— *Echoes from Old Cricket Fields* (London, 1896).
Gale, N. *Cricket Songs* (London, 1894).
Gaston, A.J. *Curiosities of Cricket* (London, 1897).
Gibson, A. 'Lillywhite's Men', *Listener*, 97: 340.
———— *Jackson's Year* (Sportsmans Book Club, 1966).
———— *The Cricket Captains of England* (London, 1979).
Giffen, G. *With Bat and Ball* (London, 1898).
Gilligan, A.E.R. 'Sussex Through the Years', *Wisden 1954*, 109–13.
Glanville, B. *People in Sport* (London, 1970).
Golby, J. and Purdue, A.W. *The Civilisation of the Crowd: Popular Culture in England 1750–1900* (London, 1984).
Golesworthy, M. *The Encyclopaedia of Cricket* (Sportsmans Book Club, 1964).
Gordon, Sir H. *Background of Cricket* (London, 1939).
Gorham, D. *The Victorian Girl and the Feminine Ideal* (Indiana, 1982).
Grace, W.G. *Cricket* (Bristol, 1891).

——— *The History of a Hundred Centuries* (London, 1895).

——— *Cricketing Reminiscences and Personal Recollections* (London, 1899).

Grayson, E. *Corinthians and Cricketers* (Sportsmans Book Club, 1957).

Greaves, G.L. *Over the Summers Again: A History of Harrogate Cricket Club* (London, 1976).

Green, B. ed., *The Cricket Addict's Archive* (Newton Abbot, 1977).

——— ed., *Wisden Anthology, 1864–1900* (London, 1979).

——— ed., *Wisden Anthology 1900–1940* (London, 1980).

——— ed., *Wisden Anthology 1940–1963* (London, 1982).

——— ed., *The Wisden Book of Obituaries* (London, 1986).

——— *A History of Cricket* (London, 1988).

Green, G. *The Official History of the F.A. Cup* (Sportsmans Book Club, 1960).

Grimble, A. *A Pattern of Islands* (London, 1952).

Grimsley, W. *A Century of Sports* (Associated Press, 1971).

Gutteridge, L.E.S. 'A History of Wisden', *Wisden 1963*, 74–88.

Haley, B.E. 'Sports and the Victorian World', *Western Humanities Review* (1968), 12: 115–25.

——— *The Healthy Body and Victorian Culture* (Harvard, 1978).

Hamilton, B. *Cricket in Barbados* (Bridgetown, 1947).

Hammond, J.L. *The Growth of Common Enjoyment* (London, 1933).

Harbottle, G. *A Century of Cricket in South Northumberland 1864–1969* (Newcastle upon Tyne, 1969).

Hardy, A. *Queen Victoria was Amused* (London, 1976).

Hargreaves, J. *Sport, Power and Culture* (Cambridge, 1986).

Harrington, H.R. 'Charles Kingsley's Fallen Athlete', *Victorian Studies* (Autumn, 1977), 21: 73–86.

Harris, H.A. *Sport in Britain: Its Origin and Development* (London, 1975).

Harris, Lord *A History of Kent County Cricket* (London, 1907).

——— *A Few Short Runs* (London, 1921).

Harrison, B.H. 'Religion and Recreation in Nineteenth Century England', *Past and Present* (December 1967), 38: 98–125.

——— *Drink and the Victorians: The Temperance Question in England 1815–1872* (London, 1971).

Harte, C. *The History of the Sheffield Shield* (Sydney, 1987).

——— *A History of Australian Cricket* (London, 1993).

——— and Hadfield, W. *Cricket Rebels* (Sydney, 1985).

Haygarth, A. *Scores and Biographies*. 15 vols (London, 1862–76).

Haynes, B. and Lucas, J. *The Trent Bridge Battery: The Story of the Sporting Gunns* (London, 1985).

Hemyng, B. *Jack Harkaway at Oxford* (London, 1872).

Higgins, F. *Findon Cricket Club 1867–1967* (London, 1967).

Hignell, A. *The History of Glamorgan County Cricket Club* (London, 1988).

Hoberman, J.M. *Sport and Political Ideology* (London, 1984).

Hodgson, D. *The Official History of Yorkshire County Cricket Club* (London, 1989).

Holmes, R.S. *The County Cricket Championship* (London, 1894).

———— *Surrey Cricket and Cricketers* (London, 1896).

———— *History of Yorkshire Cricket* (London, 1904).

Holt, R. *Sport and the British: A Modern History* (Oxford, 1989).

Houghton, W.E. *The Victorian Frame of Mind* (Yale, 1966).

Howat, G. *Village Cricket* (London, 1980).

Hughes, T. *Tom Brown's Schooldays* (London, 1857).

———— *Tom Brown at Oxford* (London, 1869).

———— *The Manliness of Christ* (London, 1879).

———— *James Fraser: A Memoir* (London, 1889).

Huizinga, J. *Homo Ludens: A Study of the Play Element in Culture* (London, 1949).

Hurst, J.L. *Century of Penrith Cricket* (Cumberland, 1967).

Hyam, R. *Britain's Imperial Century, 1815–1914* (London, 1976).

Ibrahim, H. *Sport and Society* (California, 1976).

Inglis, F. *The Name of the Game: Sport and Society* (London, 1977).

Inglis, K.S. *The Churches and the Working Classes in Victorian England* (London, 1963).

Jackson, N.L. *Sporting Days and Sporting Ways* (London, 1932).

James, C.L.R. 'Cricket in West Indian Culture', *New Society* (1963): 8–9.

———— *Beyond a Boundary* (Sportsmans Book Club, 1964).

Jessop, G.L. *A Cricketer's Log* (London, 1926).

Jeyes, S.H. 'Our Gentlemanly Failures', *Fortnightly Review* (1 March 1897).

Joy, N. *Maiden Over: A Short History of Women's Cricket* (London, 1950).

Joyce, P. *Work, Society and Politics: The Culture of the Factory in Late Victorian England* (London, 1980).

Kaplan, M. *Leisure: Theory and Policy* (New York, 1975).

Kay, J. 'League Cricket', in E.W. Swanton, ed., *The World of Cricket* (London, 1966), 680–711.

———— *Cricket in the Leagues* (London, 1970).

———— *A History of County Cricket: Lancashire* (Newton Abbot, 1974).

———— 'League Cricket – the North and the Midlands: the Story to 1964', in E.W. Swanton, ed., *Barclays World of Cricket* (London, 1986) 571–75.

Kilburn, J.M. *A History of Yorkshire Cricket* (Sportsmans Book Club, 1971).

———— 'Over 100 Years of Scarborough Festivities', *Wisden 1977*, 151–53.

Kingsley, C. *Health and Education* (London, 1874).

Knight, A.E. *The Complete Cricketer* (London, 1906).

Kynaston, D. *Bobby Abel: Professional Batsman* (London, 1982).

Laborde, E.D. *Harrow School Yesterday and Today* (London, 1948).

Lansbury, C. 'A Straight Bat and a Modest Mind', *Victorian Newsletter*, 49: 9–18.

Ledbrooke, A.W. *Lancashire County Cricket: The Official History: 1864–1953* (London, 1954).

Lee, A.J. *The Origins of the Popular Press, 1855–1914* (London, 1976).

Lee, C. *From the Sea End: The Official History of Sussex County Cricket Club* (London, 1989).

Lemmon, D. *'Tich' Freeman and the Decline of the Leg-Break Bowler* (London, 1982).

———— *Cricket Mercenaries: Overseas Players in English Cricket* (London, 1987).

———— *The Official History of Middlesex County Cricket Club* (London, 1988).

———— *The Official History of Surrey County Cricket Club* (London, 1989).

———— *The Official History of Worcestershire County Cricket Club* (London, 1989).

Lester, J.H. *Bat vs Ball, 1864–1900* (London, 1900).

Leveson Gower, Sir H.D.G. *Off and On the Field* (London, 1953).

Lewis, T. *Double Century: The Story of MCC and Cricket* (London, 1987).

Lewis, W.J. *The Language of Cricket* (Oxford, 1938).

Lilley, A.A. *Twenty-Four Years of Cricket* (London, 1912).

Lillywhite, F. *The English Cricketers' Trip to Canada and the United States in 1859* (London, 1860: repr., with a long introduction by Robin Marlar, London, 1980).

Lloyd, T. *The British Empire 1558–1983* (Oxford, 1984).

Lorimer, D.A. *Colour, Class and the Victorians* (Leicester, 1978).

Lowerson, J. and Myerscough, J. *Time to Spare in Victorian England* (Sussex, 1977).

Loy, J.W. and Kenyon, G.S. eds, *Sport, Culture and Society* (Toronto, 1969).

Lubbock, P. *Shades of Eton* (London, 1929).

Lyttelton, R.H. *Cricket* (London, 1898).

———— et al., *Giants of the Game* (London, 1899: repr., with an introduction by John Arlott, Newton Abbot, 1974).

Mackenzie, J. ed., *Imperialism and Popular Culture* (Manchester, 1986).

Malcolmson, R.W. *Popular Recreations in English Society*, 1700–1850 (Cambridge, 1973).

Mandle, W.F. 'The Professional Cricketer in the Nineteenth Century', *Labour History* (1972), 23: 1–16.

———— 'Games People Played: Cricket and Football in England and Victoria in the Late Nineteenth Century', *Historical Studies* (1973), 15: 511–35.

———— 'Cricket and Australian Nationalism in the Nineteenth Century', *Journal of the Royal Australian Historical Society* (December 1973), 59: 225–46.

———— 'W.G. Grace as a Victorian Hero', *Historical Studies* (1981), 19: 353–68.

Mangan, J.A. 'Eton in India: The Imperial Diffusion of a Victorian Educational Ethic', *History of Education* (1978), 7: 105–18.

———— *Athleticism in the Victorian and Edwardian Public School* (Cambridge, 1981).

———— 'Grammar Schools and the Games Ethic in the Victorian and Edwardian Eras', *Albion* (1983).

———— 'Christ and the Imperial Games Fields: Evangelical Athletes of the Empire', *The British Journal of Sports History* (September 1984), 1: 184–201.

———— *The Games Ethic and Imperialism* (London, 1986).

———— ed., *Pleasure, Profit and Proselytism: British Culture and Sport at Home and Abroad, 1700–1914* (London, 1988).

March, R. *The Cricketers of Vanity Fair* (Exeter, 1982).

Marder, J.I. 'Buying Back One's Past', *Wisden 1975*, 143–49.

Margetson, S. *Leisure and Pleasure in the Nineteenth Century* (Newton Abbot, 1971).

Marrus, M. *The Rise of Leisure in Industrial Society* (St Charles, 1974).

Marshall, J. *Sussex Cricket: A History* (London, 1959).

———— *Lord's* (Sportsmans Book Club, 1970).

———— *Headingley* (Newton Abbot, 1972).

———— *Old Trafford* (Newton Abbot, 1973).

Martens, J.W. 'Rugby Union Football and English Society 1871–1914', PhD Thesis submitted to the University of Manitoba, 1988.

Martineau, G.D. *Bat, Ball, Wicket and All* (Sportsmans Book Club, 1954).

———— *The Field is Full of Shades* (Sportsmans Book Club, 1954).

———— *They Made Cricket* (Sportsmans Book Club, 1957).

Martin-Jenkins, C. *The Complete Who's Who of Test Cricketers* (London, 1983).

Mason, T. *Association Football and English Society 1863–1915* (Sussex,

1980).

McCrone, K.E. *Playing the Game: Sport and the Physical Emancipation of English Women 1870–1914* (Lexington, 1988).

McIntosh, P.C. *Physical Education in England since 1800* (London, 1952).

———— *Sport and Society* (London, 1963).

McKenzie, Sir C. 'Shillings for W.G.: Looking Back Eighty Years', *Wisden 1973*, 103–07.

Meacham, S. *A Life Apart: The English Working Class, 1890–1914* (London, 1977).

Meller, H.E. *Leisure and the Changing City, 1870–1914* (London, 1976).

Menke, F.G. *The Encyclopedia of Sports* (New York, 1977).

Metcalfe, A. 'Organised Sport in the Mining Communities of South Northumberland, 1880–1889', *Victorian Studies* (Autumn, 1982).

———— *Canada Learns to Play: The Emergence of Organized Sport, 1807–1914* (Toronto, 1987).

Midwinter, E.C. *W.G. Grace: His Life and Times* (London, 1981).

Mitchell, B.R. and Deane, P. *Abstracts of British Historical Statistics* (Cambridge, 1971).

Monro, F.R. D'O. *The History of the Hampstead Cricket Club* (London, 1949).

Moore, D. *The History of Kent County Cricket Club* (London, 1988).

Moorhouse, G. *Lord's* (London, 1983).

Moses, E.W. *To Ashbrooke and Beyond: The History of the Sunderland Cricket and Rugby Football Club 1808–1963* (London, 1963).

Mott, M. 'The British Protestant Pioneers and the Establishment of Manly Sports in Manitoba, 1870–1886', *Journal of Sport History* (Winter 1980), 7: 25–36.

Moult, T. ed., *Bat and Ball: A New Book of Cricket* (London, 1935).

Moyes, A.G. *Australian Batsmen* (London, 1954).

———— *Australian Cricket: A History* (London, 1959).

Muir, R. *A Short History of the British Commonwealth* (London, 1962).

Mullin, P. and Derriman, P. *Bat and Pad: Writings on Australian Cricket 1804–1984* (Oxford, 1984).

Murphy, P. *E.J. 'Tiger' Smith of Warwickshire and England* (Newton Abbot, 1981).

Newnham, L. *Essex County Cricket 1876–1975* (Colchester, undated).

Newsome, D. *A History of Wellington College 1859–1959* (London, 1959).

———— *Godliness and Good Learning: Four Studies on a Victorian Ideal* (London, 1961).

Nyren, J. *The Young Cricketer's Tutor* (London, 1833).

———— *Cricketers of My Time* (London, 1833).

Oman, Sir C. *Memories of Victorian Oxford* (London, 1941).

Parker, E. *The History of Cricket* (London, undated).

Parker, G. *Gloucestershire Road: A History of Gloucestershire County Cricket Club* (London, 1983).

Parker, S. *The Sociology of Leisure* (London, 1976).

Parkin, G.R. *Edward Thring's Life, Diary, and Letters* (London, 1900).

Parsons, A.L. *Durham City Cricket Club History* (Durham, 1972).

Patterson, W.S. *Sixty Years of Uppingham Cricket* (London, 1909).

Peebles, I.A.R. 'A Middlesex Century', *Wisden 1965*, 128–34.

———— *The Watney Book of Test Match Grounds* (London, 1967).

Preston, H. 'W.G. Grace Centenary', *Wisden 1949*, 101–06.

Price, R. *An Imperial War and the British Working Class: Working Class Attitudes and Reactions to the Boer War 1899–1902* (London, 1972).

Pullin, A.W. *Talks with Old English Cricketers* (London, 1900).

Pycroft, J. *The Cricket Field* (London, 1851).

———— *Oxford Memories* (London, 1886).

Quigley, I. *The Heirs of Tom Brown* (Oxford, 1984).

Quin, G. *Cricket in the Meadow: A Short History of the Amersham Cricket Club 1865–1955* (Chesham, 1956).

Rait-Kerr, R.S. *The Laws of Cricket* (London, 1950).

Ranjitsinhji, K.S. *The Jubilee Book of Cricket* (London, 1897).

Read, W.W. *Annals of Cricket* (London, 1896).

Redmond, G. *The Sporting Scots of Nineteenth Century Canada* (New Jersey, 1982).

Rees, J.H. *One Hundred Years of Cricket in Gowerton 1880 to 1980* (Swansea, 1980).

Rippon, A. *The Story of Middlesex County Cricket Club* (Ashbourne, 1982).

Roberts, D. *Midland Bank Cricket Club: A Centenary History* (London, 1970).

Roberts, D. *Paternalism in Early Victorian England* (New Jersey, 1979).

Roberts, K. *Contemporary Society and the Growth of Leisure* (New York, 1978).

Roberts, R. *Sixty Years of Somerset Cricket* (London, 1951).

Robinson, R. *On Top Down Under: Australia's Cricket Captains* (Brisbane, 1975).

Roebuck, P. *From Sammy to Jimmy: The Official History of Somerset County Cricket Club* (London, 1991).

Rogerson, S. *Wilfred Rhodes* (London, 1960).

Ross, A. ed., *The Cricketer's Companion* (London, 1963).

———— *Ranji: Prince of Cricketers* (London, 1983).

Ross, G. *The Surrey Story* (London, 1957).

———— '200 Years of Laws – and LBW still the most controversial',

Wisden 1975, 128–36.

———— 'The Greatest Centenary of Them All', *Wisden 1976*, 96–106.

———— *A History of West Indies Cricket* (London, 1976).

Rouse, W.H.D. *A History of Rugby School* (London, 1898).

Rowell, G. *Queen Victoria Goes to the Theatre* (London, 1978).

Rundell, M. *The Dictionary of Cricket* (London, 1985).

Russell, C.E.B. *Manchester Boys* (Manchester, 1905).

Saltaire Cricket Club *Souvenir Centenary Booklet 1869–1969* (Saltaire, 1969).

Sampson, A. *Grounds of Appeal: The Homes of First-Class Cricket* (London, 1981).

Sandiford, K.A.P. 'The Victorians at Play: Problems in Historiographical Methodology', *Journal of Social History* (Winter 1981), 15: 271–88.

———— 'Sport and Victorian England: a Review Article', *Canadian Journal of History* (April 1983), 18: 111–117.

———— 'The Professionalization of Modern Cricket', *British Journal of Sports History* (December 1985), 2: 270–89.

———— 'Cricket and the Barbadian Society', *Canadian Journal of History* (December 1986), 21: 353–70.

———— and Stoddart, B. 'The Elite Schools and Cricket in Barbados: A Study in Colonial Continuity', *International Journal of the History of Sports* (December 1987), 4: 333–50.

———— and Vamplew, W. 'The Peculiar Economics of English Cricket Before 1914', *British Journal of Sports History* (December 1986), 3: 311–26.

Sanyal, S. *40 Years of Test Cricket* (New Delhi, 1974).

Schumpeter, J.A. *Imperialism and Social Classes* (Oxford, 1951).

Scott, P. 'Cricket and the Religious World in the Victorian Period', *Church Quarterly* (July 1970), 3: 134–44.

Seaman, L.C.B. *Victorian England: Aspects of English and Imperial History 1837–1901* (London, 1973).

Sewell, E.H.D. *Cricket Under Fire* (London, undated).

Shawcroft, J. *A History of Derbyshire County Cricket Club* (London, 1972).

———— *The Official History of Derbyshire County Cricket Club* (London, 1989).

Simon, B. and Bradley, I. *The Victorian Public School* (London, 1975).

Simon, R. and Smart, A. *The Art of Cricket* (London, 1983).

Simpson, R.T. 'Nottingham's Notable Part in the Growth of Cricket', *Wisden 1967*, 134–42.

Sissons, R. *The Players: A Social History of the Professional Cricketer* (London, 1988).

———— and Stoddart, B. *Cricket and Empire* (Sydney, 1984).

Slusher, H.S. *Man, Sport, and Existence: A Critical Analysis* (Philadelphia, 1967).

Snow, E.E. *A History of Leicestershire Cricket* (London, 1949).

———— '100 Years of Leicestershire Cricket', *Wisden 1978*, 151–55.

Spencer, H. *The Principles of Psychology* (London, 1890).

———— *Facts and Comments* (New York, 1902).

———— *Education: Intellectual, Moral and Physical* (London, 1949).

Squire, H.F. and A.P. *Henfield Cricket and its Sussex Cradle* (Hove, 1949).

Standing, P.C. *Cricket of Today and Yesterday* (London, 1902).

Stanley, Col. K.B. 'Centenary of Free Foresters', *Wisden 1965*, 226–28.

Steadman Jones, G. *Outcast London: Studies in English Working Class History, 1832–1982* (London, 1983).

Steel, A.G. and Lyttelton, R.H. *Cricket* (London, 1888).

Stoddart, B. 'Cricket, Social Formation and Cultural Continuity in Barbados: A Preliminary Ethnohistory', *Journal of Sport History* (Winter 1987), 14: 317–40.

Stone, N. 'The Rise of Worcestershire', *Wisden 1963*, 124–33.

Storch, R.D. ed., *Popular Culture and Custom in Nineteenth Century England* (London, 1982).

Strutt, J. *The Sports and Pastimes of the People of England* (London, 1801).

Swanton, E.W. ed., *The World of Cricket* (London, 1966).

———— ed., *Barclays World of Cricket* (London, 1980; rev. and repr., London, 1986.

Taylor, A.D. *Sussex Cricket in the Olden Time* (Hove, 1900).

Taylor, W.T. 'History of Derbyshire Cricket', *Wisden 1953*, 104–14.

The Times M.C.C. 1787–1937 (London, 1937).

Thomas, A.W. *Cardiff Cricket Club 1867–1967* (Cardiff, 1967).

Thomas, K. 'Work and Leisure in Pre-Industrial Society', *Past and Present* (December 1964), 29: 50–62.

Thomas, P.F. *Old English Cricket* (London, 1929).

Thomson, A.A. *Pavilioned in Splendour* (London, 1956).

———— *Odd Men In: A Gallery of Cricket Eccentrics* (Sportsmans Book Club, 1959).

———— *Hirst and Rhodes* (Sportsmans Book Club, 1960).

———— *Cricket Bouquet* (London, 1961).

———— *Cricket: The Golden Ages* (Sportsmans Book Club, 1962).

———— *The Great Cricketer: W.G. Grace* (London, 1968).

———— *Cricket: The Wars of the Roses* (Sportsmans Book Club, 1968).

Thompson, E.P. *The Making of the English Working Class* (New York, 1963).

Thornton, A.P. *The Imperial Idea and its Enemies* (London, 1959).

———— *Habit of Authority* (London, 1966).

Tozer, M. *Physical Education at Thring's Uppingham* (Uppingham, 1976).

Trevelyan, G.M. *Illustrated English Social History* (London, 1952).

Trevelyan, G.M. *English Social History* (London, 1958).

Trollope, A. ed., *British Sports and Pastimes* (London, 1868).

Twigg, J.D. 'The Players of the Game: R.G. Barlow and the Stonewalling Tradition', *Journal of the Cricket Society* (Autumn 1987), 13: 6–10.

Vamplew, W. *The Turf: A Social and Economic History of Horse Racing* (London, 1976).

————— 'Sports Crowd Disorder in Britain, 1870–1914: Causes and Controls', *Journal of Sport History* (1980), 7: 5–20.

————— 'The Influence of Economic Change on Popular Sport in England, 1600–1900', in R. Crawford, ed., *Proceedings of the First Australian Symposium on the History and Philosophy of Physical Education and Sport* (Melbourne, 1980), 126–51.

————— 'The Economics of a Sports Industry: Scottish Gate-Money Football, 1890–1914', *Economic History Review* (November, 1982), Second Series, XXXV: 549–67.

————— 'Profit or Utility Maximisation? Analysis of English County Cricket before 1914', in Vamplew, W. ed., *Economic History of Leisure*. Papers presented at the Eighth International Economics History Congress (South Australia, 1983), 38–60.

————— 'Playing for Pay: The Earnings of Professional Sportsmen in England 1870–1914', in Cashman, R. and McKernan, M. eds, *Sport: Money, Morality and the Media* (New South Wales, 1982), 104–30.

————— 'Close of Play: Career Termination in English Professional Sport 1870–1914', *Canadian Journal of the History of Sport* (1984), 15: 64–79.

————— 'Not Playing the Game: Unionism in British Professional Sport 1870–1914', *British Journal of Sports History* (December 1985), 2: 232–47.

————— *Pay up and Play the Game: Professional Sport in Britain 1875–1914* (Cambridge, 1988).

Vockins, M.D. *Worcestershire County Cricket Club: A Pictorial History* (London, 1980).

Wadsworth, A.P. 'Newspaper Circulations, 1800–1954', *Manchester Statistical Society* (March 1955).

Waghorn, H.T. *Cricket Scores 1730–1773* (London, 1899).

————— *The Dawn of Cricket* (London, 1906).

Wakley, B.J. *The History of Wimbledon Cricket Club 1854–1953* (Bournemouth, 1954).

Walton, J.K. *The English Seaside Resort: A Social History 1750–1914* (New York, 1983).

Walvin, J.A. *The People's Game: A Social History of British Football*

(Newton Abbot, 1975).

———— *Leisure and Society, 1830–1900* (London, 1978).

———— 'Dust to Dust: Celebrations of Death in Victorian England', *Historical Reflections* (Fall 1982), 9: 353–71.

Waring, A.J. *'W.G.', or the Champion's Career* (Bristol, 1899).

Warner, Sir P.F. *Cricket in Many Climes* (London, 1900).

———— *Book of Cricket* (London, 1946).

———— *Gentlemen vs Players* (London, 1946).

———— *Lord's 1787–1945* (London, 1946).

———— *Long Innings: An Autobiography* (London, 1953).

Webber, R. *The Australians in England* (London, 1953).

———— *The County Cricket Championship* (Sportsmans Book Club, 1958).

———— *The Phoenix History of Cricket* (Sportsmans Book Club, 1961).

Wellings, E.M. *A History of County Cricket: Middlesex* (Newton Abbot, 1973).

West, G.D. *The Elevens of England* (London, 1988).

Weston, G.N. *W.G. Grace: The Great Cricketer* (Liskeard, 1973).

Wiener, M.J. *English Culture and the Decline of the Industrial Spirit* (Cambridge, 1981).

Williams, M. ed., *The Way to Lord's: Cricketing Letters to 'The Times'* (London, 1983).

———— ed., *Double Century: 200 Years of Cricket in 'The Times'* (London, 1985).

Wohl, A.S. *Endangered Lives: Public Health in Victorian Britain* (Harvard, 1983).

Wolfe, H.A. *Wallasey Cricket Club 1864–1964* (London, 1964).

Woodhouse, A. *The History of Yorkshire County Cricket Club* (London, 1989).

———— *et al.*, *Cricketers of Wombwell* (Bradford, 1965).

Woodward, Sir E.L. *The Age of Reform: 1815–70* (Oxford, 1962).

Worsley, T.C. *Barbarians and Philistines* (London, 1940).

Wrigley, A. *The Book of Test Cricket* (London, 1965).

Wye, A. *Dr. W.G. Grace* (London, 1901).

Wymer, N. *Sport in England* (London, 1949).

Wynne-Thomas, P. *England on Tour* (London, 1982).

———— *The History of Hampshire County Cricket Club* (London, 1988).

———— *The History of Lancashire County Cricket Club* (London, 1989).

———— *The Complete History of Cricket Tours at Home and Abroad* (London, 1989).

Yeo, S. *Religion and Voluntary Organizations in Crisis* (London, 1976).
———— and E. eds, *Popular Culture and Class Conflict 1590–1914: Explorations in the History of Labour and Leisure* (Brighton, 1981).
Yiannikis, *et al.*, *Sport Sociology* (Iowa, 1976).
Young, G.M. ed., *Early Victorian England 1830–65* (Oxford, 1934).
Young, P.M. *A History of British Football* (London, 1969).

Index

Typeset by Poole Typesetting (Wessex) Ltd, Victoria Chambers, Fir Vale Road, Bournemouth and printed in Great Britain at the University Press, Cambridge.